Invisible in Plain Sight

Invisible in Plain Sight

Voices from the By-Lanes of Kamathipura

Swati Pandey

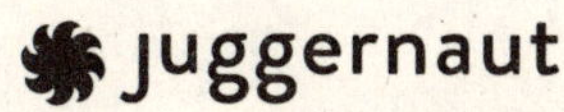

JUGGERNAUT BOOKS
C-I-128, First Floor, Sangam Vihar, Near Holi Chowk,
New Delhi 110080, India

First published by Juggernaut Books 2025

10 9 8 7 6 5 4 3 2 1

P-ISBN: 978-93-5345-296-4
E-ISBN: 978-93-5345-496-8

Typeset in Adobe Caslon Pro by Mukul Chand

Printed at Thomson Press India Ltd

The author's royalties from the sale of this book will be contributed to the women of Kamathipura featured in the book.

For my father, Dr Jnanesh Ranjan Roy, who let me dig for worms, and crush leaves and flowers, believing that a child's messy potions were just a different kind of a playground of wonders, far beyond any single definition.

Contents

Prologue

The rule of the jungle has always been the same; either you become the beast or you get killed by the beast – the hunt is always on. The rule of the jungle has always been the same since the evolution of species; either you are the big cat or the sly fox, powerful and feared or cunning and dangerous or be part of a skulk. The rule of the jungle is fatally savage, with little empathy for the weak. The only strength for the weak is to be part of a horde and revel in the security of numbers. In the jungle, the weak are not – or should not be – protected; there is always an active purge of the weak. There are no ethics, no gratitude, no morality; the artificial constructs of protection that society defines. As soon as it turns dark, the predators unleash their bloodthirsty canines and go hunting. The law of the jungle is ferocious. The philosophy of survival is not a choice. Outside the jungle, we – the evolved society who live within the comfort of our rules and structures, and offer protection for our weaker constituents – often forget the law of the jungle.

The apparently harmless metropolis of Mumbai too has a jungle in it; an impenetrably thick and dangerous jungle, ruled by predators and survived by many. If you ever step into it, you will be sucked into the vortex, it will play a mind-altering conspiracy against you from which there is no escape. Survival, with only basic instincts at play, is part of the game. Surrounding this jungle from all sides, lies the oasis that is the epitome of societal refinement, of values, of moral lines and barriers, of affluence and acceptance.

Two disparate worlds coexist – one within the womb of the other without giving a thought to each other. 'Oh, East is East, and West is West, and never the twain shall meet,' wrote Rudyard Kipling. When these worlds intersect, the real story of interest emerges.

It was a special day in the life of a Bengali household – celebrating the New Year, the first day of the Hindu month of Baisakh, roughly mid-April. An uncomfortable and humid summer had set in. Mumbai had never been so hot, and that too in April itself. Muttering under her breath, the woman of the house – adorned in all her finery – had just fed her family a hearty meal complete with delicacies both Bengali as well as Maharashtrian – *gorom bhaat* (steamed rice), *ilish bhapa* (steamed Hilsa fish), *cholar dal* (Bengal gram cooked with coconut and spices) and *shorshe ilish* (Hilsa fish cooked in a mustard gravy), along with the ubiquitous puran poli (a flat wheat pancake with sweet gram flour stuffing) and the must-have *amrakhand* (a mango-flavoured yogurt to celebrate the king of fruits in India). The woman – born a Bengali with Odiya roots – was a 'practising Maharashtrian' who enjoyed this amalgamation that defined the core of India. Her large-sized government apartment was adorned with strings of jasmine blossoms that made the summer heat somewhat bearable. The night before, she had made a fine-ground paste of rice powder and had soaked it in water to draw the Bengali rangoli known as *alpana* to pray to Laxmi, the goddess of good fortune, to bless her family – a practice that had been passed down through the generations from mother to daughter. Would I call the woman religious? I am not sure, for religion is different from tradition. This woman was steeped in tradition. It had been a day well spent with the jolly banter of her family – her ageing mother, the one who had given her her Odiya roots; her quiet and soft-spoken husband and her very argumentative son. But a feeling of trepidation had also flooded her mind.

It was a feeling akin to walking along the outer margins of societal acceptability; of being on the cusp of committing a crime, desperate to hide it from the world. Something she wanted to do but also wanted to avoid at the same time. She was what may be commonly expressed as in between worlds, or about to walk into the bowels of the jungle that she had been a cursory observer of until now but it was time to cross the Laxman Rekha and walk into the other world. Laxman Rekha is a mythological phrase adopted from the Indian Hindu Epic Ramayana where it is said that, Lakshman, the younger brother of Lord Ram, draws a protective line around their hut and requests Sita not to cross it, in their absence. Lakhsman Rekha symbolizes a boundary of safety and protection that results in dire consequences, when crossed, as in the epic when Sita crosses it, the demon king Ravana abducted her.

She filled an earthen pot with delicious rosogullas (a Bengali sweet made of jaggery and cheese), gave herself a moment to breathe, adjusted the jasmine garland pinned to her neat bun and set off. As she left her home, she called out loud to no one in particular that she was stepping out for a while, and would be back after a couple of hours. However, she had made sure that each member of her family was busy elsewhere so as to not hear her. Not that anyone had ever questioned her about her whereabouts. Maybe it was the agony tearing at her heart that made her turn and look back into the comfort of her own home, perhaps wishing that someone would stop her. The workings of the human mind remain a mystery.

Off she went into the forbidden forest. It was a balmy afternoon. A milk-white car hesitatingly stopped a few steps ahead of the wide, dingy lane that opened into a few narrow smaller by-lanes. The streets were lined with makeshift shops selling gaudily sequined garments, or maybe they only appeared gaudy to her. Hawkers along the footpath looked like a line of ants – all overloaded with wares of various kinds. Most of the shops had tin walls which reflected the harsh glare of the sun, turning the place into a bright furnace. Men crowded the small eateries, bars and cigarette, beedi and paan stalls that stood by the side of the street. Betel nut-spit stains and beedi stubs littered the ground. A peculiar smell of cheap country liquor engulfed the place. The neighbourhood did not appear to be out of the ordinary. Millions of by-lanes with similar sights and people criss-crossed the country. Yet there was something dark about it, as if it were shrouded by something, like an omnibus funeral scarf that wraps the face of a dead body. Fear and apprehension had taken over her mind. Yet, overtly, it typified impoverished neighbourhoods

– like many small ones dotting Mumbai – which one passed by without so much as giving them a second glance. She remembered how quickly she used to roll up her car windows every time she passed through this area. And if her mother or son were travelling with her in the car, she would invariably ask the driver to take another route instead of passing through this particular zone of the metropolis.

With a palpitating heart, she stepped out of the car, the glare of the sun hitting her full blast. She looked delicate even though she had steely eyes. Her perfectly pleated soft yellow silk saree glowed in the bright sunlight, complementing the beaded mojari sandals and small diamond ear-studs that glinted in the sun. Every time the wind caressed her face, the scent of jasmine perfumed the air around her. She lowered her gaze, maybe to avoid the harsh sun, or maybe to deflect many an unwanted gaze that made her nervous and also acutely aware that here she was being judged by one and all. And indeed, all eyes had turned towards her, screaming at her intrusion. She looked like an alien amongst them, the odd one out. Beads of sweat ran down the sides of her face. Her stomach was all knotted with unease, the deep stench of human excreta disorienting her further. This unease was so unlike her normal, confident self. She was used to being in command of situations and her emotions. But today this confidence had deserted her at a time when she had needed it the most. She was in the heart of 'their' territory, which she had only heard of while visiting the nearby post office frequently over the past three months. It was a place that she had only envisioned in her imagination from the cocoon of the post office when she was there for meetings, or other planned activities. Her world far from the world that was Kamathipura.

The woman in question was the postmaster general of Mumbai with more than 5,000 men and women working beside her, and she the commander of this ubiquitous force. And command she did this ubiquitous force. Fearless and forward looking, it seemed like only yesterday – rather than 26 years ago – when she joined the civil services, where she had told the interview board that she wanted to be amongst the people and become an agent of positive change. Many things about her had changed, but the fire in her eyes to be that catalyst never did. This fire was the reason why she even happened to chance by this area in the first place – to ensure that people without the papers to prove their identity were brought into the formal fold of financial inclusion. She had been tirelessly working towards this goal for the past five months, spending hours in the tiny, claustrophobic post office at the mouth of a lane. Sending her dedicated bunch of postmen and women to bring in women who did not want to leave their comfortable corners was one thing. Being able to talk to them was one humongous task; explaining financial inclusion was quite another. Every time she was in that area, of course, her post office was the epicentre from where she reached out and engaged in countless hours of ice-breaking with them, always aided by the staff of the post office. During this time she had completely upgraded this tiny, dilapidated post office into a modern, digital, people-friendly, all-women post office. Aiding the women here had become her mission; be able to protect them, to give them a voice and to educate them in financial inclusion so that they might command their own finances and, in a small way, have a right over their own wants in life. In this flow of work, as it happens with humans, an emotion of fondness had crept in for one particular 'gang' of women.

A gang that was boisterous and temperamental but also loving, led by a fearless woman who had no filters while talking. She said what she felt. Society had not been able to suppress her ability to express her thoughts, even though at times it caused a great deal of embarrassment to others. Kajol, the woman, would be her primary host for the day. This time the postmaster general's foray into the area was different. She was alone, heading into the unknown; she was 'going native', a typical anthropological term that had stuck with her from the time when she was a practising anthropologist years ago, before her avatar as a civil servant. There was something romantic about the term 'going native', suggesting an immersive experience where one sheds one's prejudices and rigid mindset and adopts the environment of the other. Wait a minute, why were these thoughts coming to her? Was she going as a guest or an anthropologist? Or is that what reality is without one's knowledge? A new interaction is also a chance for study and learning; we do not merely term it anything other than a visit. She ventured into the belly of the jungle – an area she had not dared to go before, only glanced at when passing by – but this time it was different, she was alone. No staff members accompanied her for assistance or protection.

There had been no reconnaissance, no forward planning; just a leap into the unknown. For today, to celebrate the New Year, she had been invited for the first time into the 'homes' of the women whom she lovingly called the 'toofani' girls. Her term for them truly reflected that sisterhood of women, but the world had a very different and ugly label for them – one that stamped a woman forever and showed no mercy. The Italian Marxist critic Antonio Gramsci coined the term 'subaltern' for people like them. They are the people who are left out or ignored by the annals of popular history. They are powerless in an absolute sense of the term.

She halted at a distance, almost turning back, her mind fertile with excuses for cancelling the plan, but a sense of duty, of a promise made, made her hold steady. She chided herself for having accepted Kajol's invitation. The toofani girls were opening their homes to her. It was a rare invite, one that is rarely extended and even more rarely accepted. Nevertheless, it being the first time that she was visiting someone's house, she had carried out the social formality that she had been taught – of bringing sweets for them. The pot of rosogullas she had brought along was to be the ice-breaker, Kajol was a Bengali after all! With that she started walking towards one of the serpentine by-lanes. That was the initial pull, the start of this story, the common bond of melodious Bengali.

Language is known to shape culture and behaviour. Speaking to people in their preferred language establishes an emotional connect with them. It seems like magic that people who have absolutely nothing other than a language in common can feel comfortable with each other despite the chasm of societal differences.

She stepped silently ahead to see Reshma – one of the women she had exchanged many a light moment with and had also scolded as if she had been an errant child – standing with three other women. She was decked up in a dazzling and gaudily colourful saree with a deep-cut sleeveless blouse that had tiny sparkling mirrors all over, cheap stone jewellery and a garland of jasmine flowers in her hair. Her bun had been done in a bouffant style popular with the heroines of 1960's mainstream Hindi cinema. Her face glittered with overdone garish make-up. Her lips were blood red with uneven coats of lipstick, and her eyes were hardly visible, masked by the dark magenta eye shadow.

This was the way our postmaster general had always seen Reshma – on overkill. A familiarity had bred in this tawdry. What struck the woman was how the jasmine garland was perceived and the connotations it carried despite being a neutral element. But nothing could have been further from the truth for the garland that lent grace and femininity to one, made the other look like an object of cheap enticement. The other women with Reshma were dressed like other heroines of the Hindi movies. One stood apart. Dressed in a black chintzy gown, big, round junk earrings and dark, blackish-maroon lipstick, she looked like a goth. Her hair was open and coloured a glaring blonde. Her eyes were painted with thick layers of kohl.

Reshma saw her Officer Didi approaching and ran towards her, hugging her so tight and with a force so strong that the woman was pushed back a little. The postmaster general was taken aback by the funk of tobacco and alcohol from Reshma's mouth. She looked at her angrily and said, 'You are drunk again, in spite of the doctor's warning!' She knew that Reshma struggled with chronic gastritis and frequented the local doctor's clinic or Hakim's. The broad smile on Reshma's face disappeared at once and her face turned white as a sheet. She looked down and stood silently. But before Reshma could reply, the other women came running up hugged their guest.

The one in the gown snatched the pot of rasgullas from her hands and shouted out of excitement, 'With us around, why are you carrying this load? By the way, what's this? A gift for us?' Her eyes lit up with joy. Seeing their enthusiasm, she smiled and told them that she had brought rasgullas for all of them and asked the woman in the gown to distribute the sweet amongst themselves. As per the Bengali law of bonding and celebration, when fellow 'bongs' meet – and God forbid if they are all women – there has to be a deafening cacophony, with all of them speaking at once.

In the hullabaloo – and unnoticed by the postmaster general – a drunk and unkempt-looking middle-aged man had crept towards them. He asked her in a voice that resembled sandpaper grinding against metal, '*Kitna hai?*' The postmaster general either did not hear him well or did not understand that he was asking her how much she would charge, but she got a sense of someone defiling her space and was assailed by a foul, nauseating odour. As if at the cracking of a whip, the atmosphere of camaraderie vanished and there was a micro-second of deathly silence. And then reality sank in. The postmaster general found herself being pushed into the inner recesses of a building nearby and heard Guriya's rancid voice screaming unheard profanities at the man.

Reshma's rave was followed by one tight slap on the left cheek of the now bewildered man, and numerous other swear words and slaps from the toofani women. The postmaster general could still not fathom what exactly was going on. She stood there flabbergasted, seeing the women physically abuse the man. The man, now mildly injured, was asking for forgiveness with folded hands. It was such a paradox – these were women that she thought needed saving, but whatever was happening, it appeared that they were quite a powerful bunch and that it was the poor man who needed saving. There wasn't much to distinguish between the hunter and the prey. The hunter at this very moment looked like a hapless prey. In the midst of this terrible chaos, the postmaster general saw Kajol and Salma, who was fondly known as Aapa, running towards her.

As she came closer, Salma, half amused, half cross, pushed her towards a dark, musty, narrow flight of steps leading further up into the darkness. Turning back, Salma shouted, addressing Guriya with a wink, indicating that she should take care of the man, using an abusive, filthy, colloquial version of Bengali that the postmaster general had only heard drunk rickshaw wallas of Kolkata speak. Her head was now buzzing with a sudden ache. Too much was happening too soon, over which she had no control. She couldn't see much but could only hear the foulest of language being spoken, and that stung her ears. Within a blink of the eye, Salma and Kajol caught her hands and took her up the dilapidated four-storeyed building. As the three of them walked up hastily, she turned around and saw several women lining the street, to partake in the drama of the day. It looked like an ordinary day for them.

The postmaster general silently walked with them into the darkness, which was both literal and figurative. A foul smell of urine and sweat pervaded the staircase. She tripped on her saree, fumbled and fell as she could hardly see anything. Aapa switched on the flashlight of her mobile phone to show her the way. Everything was broken and rotting. Everything and everyone.

As they climbed up a few steps she saw a shadow rushing towards her. She was nervous. Salma screamed at the top of her voice to the shadow – a few more profanities – asking the shadow to reveal herself. A female voice, soft, laced with shame, as if it did not belong there, cooed back. She immediately recognized Rani's gentle voice. Salma and Kajol smiled a smile of relief.

The postmaster general had reached their sanctuary, their home. She saw a line of numerous pocket-sized rooms, made of plywood and 'decorated' with newspapers for wallpaper. All the doors were shut. Some walls were rotting, leading to gaping holes through which you could look from one room into the other. Some rooms were lit by the same dull yellow light. There was not a single opening for ventilation. A cat was nosing through the piles of garbage that lay on the ground, emitting an odour of human vomit.

The postmaster general saw Rani standing with a wide smile on her face and hugged her. Rani led the way to one of the nondescript rooms and made the shivering woman sit on the bed, which had no linen on it. The neon bulb in Rani's tiny, claustrophobic room blinked randomly, creating psychedelic patterns on the damaged, dilapidated walls. The mattress was of ancient provenance, with the cloth covered in grime. It had given way in some places and the cotton stuffing was bursting out and playing hide and seek. There were large stains on the mattress which gave off a musty smell, like that of human sweat and semen. The postmaster general felt giddy. She could barely hold back the puke that had risen to her mouth. It was as if this filth would be hers forever and could never be washed off her body. She tried to keep the vomit in and also maintain her composure for the three women were watching her pale face intently. They were testing her, looking at her leeringly, while also acting like protective mother hens. No rules of normal human behaviour were applicable here.

The jungle has its own rules. You camouflaged yourself to survive. But right now the postmaster general was an orange in an orchard full of apples. 'Didi, Didi,' Rani's intoxicating voice woke her up from her mental stupor. '*Didi, mein Reshma ka chillana suni upar se, woh harami buddha aapko aapka* rate *pooch raha tha! Maine Aapa aur Kajol ko bheja aapko lane!*

Uski toh treatment chal rahi hai. Yahan kabhi koi aadmi aap ke aur nahi dekhega.' Rani had heard the old man asking the visitor her 'price' and had sent Salma and Aapa to bring her here. That man was getting 'treatment'. That meant he was being beaten mercilessly by women who themselves were abused everyday. What an irony! No man here would bother her again.

And here their officer didi thought she was the protector of these women. Never before had she felt so enraged, so small, so powerless or so commodified as she felt in that moment. The 'bubble' in which she lived her life had kept her in a structured, protected world indeed. A world of clear rights and wrongs, a world of education and refinement, a world of respect where women empowerment, empathy, chivalry, sensitivity to the issues of women, etc., were the ideals of achievement that everyone aspired to. But none of those rules and mores of the 'normal world' existed here. This world was unabashed and did not offer any excuses for it. None whatsoever.

She was dumbstruck, as if she had been slapped hard by some invisible hand. Silent and frozen, she sat there, goosebumps showing on her skin and tears streaming down her lightly kohl-lined eyes. Her rate, her price! It was one of those moments when you understood the words but could not fathom fully what they conveyed. Perhaps that was a way of escape to maintain one's sanity. The only way to survive was to cultivate an alter ego to which bad things happened, keeping the real you safe. A deep sense of rage and the bile of hatred rose deep in the pit of her stomach. She shakingly stood up to leave, but Kajol's strong reassuring hands held her back. Kajol looked deeply into her eyes, as if commanding her to sit down, silently saying that it was going to be all right. Meek and docile as a mouse, this woman who commanded a few thousand people with her voice of steel, sat down quietly in obedience. The roles had reversed. Aapa came in with a glass of water. The postmaster general was exhausted and spent. Salma stood silent for a minute, watching her with an unfathomable gaze, as if she were a biological specimen, almost teasing and chiding her at the same time. With a momentary pause and a devil-may-care attitude, but in a soft, hesitating voice, Salma asked, '*Humaare hath ka paani piyoge na, didi?*' ('You'll drink water from my hands, won't you, sister?') Of course the postmaster general would accept water from them. She, without any emotion, a deer in the headlights with a blank look and the movements of an automaton, took the tumbler and drank the water quietly. There was comfort in the mundane. She felt calmer. She had shifted from her sympathetic nervous system to her parasympathetic system.

She was by now completely overwhelmed by the protection and respect she was being given by these women who had been vilified with many slanderous words, the most sanitized of them being 'sex workers'. They had been disowned by their families, by society, by the so-called civilized human race. They were looked down upon and hated by the world, which regarded them with righteousness, passed judgement on their character and intentions. Vilify them if you must, but does one ever talk about the men, their clientele? Men with families who lurked here in the darkness, depraved men who often abused these women? Yet the world was silent about them. The tales were only of the women, otherwise invisible to society, women who had the exact qualities and follies as any other woman, who were daughters, wives and mothers – just like any of us. And they had surrendered to this forced invisibility, to this grossly unfair rejection by society without resistance. They had borne the weight of all the stigma of the profession they had been forced into and carried their scars, all by themselves, and for years. Perhaps they were too exhausted, too worn down to stand up and fight for their rights in a society that even refused to acknowledge their existence.

Tears ran down the postmaster general's eyes to be with them, to see their 'homes' in that ocean of immense filth and muck, and be granted their love and protection. Their affection, empathy and strange camaraderie seemed to block out the foul and 'immoral' odours of sin, urine, alcohol and sweat that pervaded her nose. It was the comfort of an unlikely sisterhood. It was a collision of different worlds, but which were bound by one common factor – of their being women.

It was an extraordinarily ordinary April afternoon for her, in that tiny room in the fourteenth lane of Kamathipura. It was a day that changed her forever. There would be no looking back for her from here on in life.

Kamathipura, one of the largest, darkest and scariest jungles of human trafficking in the world, is a forbidden zone located in the southern part of Mumbai. Perhaps some of the most spine-chilling incidents of human trafficking, prostitution and heinous criminal offences in whole world too have happened here, where every day hundreds of innocent girls are trafficked from different parts of the country, sold and forced into sex work. Any one attempting to escape is either forcefully drugged, made to get inebriated or is sexually abused. They are compelled to adopt prostitution as their means of living.

Kamathipura breathes in evil and breathes out terror; the terror created by gruesome creatures who cannot be called 'human beings' anymore, who inflict horrifying torments on innocent girls to turn them into prostitutes. They are at it relentlessly, and the girls, reduced to human corpses or, rather, sex machines, die every single day of their lives. But Kamathipura was not always a shelter to prostitution. The historical records say that it was during the latter half of the eighteenth century that William Hornby, the then governor of Mumbai, initiated the massive project of uniting the seven islands of Mumbai on the pretext of administrative necessity. This demanded a huge labour force, a large proportion of which was outsourced from the state of Andhra Pradesh. The labourers who worked on the construction sites started dwelling in the low, marshy and cheap areas of the city, like Byculla, Mahalaxmi and Kamathipura, the last being the most densely populated ghetto in the city where the 'Kamathis', the migrant labourers of Andhra Pradesh who played a significant role in the development of the area during the early years of its establishment lived. Kamathipura, originally known as Lal Bazaar, underwent a massive transformation. The Andhra labourers renamed it as Kamathipuram, which later became Kamathipura, in resonance with the local diction. Naturally, there were many things Andhra in Kamathipura – Andhra temples, Andhra restaurants and Andhra community halls where the religious and social festivities of the community used to be conducted. During this era, Kamathipura had the highest number of 'pocket rooms' in the city, available at affordable rates, which mainly attracted labourers arriving from different states of the country. These labourers, who worked in the city's construction sites, had their families back home in their native villages or towns. Gambling, alcohol and sex were their stress busters after a hectic day of work. This was the chief reason for the rapid emergence of Kamathipura as the largest red-light area in the city. Ninety per cent of the sex workers from the localities of Girgaon, Oomburkharee and Phanaswadi in the city too relocated here, post 1865.

There was also intense trafficking of European, Japanese and Chinese women to this area, which had the most exotic sex workers in all of the city, eventually leading to their racial segregation in localities variously known as 'Safed Gulli', 'China Town' or 'Desi Randi-khana'. Along with the influx of domestic migrants from across the country, immigrants from the Chinese and Japanese communities too played a pivotal role in the flourishing of sex trade in the area, which soon consisted of numerous brothels and dance bars. Street prostitution here attracted a wide range of customers from various walks of life. The sex trade of Kamathipura spread its wings up to the localities of Grant Road and Madanpura. The transformation of Mumbai as the commercial capital of India post-Independence increased the rate of influx of people into the city from across the country in search of jobs, and that in turn increased the demand for commercial sex. The country's poor economy too had a role to play in the large-scale prostitution and pimping that resulted, eventually leading to Kamathipura becoming Asia's second largest sex district and the densest jungle of human trafficking in the world.

1

The Bloodthirsty Hyenas

'Every word has consequences,
every silence too.'

Jean-Paul Sartre

Salma was woken up by the sound of the azaan. It was almost dawn and time for the *fajr*, the first morning prayer. She opened her eyes slowly. She was still feeling dizzy. The rotten smell that pervaded the tiny room in which she had been kept for the last few days was intolerable. She felt the vomit rising in her stomach. She tried to get up from the crummy bed where she was lying naked, but a writhing pain erupted all over her body, especially in her lower abdomen and did not even let her sit up. It seemed as if someone had pierced a thousand nails into her body. Salma could see teeth and nail marks on her body. The bruises from burnt cigarette-ends were still raw. She could feel her womanly organ down there bleeding profusely. There was blood all over the bed. She was terribly hungry and thirsty. She felt like screaming for help, but all that she could do was to lie helpless on the bed.

And while still in bed, she heard a noise. Someone opened the door, letting in a gust of wind. There were three men. They grinned at her nastily. All three were unusually tall, dark and bearded. Salma was dreadfully scared.

She knew one of them. Her Abbu had regarded him as his 'Maalik'. Maalik bent towards her and exclaimed, '*Tujhmein bohot jaan hai*!' (You have a lot of life.) At that, all three looked at her and laughed like devils. They came closer. Salma shivered out of fear; the foul smell of beedi and alcohol was unbearable. The men looked like wild, bloodthirsty hyenas with ferocious teeth and sharp nails. Salma shut her eyes. They attacked her with all their might, with all their lust; ripping her apart with their nails and teeth and penetrating their lecherous male organs ruthlessly into her body. Salma tried to resist them, but is it possible for a girl of mere fifteen to fight against those demons? Salma's heart palpitated wildly. She felt she would die out of pain. She could not comprehend why her Abbu went away, leaving her in the hands of these devils. Salma tried to recall the course of incidents that had occurred during the last couple of days while the hyenas kept tearing at her.

Salma was the eldest of seven daughters. They used to live in Pharsatar, a small village in the Ballia district of Uttar Pradesh. Pharsatar was a very small village and its people were terribly poor. The villagers had to go to the nearest town of Belthara for their essential needs and for employment. The entire landscape of the district was quintessentially eastern Uttar Pradesh in terrain and milieu. The fertile plains of Ballia, nestled in the heart of eastern Uttar Pradesh, stretched endlessly under the golden sunlight, with the Ganga and Ghaghara rivers flowing serenely through it. Its alluvial soil, rich and dark, breathed life into its sprawling fields of rice, wheat and sugarcane; and mango orchards dotted the landscape, their leafy canopies swaying gently in the breeze. The people of this region lived simply, their daily meals a harmonious spread of roti, dals and steaming plates of rice, often accompanied by tangy pickles and fresh curd. Litti-chokha, a cherished delicacy, carried the smoky aroma of tradition, while sweet jalebis and samosas were sold in every bustling bazaar in the district.

Bhojpuri, the soul of the region and the mother tongue of the people here, flowed effortlessly in the speech of the people, its cadence warm and lyrical, carrying the weight of age-old wisdom and humour. The melody of Bhojpuri wove through their conversations like a thread of shared history, binding them to the land they called home. Alongside, Hindi served as the language of the schools and administration, while Urdu, with its poetic elegance, found its voice in the Muslim households and the daily azaan from the local mosques. The influence of Muslim culture in the region lingered in the aromas of its biryanis and kebabs at festive gatherings, in the shimmering embroidery of zardozi on sarees and the reverent greetings of '*adaab*' exchanged in the narrow lanes. This blend of Bhojpuri fervour and Muslim grace wove a tapestry of culture, where each word and custom told a story of shared roots and enduring harmony. Bhojpuri songs echoed through the air during festivals like Holi and Chhath Puja, which brought the community together in vibrant celebrations. It was a culture deeply rooted in family and faith.

This simple life with its frugal bearings was but a dream for Salma. She was born into one of the poorest families in Pharsatar. The mud hut in which she lived was undoubtedly one of the most dilapidated there. It was almost on the verge of collapse after having resisted decades of battering by the monsoon and without maintenance. It comprised a single room with a kutcha thatched roof and mud floor. The walls and the floor had cracks. Sometimes Salma felt her fate was synonymous with the multiple cracks in their mud hut. The house did not have a bathroom and the family had to depend on the open land next to their hut for their daily ablutions. Salma's mother Saziya had died giving birth to Saamiya, the youngest of the sisters, and the mud hut was left mother less and thus shattered. They had only one piece of furniture – an age-old wooden chest that had been gifted to Saziya by her mother. Salma had heard from the oldies of the village that all their furniture was sold one after the other by her Abbu, Ismail, to satiate his craze for alcohol and ritualistic gambling. Ismail used to work in the village tannery as a labourer. An alcoholic by choice, the tall, lanky and fair Ismail was in his mid-fifties. He had dense grey hair all over his head, and it covered his forehead too. He had a cut mark on his left cheek. He had acquired it while fighting with some man in the village shop selling *desi-tharra,* a locally brewed alcoholic drink made from yeast, fermented sugarcane or wheat husk found mostly in the states of Punjab, Uttar Pradesh and Bihar. Ismail exuded an intolerable smell of dead and rotten animals from his body from working in the tannery. It was a smell that could make someone puke instantly.

Ismail was drunk most of the time, abused his daughters and beat them brutally. Salma and her sisters would often be left with bruises on their bodies. Their terrible poverty, regular starvation and occasional meals should have made them skeletal, but Salma and her sisters had inherited their mother's genes. They were immensely beautiful. Her friends used to call Salma Waheeda Rehman, the famous yesteryear actor from Hindi cinema. Like Waheeda, Salma too was a great dancer. She used to blush at their comments. She had also convinced herself that she resembled the actress, in her beauty and demure charm. She had seen Waheeda in the movie *Guide*, which was screened during the previous Eid at their village playground. The actor was gorgeous. In the movie her name was Rosy, and she danced like a diva. Salma felt enraptured to be told that she looked like her! The song '*Aaj phir jeene ki tamanna hai*' had evoked an euphoric sense of liberation and renewal in young Salma. The protagonist, draped in a vibrant saree and dancing with effortless grace and joyous abandon, had transported Salma to another world.

Salma secretly compared herself with the diva on the screen. She dreamt of twirling barefoot on the rugged ground of her village, her laughter and radiant expressions breathing life into the scenery, and herself full of the sheer ecstasy of living in the moment. That song transformed the barren landscape of her life into a canvas of emotional depth, where every step she took felt like a declaration of her independence and the unshackling of her soul. In this kaleidoscope of images in her head, she found her escape, however transient it was.

During the *nikah* of the girls of her village, Salma would invariably be requested to dance to entertain the women invitees. Salma appeared to have the divine boon of being able to dance spontaneously to any tune played before her!

Wearing a colourful sharara or ghagra given to her by the groom or bride's family, she would dance in ecstasy. But Salma's Abbu would later snatch those clothes from her and sell them in the town market on the following day to pay for his drinks and his bouts of gambling. A wedding in a poor Muslim family in those areas unfolded as a simple yet heartfelt affair, steeped in tradition and communal warmth. The setting was often a modest courtyard or an open space near the groom's home, where a makeshift canopy of colourful cloth or white tarpaulin would be put up, held precariously aloft by bamboo poles. Strings of yellow marigold garlands and humble fairy lights would lend a festive charm to this scene, casting a soft glow over it as evening fell.

Women in faded yet carefully pressed sarees or salwar kameez would gather in groups, their dupattas draped or rather wrapped around their whole being, while men in simple kurtas and skull caps sat cross-legged on woven mats, chatting and sipping sweet tea. The air would be filled with the aroma of home-cooked biryani, fragrant with clove and cardamom, and the sizzling sounds of kebabs on a charcoal stove. Plates of sevaiyan – sweet vermicelli cooked in milk, would be passed around for dessert, signifying the sweetness of the occasion. The bride, in a simple but brightly coloured lehenga, her hands adorned with henna, would sit shyly in a corner, surrounded by her sisters and aunts. Her minimal jewellery was mostly of low-grade silver, but would sparkle under the dim light. It was very often a borrowed necklace, and sometimes a treasured family heirloom. The groom, dressed in a plain sherwani and wearing a garland of flowers, would be escorted in by relatives chanting blessings.

The ceremony itself would be brief but solemn, with the local maulvi or priest reciting the nikah in quiet reverence while family and friends nodded in approval. Accompanying this would be the laughter of the children running around and the warm smiles exchanged among the guests, reflecting the essence of the celebration – love, togetherness and hope for a brighter future. While the bridegroom and the bride, their faces veiled by strings of flowers, waited eagerly for the kazi to chant the sacred vows of wedlock and the final *qubulhai*, Salma would blow the audience away with her dance. People who did not know her thought that she must have had some professional training in dance. Forget training, except for that film featuring Waheeda Rehman, Salma had never even watched films to be so familiar with dance moves. She had replayed the dance from the film innumerable times in her young head, and she knew every lyric and every move by memory. Fareeda Khala, their village madrasa teacher, often said that Salma must have been a great dancer in her past life who had been cursed by Allah and was hence reborn amidst such terrible poverty. Salma did not believe all this. She believed she was the most favourite child of Allah, who had created her using the most refined sense of aesthetics, and thus it was that whoever saw her for the first time complimented her using the phrase *jannat ki hur* (heavenly beauty).

As Salma grew older, her beauty became more and more resplendent. Salma was almost fifteen years old when she started working as a domestic help at the house of Fareeda, whom she called Khala. None of the girls in the family were sent to the village madrasa, despite Fareeda's repeated requests to Ismail to send them there. However, when the village panchayat asked for one girl child from each family to be mandatorily sent to the madrasa to be educated, Ismail chose Fatima, Salma's younger sister, instead of Salma. The reason behind this was obvious, since Salma had been assigned the duties of taking care of her very young siblings and doing all the household chores of cooking, cleaning, washing and even filling the buckets from the common water tap in the village and carrying them home.

Salma had to wake up at four in the morning to get a place ahead in the daily queue to get water from the village tap. She would then finish all the house work, feed her sisters and go to Fareeda's house. There she would sweep the house clean, wash Fareeda's clothes and cook for her. Fareeda Khala paid her a reasonably fair sum for the household chores she did. However, this money was invariably grabbed by Ismail to spend on cheap roadside alcohol and gamble at the local brothels. Fareeda tried to support Salma and her sisters with food and clothes, for which Salma was grateful. At times Fareeda would narrate to her stories from the Quran, the story of Ibrahim and the fire, the story of the depressed camel, the story of Abdul Qaudir's treasure, and many more. Salma was particularly enamoured by the story of Leila the sparrow. It was a tale of a fragile bird, her tiny wings trembling in the confines of a crude cage, her song silenced by captivity. The Prophet Muhammad, with his boundless compassion, saw her plight and gently persuaded her captor to release her. When the cage door was opened, Leila fluttered out hesitantly, her frail body trembling with the unfamiliar taste of freedom, as if the vast sky itself was too grand for her small, broken spirit.

Salma's life mirrored Leila's sorrowful captivity. Her hands were calloused and worn from the endless scrubbing of floors, and her dreams lay crumpled like forgotten paper in a dusty corner of her reality. At night, she gazed through the cracked window of her tiny home, imagining the stars as the bars of a celestial cage, keeping her tethered to her drudgery.

Yet, like the sparrow, she yearned for the open skies so her weary soul could stretch and breathe and she could claim for herself the song of a life she'd never known. Every time she heard the story, she felt the mercy and benevolence of the Prophet, who rescues every living being from trouble and sets them free. Salma believed that one day she would also be free from the bondage of slavery and poverty that her father had got her entangled in. Yet she prayed for the *khyariaat* of her father before Allah. Whatever he may be, Ismail was her father and she adored him.

Apart from her father and siblings, there was also one more person Salma adored. That was her friend Faheen. Faheen was the son of Rehman Miyaan, an affluent businessman in their village. Faheen was around four years older than Salma and was studying in a city college, but they shared a unique bond of friendship. Faheen was tall and stout and soberly handsome. Faheen claimed to love Salma and made vows of doing nikah with her someday. He was enthralled by Salma's large doe eyes, spotlessly fair, creamy skin, long, pitch-black hair that emitted the radiance of newly extracted coal, and luscious lips that would turn redder when he sucked them. Often, around midnight, Salma would sneak out of her house and meet Faheen at the playground. Faheen would narrate to her tales of immortal lovers, and she would listen with utmost attention. Most of these tales were taken from contemporary Hindi films. Faheen would then kiss her passionately and hold her in his arms for a long time. Faheen was the only ray of hope in Salma's life, otherwise full of despair. Her cherished possession was a multi-coloured dupatta that Faheen had lovingly picked up for her from the town market of Belthara. He had draped it over her shoulders when presenting it. The dupatta, in vibrant hues of red, yellow and emerald, had intricate golden flowers that shimmered like captured sunlight. It was a gift of love, tenderly given, a token of promises whispered in quiet corners and laughter shared under the endless skies in the playground. The fabric, soft yet sturdy, carried his scent for days, a lingering reminder of his warmth.

Salma's second sibling, Fatima, was fourteen; she was adopted at the age of eight by a distant relative of Salma, Mansoor Chacha and Azeema Chachi, who did not have children. They were fairly affluent and sympathized with the piteous condition of Ismail's children. Thus even though Fatima knew about her biological parents and siblings, she lived with her foster parents in their house in Belthara but visited Pharsatar rarely.

Salma loved Fatima and used to wait for her visits eagerly. Being almost of the same age group, she was Salma's confidant. With time, they developed an intense bond of friendship with each other. They chatted till midnight when Fatima visited Pharsatar. Fatima hated their Abbu and the way he treats her sisters. Once she had suggested Salma to run away with Faheen and marry him. She said that was the only way Salma could escape the miseries of her life. However, Salma thought of Roshni, Zeenat, Shabnam and Milap who were only nine, eight, six and five years old and Saamiya who was only three and discarded the thought of eloping with Faheen. Meeting Faheen every night was her way of beating the abominable smell of tannery and local alcohol that came from Ismail's body as he slept on the floor and snored after satiating his frustrations by beating his daughters. To protect her sisters, Salma would take the brunt of his brutality most of the days and then weep in the embrace of Faheen to find some solace. Faheen would be terribly annoyed with Ismail and swore to kill him one day. He could not understand how someone could beat his own children like a beast.

It was the sacred time of Ramadan. The days began with *suhur* and ended with the iftar festivities. Salma had heard about the *thawab* of *fard*, the spiritual rewards of fasting during Ramadan, and religiously observed all the customs. Salma used to wait eagerly for Eid. This time she had managed to save a little money despite her Abbu having extorted most of it from her. She had entrusted it with Fareeda Khala. She wanted to get new dresses stitched for her sisters on Eid and gift Ismail a new kurta. She felt upset to see her Abbu in the same torn kurta that he had worn for several years. She knew her Abbu hated his daughters, but unlike Fatima she didn't hate her Abbu; she didn't blame him for being a tyrant. What more could a man do, torn between poverty and the liability of seven daughters. Salma could not match the wrinkled face of her Abbu with the broken-framed photograph that hung on the wall of their room showing Abbu when he was a teenager. He looked like a Shehzada. Salma prayed before Allah on each day of Ramadan to give *khushhali* to Ismail, even if it was to be in exchange for her own happiness.

One morning before Eid, Ismail said he had to go to Bambai to attend his friend Sulaiman's son's nikah. Sulaiman had sent two train tickets for them so that Salma could go too. If she went, she could take part in the dance and festivities at the wedding and Sulaiman would gift her a lump-sum *eedi*, the cash gift given to younger members of the family by parents and relatives during Eid. Salma had been hearing of Sulaiman chacha often from her Abbu. They had been childhood friends. She had heard about how Sulaiman chacha had stolen his Ammi's treasure and run away to Bambai, where he had made a fortune for himself. Sulaiman chacha ran a chain of businesses in Bambai and was a rich man. All of Pharsatar talked about his success.

Salma was thrilled. For once she wanted a break from her dull, monotonous life of slogging like a donkey all day, from taking care of her sisters. She happily agreed to go along with Ismail. Her father sent a smirk her way and asked her to dress well, pretending to be unaware of the fact that Salma did not have even a single decent dress to wear. Salma nodded and kept quiet. On hearing that Ismail had asked Salma to go with him to Bambai, both Fareeda Khala and Faheen became suspicious. They did not want Salma to go anywhere with her rogue father. They did not trust Ismail's intentions. After all, he had been selling Saziya's jewellery and the furniture in his house, and had been caught many a time stealing at the tannery to buy alcohol. Faheen warned Salma about her father. He could slip to the worst level of treachery to satiate his addiction. Salma tried to convince them that Ismail was her Abbu, after all, and he would do no harm to his own child, who was his own blood, that too during the sacred time of Ramadan.

Fareeda Khala did not say anything. She gave Salma a beautiful dress to wear for the wedding and asked her to be very careful since Bambai was a very big city with thousands of people. Salma smiled and thanked Fareeda. She requested Fareeda to look after her sisters till her return, to which she happily agreed. The night before Salma was supposed to leave with Ismail, she met Faheen at the playground and hugged him tight. Faheen requested her, for one last time, not to accompany her Abbu and to stay back, but Salma's faith in her father was so strong that she turned a deaf ear to Faheen's warnings. She pecked him on his cheek and asked him to miss her till she returned.

The next morning Salma woke up at dawn. Fatima had arrived the night before to stay with their sisters till Salma was back from Bambai. It was only a matter of seven days, so no one took it as a big deal. Salma briefed Fatima about the work to be done. There were days when there was nothing at their house to cook or eat, and Salma and her sisters would starve together till Fareeda Khala sent some food or Faheen stole some money from his Abbu's wallet and gave Salma. Salma knew the pain of starvation so well that she asked Fareeda for some money, which she promised to repay by working a few extra hours for her after she came back, and left enough food in the house for at least three to four days so that Fatima would not go berserk hearing the helpless screams of her sisters for a little food or milk.

Salma wore Fatima's salwar kameez. It was a bit small for her, but she somehow managed to squeeze into it. She followed Ismail on the narrow road of their village that led to the bus stop. As she left their mud hut, she hugged her sisters, especially Roshni, who wept bitterly and insisted on going with her. Salma's heart sank to see her cry so helplessly, and for a fleeting moment she thought of not going with Ismail and staying back. But the temptation of a lump-sum *eedi* was too great for her to resist. She followed Ismail silently down the dusty, rugged road of their village.

They reached the bus stop and waited for the bus to arrive. Salma saw many villagers standing in a queue and waiting. As the bus came, they started boarding it hurriedly. As Salma walked towards the bus, Ismail took her to the back of the bus, showing her a ladder that stood by the side of the bus. He asked her to climb the ladder and go to the top of the bus. Salma was scared. She was already nervous to see how overcrowded the bus was and how the people pushed each other still to make it inside the vehicle, like bees crowding together to build a hive. Though it was the early hours of the day, it was swelteringly hot. Ismail screamed at Salma. As Salma approached the ladder a man pushed her rear upwards very roughly, and she had no option but to climb the ladder. The top of the bus was also crowded, but Ismail, who climbed up the ladder right after Salma, managed to get a place for both of them to sit.

The next two hours were horrible. The ride was very jerky on account of the rough road and the frequent, sudden braking of the bus to avoid hitting herds of domestic animals that often crossed the road. The scorching sun made Salma perspire badly and left her back burning. There were drops of sweat all over her tender face, sharp nose and velvet lips. Her deeply oiled hair fluttered in the summer heat and blustery wind, as if Allah was blowing away her dreams and aspirations. Salma felt weird. Intuitively, she felt something eerie was about to happen. Her salwar kameez was stuck to her body from the profuse sweating. She hardly knew that the clothes clinging to her body were a metaphor of the tragic fate that was to stick to her body and soul throughout her life.

Reaching the tiny railway station of Pharsatar and seeing their train waiting for them was pure bliss. As Salma boarded the train to Mumbai with Ismail, she gazed at the skies from the compartment's window and breathed the air of her village which bade her adieu. She saw Faheen standing by the station clock and waving at her. Salma hummed, '*Aaj phir jeene ki tamanna hai/Aaj phir marne ka iradaa hai*!' as if to remind herself of her exalted status of diva. Faheen stood on the crowded platform, hidden among strangers, his body blending into the throng but his heart tethered to her. His eyes, desperate and searching, found her through the blur of the movement and noise all around. She was a vision of innocence, her delicate beauty framed by the fading light of dusk. The multi-coloured dupatta he had once draped over her shoulders fluttered faintly in the breeze. That sight would be a cruel reminder of all that would soon be lost. His chest ached with an unbearable weight, a desperate longing to call her name, to run to her, to hold her one last time. But he remained frozen, rooted in the moment, knowing that this was the end. The girl he loved – her laughter, her softness, her unguarded joy – would slip away from his life forever, swallowed by the distance that the train would carry her into.

She turned, just for a fleeting second, and their eyes met. Her gaze held everything she couldn't say, an unspoken apology wrapped in sorrow, a goodbye that neither of them wanted to say. In that moment, time slowed and the world shrank to just the two of them, two hearts breaking silently amidst the clamour of strangers.

The train lurched forward, its wheels screeching against the iron tracks, as if protesting the inevitability of their parting. She sat by the window, her face turned outward, the wind teasing strands of her hair. Her eyes, though fixed on the passing fields, betrayed a quiet storm. It had unshed tears pooling at the edges, refusing to fall. She didn't look back, not yet, for fear that one glance would break her resolve and undo her entirely.

As the train gathered speed, her face blurred behind the dust kicked up by its motion. Faheen raised his hand in a futile gesture, but the distance was already too great for her to see him. Her form disappeared into the horizon, leaving him with nothing but the scent of her memory and the echo of all they could have been. His love, fierce and unyielding, would remain forever in the shadow of that moment – she would be an untouchable beauty lost to time, a fleeting innocence he would never hold again.

The journey was long and tedious. Salma sat quietly in her seat looking out at the stations, fields and roads that disappeared within moments. The compartment was badly crowded and Salma could feel many men staring at her. She sat uneasily. She broke her fast post sunset on the train and had bread and water that she had brought from home. Ismail kept drinking alcohol from a bottle he had kept by his side. As the night grew older, Salma fell off to sleep.

She woke up with a jolt as the train suddenly braked and came to a stop. Her head was spinning badly. She slowly sat up in her seat, rubbed her eyes and peeped out through the caged window of the compartment curiously. It was not any railway station, but somewhere in the middle of the earth – a piece of land with hard, brown soil, cracked at frequent intervals. There were no trees or people anywhere in this deserted place. She saw a flock of sparrows chirping, sitting on the wires that ran parallel to the railway track and thus to their train. Now it started to rain and the birds were drenched wet. It appeared as if they were arguing over some serious agenda. Salma noticed drops of water falling down from the wires. She could now clearly smell the exotic fragrance of rain and soil, which overpowered the foul odour of country liquor and tobacco that suffused the entire compartment. She closed her eyes, took a deep breath to take in the smell of petrichor and looked at the sky. The colour of the sky was a blend of black and grey, a mysterious veil of mighty clouds hiding the lustre of the infant sun. Salma had been waking up at dawn every day, but she had never witnessed such an enigmatic sight before at this hour. The train was moving slowly now after a brief halt. Salma gazed at the sultry landscape; she thought the earth must be feeling as thrilled as she did every time Faheen touched her. She felt coy and blushed. Suddenly, she felt a push on her shoulder; '*Khirki kya tera baap bandh karega? Paani aa raha hai*!' Salma turned back and looked at Ismail. He was drunk and his eyes were red. Shouting at Salma, he shut the window with a bang and went back to sleep in his seat.

Salma looked inside the compartment. It was a complete antithesis of the view outside. There were almost twenty people inside that she could see; a few of them were smoking beedis while the others were snoring. Their snores sounded like the guttural roars of wild animals. The compartment was dirty and messy with piles of waste scattered here and there. Salma saw a gigantic man with decaying teeth smiling at her nastily. She was scared. She pulled her dupatta quickly over her head and leant back in her seat to escape that horrible sight. Soon she fell asleep.

When she woke up, it was almost afternoon. The rains had stopped and she could see the sun shining bright. Someone must have opened the window, she thought. She saw Ismail sitting and lazily scratching his cheeks. Salma wanted to go to the washroom. She approached Ismail to show her the way. He asked her to walk towards the end of the compartment. Salma was afraid to go there by herself, but she had no option but to manage it by herself. She walked to the washroom and opened the door, only to gag at the combined fetid and pungent odour of urine and stools. Everywhere in the tiny washroom there was human excreta and saliva. There was no water at all in there. Salma ran back to her seat and sat quietly, controlling her urine. She felt like crying. She felt like going back home, but the temptation of visiting the city of Bambai was too strong for her to resist. So she sat like a stone in her seat as the train ran like a hungry cheetah. After an hour, when it became impossible for her to control herself, she just had to visit the washroom, where she both peed and vomited out of disgust. She came back to the compartment, drank some water and sat quietly.

She saw Ismail eating the bread and curry that she had brought from home. Not even once did he offer her some. Salma opened her bag, took out a banana and ate it. It was almost late evening. She leaned back in her seat and thought of her sisters and Faheen. What must they be doing now? She missed them all badly. She wanted this journey to get over soon.

The next morning, Salma woke up to a strange noise resembling a cacophony of people quarrelling. She woke up to realize that the train had screeched to a halt at a really big and chaotic station where crowds spilled out like a dam bursting its banks. No sooner did she try to discern where she was than she heard Ismail shouting at her, '*Bambai aa gya! Jaldi utar!*' Saying this, he almost pushed her towards the exit door of the compartment.

An utterly confused Salma held her bag to her bosom as she got down from the train. People were rushing about like swarms of ants. All the trains she could see were overcrowded. Salma could hear a lady shouting out platform numbers and names of the trains at the top of her voice. Salma had never seen such commotion ever in her life. She nervously followed Ismail. They walked out of the railway station and stood before the taxi stand. Salma saw the drivers of the *kaali-peeli* (black and yellow) taxis bargaining with customers. The air of the city hit her first – thick, salty, and alive with noise. Clutching her frayed cloth bag tightly, she stepped onto the platform, dwarfed by the towering iron arches of the station. Her feet moved with the tide of passengers, most like her, hailing from Bihar and Uttar Pradesh, their bundles wrapped in faded sarees or jute sacks, their faces etched with the same mix of exhaustion and guarded hope.

Outside, the scene even more overwhelming. Black-and-yellow taxis, their boxy Premier Padmini frames dented and faded from years of wear and tear, stood queued in uneven rows. The smell of diesel fumes mixed with the sharp tang of vada pav and the sweat of hundreds of jostling bodies. Taxi drivers, most of them in white kurtas or undershirts, leaned against their cars, chewing paan or calling out to the arriving passengers. Their language was a medley of gruff Marathi, snatches of Hindi and the occasional Bhojpuri, their accents thick and their words quick, like the city itself.

'*Arre, chalna hai ki nahi? Meter se hi jaunga!*' one driver barked, his hand resting on the door of his taxi. Another argued with a man from her train, a fellow from Gorakhpur, over the fare to Byculla. '*Do rupiya meter se upar lega? Yeh loot hai!*' the man shouted. The driver spat out a red streak of paan on the pavement and shrugged, his voice indifferent. '*Bhai, Mumbai mein sab mehnga hai. Chalna hai toh chalo.*'

The taxis themselves seemed tired, their black paint chipped and their yellow roofs faded from years under the sun. The interiors were no better – the torn seats were patched with duct tape, the windows fogged with grime. There were tiny plastic gods glued to their dashboards. Yet they hummed with purpose, ready to weave through the city's endless maze of traffic.

She watched all of this, with a pang of nervousness mixed with awe. This was Bambai – a place that swallowed you whole, where the din of voices and the honk of horns felt like a never-ending orchestra. She clutched her bag tighter. There was great trepidation in her heart. She knew she was stepping into a world unlike anything she'd ever known.

After a minute or so, she saw Ismail greet a man.

'*Salaam alaikum Maalik*,' Ismail grinned and hugged the man. He also asked Salma to greet him.

The man was unusually tall, dark and bearded. He looked straight into Salma's eyes, smiled wickedly, and retorted, '*Walaikume salaam*.'

Salma remembered the bloodthirsty hyenas that used to come cackling into their village hunting for pet pigeons, hens and goats. Many a time she had seen them carrying away their prey by their teeth. Salma's heart was beating fast. Ismail asked her to get into a taxi. The hyena-man sat next to her and watched her with dilated eyes and a filthy smile. Salma was feeling thirsty. He gave her a bottle of Limca and asked her to drink it. Salma drank it out of fear. After that everything turned black.

'*Aapa o Aapa! Kya huaa? Kyun ro rahi ho, Aapa*?'

Salma was woken up by Annu. Salma looked frightened and was sweating badly. It was almost two decades ago that she had been sold by her Abbu to Maalik and his brothers, who tormented her for some time and threw her unconscious in the Chauda Galli of Kamathipura, thinking her to be dead. But as Maalik had said, '*Tujh mein bohot jaan hai.*' Salma had regained consciousness. From then on, numerous hyenas had raped her and beaten her up till she learnt the craft of taking all this as a means of her survival, and with time, the quiet, calm and serene Salma transformed into a bolder and wiser version of herself, known as Aapa. Yet something of the old Salma remained deeply buried inside her – her memories of Faheen, her momories of her village, her sisters, of Fareeda Khala, of those several known faces who adored her. But time, cruel and unyielding, had unravelled her story in a different and merciless world. The days of whispered secrets and tender touches had dissolved into shadows, and fate had thrust her into a very dark reality. Their paths had diverged, yet Faheen's absence left a void she couldn't fill. As she struggled to survive, her innocence was slowly stripped away by the constant poverty and exploitation she endured. The world that once seemed hopeful and where she could dream, now turned cold and unforgiving, pulling her into the shadows of society where names were forgotten and dignity became a currency she no longer possessed.

Through it all, the dupatta gifted her by her beloved Faheen remained. Kept folded carefully in a corner of her small, dimly lit room, it was her one connection to a past life she could barely relate to now. On nights when the weight of the world pressed too heavily against her chest, she would take it out, letting the fabric spill over her lap like a river of lost time. The golden flowers, though faded and tarnished, still glimmered faintly in the flickering light of the single bulb in her room, whispering of the girl she once was – a girl who had believed in love, in tomorrow, in herself.

She would press the dupatta to her face, the faint scent of her past still clinging to it, and for a moment she felt she could feel his touch, hear his voice and remember what it was to be cherished. Though life had stolen her innocence and dragged her into a world she could never have even imagined, the dupatta remained her talisman – a fragile reminder of a love that once made her feel whole, and of the person she had been before the world turned her into someone else.

2

The Jungle is Alive

The phenomenon of predation has a bizarre history of evolution. Dating back to more than a billion years from now, predation has been an integral part of the cosmos, emphasizing the Darwinian concept of *survival of the fittest*, where the world is perhaps an impervious and pathless jungle, full of feral carnivores. The zones beyond our heads or beneath our feet are also not free from predators; they stay alert constantly searching for prey, tearing them apart by their blatant jaws or sharp claws and feasting on their flesh.

With the dominance of human species in scientific and technological innovations, society has progressed towards development and modernization, yet the curse of predation reigns superior within every layer of our society. The act of predation has taken such rampant form in this century that in each second a predator is compelled to kill a prey in some corner of the earth for the sake of survival.

The vicious game between the hunter and the hunt thus continues, shamelessly crushing the notions of humanity, relationships, ethics and compassion.

Here a father preys on his child, without so much as a shudder, for the cause of survival. Brutal is the world in which we live, where every day is a battle of survival.

Maalik and his brothers had raped Salma multiple times, leaving her half dead next to a gutter in the Chauda Galli of Kamathipura. When Salma regained consciousness, she found herself wrapped in a dirty sack. She could hardly move or even breathe. Salma thought she had died and had been transported to some hell by Allah for some sins she had committed. After a long time, someone opened the mouth of the sack. It was an animal, a dog and not a human being. The dog smelt the sack and tried to figure out if there was anything edible inside. Seeing a human body, the dog ran away. Salma peeped out from inside the sack. It was night time and she could see a long pavement in front of her. There were street lamps and buildings on both sides of the street. Under her back was a huge gutter which stank. Hundreds of mosquitoes were now biting her. She wanted to step out of the sack, but how could she, the men had left her naked. Salma put her hands on her face and wept bitterly. She remembered her sisters, she remembered her village, she remembered Fareeda Khala, she remembered Faheen. Destiny had been so cruel towards her. Poverty was the most malicious element in the world. It had made her own Abbu sell her for the sake of some money. It occurred to her that someday he might even sell her sisters. That thought chilled her to the very bone. She became so frightened at the thought of Roshni or Zeenat in her condition that she became nearly hysterical. Suddenly she heard a voice: '*Chuhiya ko andar se nikal!*' It was a strange, commanding voice. She could not make out whether it was a male or female voice. In a few seconds she saw a pair of black, densely haired hands pulling her out of the sack. She hesitated to come out of the sack but those hands forced her out of it. What Salma saw now frightened her even more. There were six people standing around her. They looked like men but were in women's attire; all of them were in sarees and started clapping madly seeing her. They were eunuchs, hijras, understood Salma. One of them came close to her and covered her body with a piece of cloth. 'JAMUNA!' shouted the one who gave her the cloth, '*Hijraa galli mein kisne yeh heera fek ke gya re!*' she giggled, '*isko Maya ke paas chhod aa*,' she ordered, and left. The others followed her. The eunuch named Jamuna helped Salma get up, offered her water and made her sit in a rickshaw, which soon rode into the darkness somewhere. Jamuna dropped Salma in front of an old, rugged building and left. Salma looked around. A thin man, possibly in his middle sixties, with a beedi in his mouth, was looking at her. Curiously, he asked Salma, '*Kaun hai be tu?*' Before Salma could reply, a coarse voice from inside the building ordered, '*Chiriya ko andar leke aa, Siraj!*' Siraj took Salma inside. Salma saw a man seated there with many women around him. The women were all decked up in sarees, garlands of mogra and caricatured make-up. They were sitting like puppets. The man was very fat, bald, whitish complexioned, and had a thick moustache. He came closer to Salma and shouted, addressing everyone in the room, '*Main isko chakkhta hoon.*' Saying that he pushed Salma on to a couch in the room and removed the cloth wrapped around her. Salma could see everyone in the room laughing and excited, as if they were about to experience something exotic. The man opened his trousers and asked Salma to take his male organ in her mouth. Salma had no power left in her. She could barely stand, forget protest. She silently took the disgusting thing in her mouth and waited for the next instruction, like a robot. The man caught her hair and jerked away. This continued for some time till Salma fainted. When she woke up she found herself in a room. Her body was still swollen and bruised all over. She noticed two women decking her up with tons of make-up. One of them told her that she had been unconscious for more than three days, that she had already been ravished and torn apart by three customers, and that Anna Shetty, the owner of the brothel, had called in the doctor, who had treated her with the necessary medications. Today she had been auctioned to two customers who had agreed to pay double the normal rate, and they would destroy her together at the same time. Salma smiled sadly. She stood up and faced the mirror. Tears rolled down her cheeks. Finally she had been turned into a professional prostitute meant to spread her legs before any man who would pay her money. She thought it would have been better had she died inside the sack that night. She could not fathom why the benevolent Allah was being so brutally unkind towards her. She had landed in a pit from where there was no escape.

Days passed like a blunt knife passes through the bones; dragging, stuck and agonizing. The rooms where she spent her blurry days were all dark and suffocating, the air thick with the stench of sweat, cheap perfume and despair. They reminded her of a snake pit she had once seen in her now almost faded village, a writhing darkness of venomous creatures, their fangs ready to strike at the slightest movement. Here, too, danger slithered in unseen, coiled in the shadows, waiting to poison what little humanity she had left in her. The men who came were no different from those snakes – hunters, predators, their touch cold and calculating, leaving behind invisible bites that festered deep within her soul. Women like her were trapped in these dungeons of satanic hell, forced to smile through their suffering, their once-bright eyes dulled like those creatures who had learned not to hope for escape. Every night she felt the venom seep further into her, numbing the girl she used to be, as if this pit were consuming not just her body but her very existence. With a cold sigh, she took the lipstick from the shelf and started the drama of painting up for public consumption.

Twenty-five years had passed. Salma had survived the netherworld of Kamathipura, selling her body day after day in exchange for money. She was the most beautiful prostitute in Anna Shetty's brothel. She had weathered the wrath of the demonic Maya, the Madam of the brothel, every single day because of her beauty, which remained untarnished despite the appalling assaults and abuses, and despite her being forcibly drugged every day. She had seen and experienced the nastiness and repugnance of the fraternity of commercial sex trade. Maya had sold her in the hustling red-light district of Khidderpore in Kolkata, where circumstances were even worse than in Mumbai, to teach her a lesson for being demure. Khidderpore was the dock town of Kolkata and housed the third largest red-light area of the city, Sonagachi and Kalighat being the first and second. Kidderpore, with its damp, narrow streets and towering warehouses, exuded the gritty essence of the sea. The port town pulsed with the relentless rhythm of labour – the creaks of rusted cranes straining under heavy loads, the shouts of dockworkers hauling bales of jute and the occasional mournful whistle of a departing steamer. The air was a heady mixture of brine, diesel fumes and the musty odour of aging wood clinging stubbornly to the crumbling colonial structures and the sweat-soaked garments of those who worked along the docks. The tangy smell of the Hooghly River lingered everywhere, mingled with the acrid smells of tar and rusting metal. Ships of varying sizes swayed gently in the harbour, their chipped paint and groaning masts telling silent tales of countless journeys. Along the waterfront, labourers moved ceaselessly, their voices raised in exertion as the metallic clinks of chains harmonized with the distant, low hum of the steamers.

From across the seas and distant lands, sailors, merchants and labourers disembarked here, their faces etched with the toll of endless days spent under the unforgiving sun or enduring the monotony of rolling waves. For these men, setting foot on land was not an occasion for celebration but a reminder of their solitude. Kidderpore's shadowy alleys offered little solace, instead amplifying the void that each man carried within. The exhaustion on their faces betrayed their vulnerability, and for many, fleeting distractions became their only refuge. The brothels of Kidderpore, tucked into dingy alleys, waited like silent sentinels, ready to offer them some fleeting respite. Their weathered doors, with their coat of peeling paint, opened into spaces where melodies played on the harmonium drifted out lazily, blending with soft laughter and murmured promises. Men entered these establishments with uneasy steps, their postures betraying a mix of longing and unease. Some strode in with exaggerated confidence, masking their shame with boisterous talk and forced laughter. Others slinked in quietly, heads lowered, their worn clothes and salt-stained boots speaking of distant lives and rough journeys. They clutched their hard-earned wages tightly to their bodies as they haggled in broken Bengali or Hindi, in accents betraying their roots from lands far beyond this city.

Inside, the women greeted them with practised smiles, their faces painted in bright colours that failed to hide the weariness beneath. Dressed in garish sarees or overly ornamented salwar kameez, they moved with a precision born of routine, offering a hollow warmth to men desperate for a reprieve from their harsh lives. For the sailors and labourers, these encounters were brief moments of escape – fleeting chances to forget the harshness and aching emptiness of their lives.

The women of Khidderpore faced hell in the name of sex trade. Salma was no exception. She had been constantly raped by gangs of men, from different tribes, some soldiers, and many of them terribly brutal. One day her pimp put her before a group of men and she ended up bleeding so profusely that she was admitted in hospital. There she ran away to escape the horrors of the brothel. But where could a woman like her escape to? Who would offer her a hand of help without exploiting her? Everywhere Salma found predators, red in tooth and claw, ready to prey on her flesh. Finding no other refuge, she returned to Kamathipura, fell at the feet of Maya and begged her to let her stay there. The vindictive Maya agreed but in return peddled Salma to the worst of customers, the most perverted of the lot in exchange of double the standard money. They were the type who feasted not only on her flesh but also on her soul. Salma soon became a machine, mechanized to satisfy the abominable lust of men. Eventually she became a living corpse as she aged and was substituted by newer groups of younger girls who were trafficked from different parts of the country, who were as helpless as she had been in her youth.

Salma hated the gods every moment of her life, yet she read all the namaz, fasted during every Ramadan and visited mosques. What she achieved as a reward was perhaps the name 'Aapa' and a band of women companions, each of whom had a heart wrenching tale of their own to tell. Thus emerged Salma's new identity – that of an older and wiser woman. As Maya asked Salma to train a bunch of new girls in the craft of prostitution, Salma started interacting with them. The girls eventually ended up calling her 'Aapa', a term of address for an elder sister, because of her kindness and generosity. She bathed their wounds, fed them and made them understand the most important bottom-line of their lives – that since there was no escape for them, they must embrace the rule of the jungle instead of trying to fight against the beasts. Salma had met hundreds of men who came to her as customers but never experienced the emotion of love or affection with any. Neither did she want a partner for herself, unlike many of the women of Kamathipura who always fell into the trap of attachment. Aapa vaguely remembered herself as Salma, having long surrendered her name to time and the life she lived. She was no longer the young girl who had arrived here with a heart full of resistance; now, her weary body and soft, lined face bore the stories of a thousand nights spent in survival. She had long ceased to dream of changing this life she lived. Yet, in the midst of this world of grime and sorrow, a connection had indeed blossomed – a connection she had neither sought nor expected – with Sujan, a bus driver from Bihar.

Sujan was a man of quiet strength, his wiry frame hardened by years of navigating the chaos of Mumbai's streets. His hands, rough from the steering wheel, belied the gentle soul within. He had a family back in Bihar: a wife who waited for him, children who saw him as their distant provider. And yet he found himself returning to Kamathipura, not for the reasons most men ventured there for but for Aapa – for her laughter, her wry humour, her stories that mirrored his own struggles. What had started as a chance encounter had grown into something neither of them could fully define.

Sujan would sit on the floor of her room, leaning against the peeling walls as Aapa perched on the edge of her cot, her saree draped loosely over her frail shoulders. The air between them was often filled with his stories of home, tales of his children's pranks and the sprawling fields of his village. She would listen, her face softening, her laughter occasionally breaking through the heavy stillness. For those moments she forgot the weight of her world – the smell of sex, the harsh whispers of the women outside, the perpetual aches in her body. With Sujan she could be someone other than Aapa. She could simply be Salma. He cared for her in ways no one else ever had. When she fell ill, he brought her medicine, sitting by her side for hours as she drifted in and out of sleep. He would bring small gifts: a tin of ghee, a bag of rice, sometimes a garland of marigold that reminded her of the life she'd left behind. These gestures, simple but profound, spoke of a love that was both tender and doomed. She never asked him why he came or what he sought from her, but she knew the answer – it was for the same thing she sought from him. Companionship. Solace. A reminder that despite everything, they were still human.

But their love, if it could be called that, was as fragile as it was impossible. Sujan belonged to another life. He had a wife and children who depended on him. His world would never accept his bond with a woman like Aapa. She knew this, as surely as she knew that Kamathipura was her cage. The life she had been forced into decades ago had stripped her of any illusion that she could have a future outside its narrow lanes. And yet she held on to the moments they shared, hoarding them like precious coins in a world that had given her little else.

Sujan's visits eventually became less frequent. She could sense that the pull of his family and the weight of his responsibilities were drawing him away. And yet, when he visited he brought light to her dim room, laughter to her silence. In another world, another life, perhaps they could have been more. But in Kamathipura, love was a flower that bloomed in the darkness, destined to wither before it could see the sun. Still, for Aapa and Sujan, it was enough to have had it at all. In a world where love was a rarity, even the impossible kind was a treasure. Salma still remembered how Sujan wept like a baby to see her bruised body after she was tormented by some perverted customer.

Even after Salma had aged, Sujan kept supplying her money and groceries, whenever she was in need of them. In her otherwise hopeless life, life-less Salma had a friend in Sujan, for which she thanked Allah.

Salma's life took yet another turn after she started spending time with the band of the new girls she had met. She had witnessed the transformation in each of them, from simple docile village girls to out-and-out professionals who adopted the trade as their means of livelihood. Salma would take care of their children, go to the thriving cloth market of Kamathipura and buy dresses for them during the early hours of evening, when the infamous red-light area of Mumbai traded the finest quality of fabrics instead of flesh at the cheapest rates. The cloth merchants across the city and suburbs of Mumbai, and even novices from the fashion industry, would gather in Kamathipura every day. The tradition of selling clothes and fabric here went back to the times when the country was under British subjugation, and was to this day the same as before. Salma saw women from every stratum of society jostling with each other in the cloth market of Kamathipura for fabric, unaware that they often brushed shoulders with that category of women they considered abhorrent. This cloth market, with its shining and shimmering satin, cheap polyester, fancy Chinese lace and deep, warm velvet, had become a melting pot.

One such day, when Salma was bargaining for a gorgeous sharara that she wanted to buy for Rani, she saw a woman walking towards her. This woman was not from her world. She looked beautiful and different. She wore a peacock-blue Bengali dhakai saree (Salma recognized the saree as she had seen a few of the same type worn by her acquaintances who were from the state of West Bengal) and high-necked blouse. Her hair was neatly tied in a bun, which had a string of mogra around it. But what attracted Salma most about the woman were her eyes. There was something very mystical about her eyes. They were sharp and stern yet beautiful but had a strange tenderness to them too. While Salma was lost in her thoughts, she felt a soft pat on her shoulder: '*Aapa, kaise ho aap?*' Salma arranged her thoughts, came back to reality and saw the same woman standing, just by her side, smiling. Now she knew who it was; it was that officer Didi, whom she and her friends had met in the big post office a few days before. Salma felt awkward. She was embarrassed to find a woman of such high stature talking to her, regarding her as her 'Aapa'. She stood in silence. The woman asked her softly, '*Aapa, aapka aur aapke saahelio ka ghar kidhar hai?*' Salma felt the stir of deep shame. She did not want this woman to know where they lived and under what circumstances. She turned and walked away hastily, not answering her. She did not want to look back and check whether the woman is still there. Salma almost ran, escaped to her room, shut the door and took a sigh of relief.

Back in her room, she sat perturbed. Salma knew that they had no identity at all. They were mere commodities in this world, and even survival was a luxury for them. She trudged along to her small, broken room she had lovingly called home for years, yet now it seemed colder, emptier. The walls, once adorned with cheap posters and over-blown images of the cinema heroines of yesteryears, had become a pale reflection of her own life – peeling, cracked, and weathered by time. She sat on the edge of the creaky cot, her dupatta loosely draped over her thinning shoulders, staring at her reflection in a broken mirror. The woman staring back at her was a stranger. The kohl that once highlighted her almond-shaped eyes now emphasized the hollows beneath them. Her cheeks were sunken, her lips cracked, and the vibrant rouge that once danced on her face now felt like a pathetic attempt to mask what time had stolen. Silently as a mouse, she rose, and from the dusty confines of her meagre possessions she took out that brown, faded, torn, hardly-there dupatta and caressed her cheeks with it. To will herself to smell a waft of what remained of her innocence and coy love – her Faheen. All the iridescence of the fabric had been lost to the passage of time.

The irony was not lost on her. Years ago, when she first stepped into this world – wide-eyed, frightened, and yet strangely hopeful – she was heralded for her youth and beauty. Men had fought over her, their gazes devouring her, their money flowing freely for even a moment in her company. Her charm was her currency, her body her ticket to survival in a life she had never chosen but had learned to endure. Back then, she had despised their hunger but had grown to rely on it. Her presence in those dimly lit rooms was celebrated, though her laughter was rehearsed and her movements deliberate. She had been someone then – desirable, needed, sought after.

But now everything had changed. Her body, once her livelihood, had betrayed her. The inevitable passage of time had turned her from an object of desire into one that fetched only disregard. Clients no longer looked at her; they chose the younger girls, fresh faces with fresh skin and the same naive desperation she once carried. The men who had once lined up at her door now avoided her completely, as though her age rendered her invisible. Even the younger sex workers in the brothel treated her with a mix of pity and disdain, almost like rebelling teenagers ridiculing their mother, whispering about her in corners, their voices laced with the silent fear of what they might one day become.

The rejection cut deeper than she cared to admit. Her existence had always been transactional, and now even that was denied to her. The irony was cruel – she had given everything she had to this profession, and now, when she needed it most, it had nothing left to offer her. Her beauty, the very thing that had trapped her, was gone. And with it, so was her sense of worth. Her pathos lay not just in the loss of youth but also in the realization that she had never truly owned herself. Her beauty had been her prison, her body her currency, and now that currency was deemed worthless. She tried to imagine a life beyond these walls but was met with nothing but a void. She had no family to return to, no skills to trade, and no place in a world that had always shunned her.

And yet there was something within her that refused to give in completely to this hopelessness. But it wasn't hope – hope had left her long ago – but a quiet determination, a stubbornness born out of the need to survive. She had endured so much already: the leering gazes, the cruel hands, the constant degradation. Perhaps there was a way forward, even if she couldn't see it now. Perhaps she could find a sliver of dignity in the world, which had offered her none so far.

For now, though, she sat in the dim light of her room, caught between the ghosts of her past and the uncertainty of her future. The path ahead was unclear, but she knew one thing: she would not let the darkness consume her. Not yet.

A flicker of defiance stirred within her – a fragile ember that refused to be extinguished. Perhaps there was dignity to be found in carving a new path for herself, however uncertain or unkind it might be. But for now she sat in that room, caught between the past that had consumed her and the future that loomed like a shadow before her, its edges frayed with doubt.

Salma realized that each of them was merely a bird with broken wings. They were physically alive but caged for eternity, denied all rights to explore the sky. Yet the very fact of their being alive gave them a dim ray of hope – of witnessing better days in the future, of gifting a better tomorrow to their children to overcome the hate and exile that they had faced all their lives.

3

And Dream of Sheep

The heritage tower clock of the Chhatrapati Shivaji Maharaj Terminus railway station, a solid reminder of the British era in India, struck twice. It had been diligently showing time to the restless metropolis of Mumbai for the last one hundred and thirty-five years. It was already two in the afternoon. The digital announcement system of the railway station intimated the departure of the Mumbai-Howrah Duronto Express exactly after seven minutes from platform number eighteen of the gigantic railway station. Annu was running towards that platform, rolling along a suitcase that ran equally fast. She could not afford to miss the train to Howrah, which would leave the station soon. She crossed innumerable stalls, trolleys, waiting rooms, ticket counters and passengers as she sped towards it desperately, like an eagle flying after its prey, cutting through fierce winds. Her uncombed hair flew all over. Her yellow cotton saree with red roses printed on it proved its loyalty to her by covering her bosom and body, like a valiant warrior protecting his ruler. Annu's oval face with its wide forehead was full of droplets of sweat that dripped off her perfect jawline. She rubbed her sweat away as she ran incessantly uttering the name of God; '*Joy Bholanath*!' Within the next one minute she reached the platform and rushed past the compartments to find hers. She bumped into a ticket collector who would have almost lost his balance and fallen, had Annu not caught him by his hand. '*O dada, yeh dabba kaunsi hai*?' she asked the ticket collector, showing him her ticket. The ticket collector grinned and replied that it was right after the compartment they were standing next to. '*Joy Bholanath*,' exclaimed Annu, touching her folded hands to her forehead and running again, till she got inside her compartment and checked her seat number. No sooner had she sat in her reserved seat than the train blew its final whistle and started to move. '*beche gechi baba!*' Annu shouted into the air to announce that she had been saved. She wore a smile of triumph.

After that nail-biting finish to the train, her hard wooden seat now seemed to her a royal throne, and she gave herself a few moments of freedom to look properly at the majestic railway station. What a grand station, thought Annu. Her entire village was smaller than this railway station, she thought. She remembered that back in her village she had been the fastest runner among the children of her age group. Running had been her passion. Even now running had been thrust upon her, she thought. As a child she had participated in the Canning Town race and the judge had offered her free training in some athletic club in the city. But her father refused to send her, saying that people from social strata below lower middle class and confronted with many financial instabilities – commonly referred to as 'poor' – could never become famous. Annu had cried a lot, hoping to convince her father to change his mind, but it was all in vain. Yet Annu could never quit running. She had been running dauntlessly on the difficult, rough track of life for the last thirty-three years, and yet her speed was not worth it. Annu could feel her eyes moisten. She rubbed them hard. The woman sitting opposite her smiled. Annu smiled back vigorously and pushed her suitcase below her seat.

Trains in India are like Pegasus for ordinary Indians. One of the greatest contributions of the otherwise tyrannical British reign in India, the railways are perhaps the only means, apart from the postal system, that connected the country from end to end and made communication easier for people. Arranging herself in the window seat of the train, Annu tried to read what was written on the door of the compartment.. The colourfully inked inscription on the door said: 'The first train in India ran between Bori Bunder (Bombay) and Thane on 16th April, 1853. Annu had studied only up to eighth standard, and reading was a huge challenge for her, but Annu was curious. She requested one middle aged man who was passing across her seat, probably towards the washroom of the train, to read that for her. He smiled, read it and left. Annu was surprised! 1853! She counted how many years ago it must have been, but every time she calculated she arrived at a different number. Irritated, she gave up her futile exercise, looked around the train and saw that it was a brand new one. The seats still retained their polish and lustre. Annu was thrilled to travel in a brand-new train. She tried to memorize what the write-up said about the first train to run in India so that she could tell Beena and Ruma back home. 'Reading is indeed a difficult job,' she thought, and drank water from the bottle that Meena had given her as she left home. Annu was perspiring. Her olive complexion shone bright with the interplay of sunlight and sweat on her skin. She was soothed by the familiar cacophony of Bengalis all around her, as most of her fellow passengers were Bengali. The woman sitting opposite her noticed her and was all appreciative of her beauty. '*Boro shundor dekhte tomaare*! *Koi zaao*?' The lady was mostly likely in her mid-seventies, grey-haired, fair-skinned and plump. '*Haan Mashima. Deshe jacchi*,' ('Yes auntie, I am going to my native place,') replied Annu, with a big smile, and then looked the other way holding her excitement. She was not supposed to talk or be friends with anyone, she remembered. Looking outside the window, seeing the railway stations along the way vanishing in the blink of an eye, Annu realized it had been almost ten years since she had last visited her native place, Bhaleya.

Bhaleya was a small village in Canning Town in the South 24 Parganas district of West Bengal. It fell within the southern fringes of West Bengal, sitting quietly at the confluence of bustling life and serene wilderness, cradled by winding creeks and mangroves that reached out like ancient fingers towards the Bay of Bengal, their gnarled roots snaking into the marshy soil. Life here unfolded at a pace dictated by the tides, unhurried and steeped in tradition. The mornings arrived gently, with a mist that rolled in from the wetlands blanketing the hamlets in a cool embrace. As the sun rose, its golden light pierced the fog, revealing a mosaic of bamboo huts, tiled roofs and fishing nets drying on the ground.

The air was rich with earthy scents – wet soil, drying fish and the faint tang of salt because of the proximity of the village to the Sundarbans. Men in simple cotton dhotis and gamchas slung over their shoulders, their faces weathered by years of fishing under the unforgiving sun, prepared to set out on their dinghies. Women, draped in brightly coloured sarees, balanced clay pots of water on their hips, their bangles clinking as they chatted in soft, lilting tones. Some were already bent over handlooms, weaving intricate designs into the soft cotton that the village was known for, while others squatted outside their homes, tending to simmering pots of rice and dal.

The children were its heart, their laughter echoing through the narrow, uneven lanes. They ran barefoot, their feet hardened from years of chasing each other over rocky paths and patches of soft mud. In the mornings, some trudged reluctantly to the village school, their satchels slung haphazardly over their shoulders, while the others stayed behind, helping their families with chores or accompanying their fathers to the river. By midday they would return, ravenous and flushed, swarming around the clay ovens where their mothers prepared humble but hearty meals. Rice, the staple of the region, was accompanied by a medley of dishes – dal tempered with mustard seeds, freshly caught fish fried in mustard oil, and if fortune favoured them, a tangy curry made with green mangoes or tamarind.

Afternoons were slow, drowsy affairs, marked by the rhythmic creak of wooden carts and the distant hum of cicadas. In shaded courtyards, elderly men and women exchanged tales of days long past while chewing on betel leaves that stained their lips a deep red. Children, free from their brief obligations, gathered in groups, their voices rising with excitement as they played games with rudimentary toys – sticks, stones and whatever else nature provided. For the older boys, the marshy outskirts were a playground where they fished with handmade traps or climbed mangrove trees in search of crabs. Girls, on the other hand, often stayed closer to home, imitating their mothers as they practised cooking or braided each other's hair.

As evening fell, the town was bathed in a golden-orange glow. Lanterns flickered to life, casting long shadows on the walls of the huts. Smoke from the cooking fires spiralled into the dusky sky, carrying the scent of puffed rice, fried fish and steaming vegetable curries. Families gathered on their verandas, sharing meals on banana leaves. The younger children dozed off in their mother's laps. The quiet hum of life was punctuated by the croaking of frogs and the distant call of night birds from the mangroves.

Life here was not one of wealth or modernity, but it thrived on simplicity and resilience. The people here carried the rhythms of nature in their blood, bending their lives to its ebb and flow. The Sundarbans loomed in the distance, both a provider and a threat, and the people lived with its duality etched into their souls. It was a life of humble joys and quiet struggles, one where survival was its own kind of triumph and the bonds of community were as vital as the breath of the tide. That was Bhaleya; not even a miniscule speck in the cosmos of the universe. But it was the entire universe for people like Annu, who did not have the privilege of knowing, learning, or understanding the world through any education or theoretical knowledge.

Annu was born to Haradhon and Kalpana Dhali, who relocated from the Sunderbans to Bhaleya in search of a living much before she was born. Haradhon was a fisherman, sober by nature and appearance. Haradhon was about five foot eight, had a lean structure and was of a stark, dark complexion. His eyes were sunken and cheeks broken.

Kalpana was short, dark and fat with a perfectly round face, blunt nose, thick, long hair and elephantine eyes. Kalpana's forefathers belonged to the Munda tribe of the Sunderbans who were dynastic *laathiyals*, strong men equipped with lathis or canes to protect the kings and zamindars. They were worshippers of Bon Bibi, the guardian spirit of the forest, and Dakshin Roy, the revered deity who ruled over beasts and demons. As children, Annu and her younger sister Beena had heard hundreds of stories about the legendary gods and beasts of the Sunderbans from their mother, Kalpana. Beena was nine years younger than Annu and the apple of her eye. When Annu was ten or eleven, she would carry Beena on her shoulders and take her around the village to amuse her whenever she cried. Annu would often visit the little pond owned by her father and see how fish was captured using a net and then swim in the pond all day long to return home drenched and exhausted. Kalpana would scream at Annu every day for her boyish ways and for her uncombed hair and dirty frocks. With her wild curls and mischievous grin, Annu was a picture of rebellion. Her bare feet were quick as she darted between mustard fields, dragging her younger sister into her impromptu adventures. Beena, smaller and quieter, followed her dutifully, her wide eyes brimming with admiration and just a tinge of exasperation at Annu's untameable spirit.

One incident from her childhood still stood out in her mind. She must be thirteen or fourteen while Beena, four or five. That day she had taken Beena to the haat, the weekly village fair. The air smelled of freshly fried pakoras and the earthy aroma of turmeric and chilies. Vendors from the nearby areas had arrived at dawn, setting up their wares under makeshift tarpaulin roofs held up by bamboo poles. The haat sprawled across an open ground. It was a riot of colours and sounds. There were stacks of earthen pots glinting in the sunlight, rows of vibrant glass bangles and heaps of seasonal fruits and vegetables arranged in artistic piles. The cacophony of bargaining echoed in the air as women haggled with the stall keepers over the price of their wares, children clamoured for sweets, all this punctuated by the occasional mooing of a restless cow tethered nearby.

Annu held Beena's hand tightly as they navigated the chaos, her eyes darting from stall to stall. 'Look at those bangles, Beena! Shall we get some for Ma?' she asked, her tone brimming with excitement. Beena nodded eagerly, but Annu's attention was already elsewhere – drawn to a group of boys rolling old bicycle tyres in a race along the edge of the haat. Her rebellious spirit ignited at the sight.

'Beena, sit here,' Annu told her sister, plopping her on a wooden bench near a vendor selling puffed rice. 'Don't move, okay? I'll be right back.' Without waiting for an answer, she dashed off, her feet kicking up small clouds of dust as she disappeared into the crowd.

Annu was determined to find an unused tyre for herself. She begged and cajoled the boys to get her one, then ran to explore the nearby stalls, searching behind carts hoping to find a discarded one. Minutes stretched into what felt like hours, but her persistence paid off when a kind shopkeeper handed her a battered tyre. Grinning triumphantly, she sprinted back to the spot where she had left Beena, clutching the tyre like a trophy.

But Beena wasn't there.

The bench was empty, the vendor too was not at his stall oblivious of what had happened to the child, and the crowd thicker than before. Panic surged through Annu's small chest as she called out for her sister, her voice barely audible above the din of the marketplace. 'Beena! Beena!' she cried, weaving through the throng, her heart pounding like the drumbeats of a distant festival.

She searched high and low. Her wild curls were now plastered to her sweaty forehead and her bare feet aching from running over pebbles and dirt. Tears pricked her eyes as fear clawed at her insides. What if Beena had wandered off? What if someone had taken her? Annu had heard stories of the infamous dacoits who were tantrics and staunch worshippers of the fierce Goddess Kali. In their fervent devotion for the goddess, they performed menacing rituals in pursuit of power and success in their ventures, one of which was the slaughtering of children before the goddess. It was called *bali pratha*, as a mark of reverence and sacrifice to fetch good luck for themselves. What if they had kidnapped Beena and taken her to their den to sacrifice her before the goddess? The thought was too terrifying to contemplate. Terribly scared and also ashamed of herself, Annu trembled, slumping behind a stack of jute sacks near the edge of the haat, hugging her knees to her chest. The tyre lay forgotten beside her.

In her despair, Annu's vivid imagination painted an escape route for herself. She would run away, far away, to the Sundarbans, where the mangroves whispered secrets to the tides and the forest hid its own mysteries. She would live there, alone, like the hermits in the stories she'd heard, who tamed wild beasts. She pictured herself rowing a tiny boat into the labyrinth of rivers in the Sundarbans, far from her mother's wrath and the guilt that now felt unbearable.

As the sun dipped lower, casting long shadows across the haat, an old fisherman found her. His face, weathered by years of battling the river, softened at the sight of the frightened child. 'What's wrong, little one?' he asked, his voice gentle. Between sobs and hiccups, Annu explained what had happened, her words tumbling out in a torrent. The fisherman patted her head reassuringly. 'Come, let's find your family,' he said, lifting her on to his shoulder and carrying her back to the village.

When they reached her home, Annu braced herself for the storm. Her mother, Kalpana, stood in the doorway, her sharp eyes scanning the horizon. Kalpana was a woman of legend in the village, a survivor of the Sunderbans, where she had once fought off a tiger with nothing but a bamboo stick. Annu had always seen her mother as a figure of awe, a mix of bravery and sternness. But the look on Kalpana's face that evening was not one of anger. It was one of immense relief.

Behind Kalpana Annu could see Beena peeping at her nervously. Was Annu fantasizing that Beena was behind her mother or it was Beena for real? Annu was confused. Within moments Beena ran towards her and hugged her tight with her little arms. Annu cuddled her and looked at Kalpana. She was relieved to see Beena, whom she thought she had lost forever in the labyrinth of the haat. But how did Beena get home before she did? Beena told her that Annu had disappeared for so long leaving her on the bench before the vendor selling puffed rice that she grew nervous and began to cry. It was almost sunset time and Annu was nowhere to be seen. Beena had broken into tears and the puffed rice vendor had asked her where she lived and why she was crying. The vendor turned out to be a relative of their neighbour Bhojo Kaka. He had brought Beena to Bhojo Kaka's, and Bhojo Kaka had brought her back home. Narrating the sequence of events breathlessly, Beena paused and looked at Haradhon, who was standing right there. Annu was too scared to look at her father. Haradhon, silent and stoic, placed a hand on her head and asked her to relax. It was a gesture of quiet forgiveness. No words were spoken, but Annu felt the weight of her parents' love in that moment, heavier and more profound than any scolding could ever be. She sobbed into her mother's shoulder, the warmth of Kalpana's arms dissolving her fears and guilt. That night, as the household settled into the comforting routine of dinner and storytelling, Annu lay beside Beena.

The incident, though terrifying, became a turning point in Annu's young life. Her mother, once a figure of unyielding strength, now seemed human – fearless yet tender, a role model who carried the weight of her family with grace and love.

The haat, with its chaos and colours, its vendors and wares, became a memory etched into Annu's heart – not just for the fearful incident that day but also for the lesson it imparted. That was the day she had got a sense of the depth of her family's love, a love that could forgive mistakes and offer solace to one even in the most frightening moments. In the soft glow of the kerosene lamp that night, Annu vowed to protect Beena and to channel her own rebellious energy into becoming the kind of woman her mother was: brave, nurturing and unbreakable.

Annu used to go to the secondary government school in Bhaleya till she was thirteen. She studied till class eight. She wanted to study further but Kalpana removed her from the school. Kalpana had her own reasons for not allowing Annu an education, and any woman of Kalpana's background would have thought the same way.

There was a particular incident in Kalpana's life that had made her very wary of the dangers that could befall young women like her. Kalpana was a teenager, staying with her parents and ten siblings in their Sunderbans house. Life was uncomplicated for children like her, who were able to experience nature in its most attractive avatar. They would bask under the unpolluted sun, play under the maternal shade of the Sundari trees, swim across the confluence of the Ganges, Brahmaputra and Meghna rivers and explore the vast and intense mangrove during the day. At night they were strictly instructed to stay inside their huts and stay alert. Any time the hungry beasts of the jungle could visit their cattle sheds in search of food. There were days when these predators took away their goats, ducks or calves. The monsoon was the time of the greatest threat, when the beasts would arrive anytime, tiptoeing their way in so their footsteps would not be heard. Then they would catch their domestic animals and drag them into the forest.

That was the Sunderbans, where on one hand every day was a boon from nature, and on the other hand every day a struggle for survival. Apart from the fierce predators from the jungle, some of whom could be man-eaters, Sunderbans also had a few gangsters who would smuggle out items illegally, exporting them to foreign countries. They would even traffic innocent girls from the settlements of the mangrove forest to the cities for prostitution. In order to check this activity, the government had deputed one of its most competent officers to the Sunderbans as the sub-divisional police officer. Devyani Roy was no less astute and majestic than the beasts of the Sunderbans. Kalpana had seen her often on her rounds of the locality late in the night.

Within a couple of months Devyani was able to bust a smuggling racket by a gang headed by the notorious Pancha Bagdi. Pancha had warned Devyani to not mess with him, and that the consequences would be dangerous. But Devyani was determined to stop the smuggling racket. She had prepared a detailed report on Pancha, which was to be submitted to the government authorities in Kolkata. The night before the day she was to travel to Kolkata, she went missing from the government quarters where she lived. Her subordinates and the local populace searched for her in every nook and corner of the island, but could not find her. She disappeared the way camphor disappears when set to fire. Some people thought she must have been preyed on by the bloodthirsty beasts of the jungle, while others thought she must have absconded to save her skin, given how controversial the case was. But everyone knew the reality. A few days after her disappearance, Kalpana overheard Pancha Bagdi telling the elderly men of the village that educated women often made a mess of their lives, and that women should not be educated: '*Joto beshi pore, joto beshi jaane, toto kom maane.*' The more they studied, the less they could be controlled by men, he was telling them. Devyani was never seen again, never found anywhere ever. It had been decades since that incident, but the words of Pancha Bagdi had hit Kalpana so hard she never forgot them. Women should not be educated and the consequences of educating them were always dire; Kalpana was rock solid about her decision not to grant much independence or education to her daughters. Thus, Annu's going to school was stopped forever. But Annu had no grudges, no complaints. She was a runner, and she relished running.

Annu's life ethos was shaped by her contrite mother living in nostalgia about the Sunderbans, literally translated as the beautiful jungles and colloquially known as the Bon. Many nights she and her sister sat cross-legged on the dusty floor of their dimly lit hut, her eyes wide with wonder as their mother told them stories of the Sunderbans. The faint glow of the kerosene lamp flickered on Kalpana's face, highlighting her strong jaw and the sharp glint in her eyes. Her voice, low and gravelly, carried the cadence of the jungle – it was both a lullaby and a warning. As she spoke, the cramped hut seemed to dissolve and Annu was transported to a world of tangled mangroves, prowling tigers and the shimmering water channels of the Sunderbans, the great 'Bon' of Bengal.

Kalpana's stories were steeped in the folklore of the land: there were tales of Bon Bibi, the goddess who protected the humble honey collectors and woodcutters from the wrath of Dakshin Rai, the tiger god. 'Bon Bibi is not just a protector,' Kalpana would say, her voice full of reverence. 'She is a mother. She listens to the cries of the lost and the frightened, guiding them to safety.' Annu imagined the goddess moving gracefully through the dense foliage, her saree trailing behind her, her hands raised in blessing. And then there were the tigers – majestic, fearsome and cunning. Kalpana spoke of their golden eyes glowing in the darkness, of how they would silently move, like shadows slipping through the trees. They were the jungle's rightful rulers, demanding respect and inspiring awe.

Annu's favourite stories, however, were the ones of ordinary men and women who had braved the jungle. Kalpana told her about honey collectors balancing precariously on the high branches of trees, their hands steady despite the buzzing swarm of bees around. She spoke of fishermen who ventured into the labyrinth of water channels, their small wooden boats disappearing into the green embrace of the mangroves.

But the tales that thrilled and terrified Annu the most were of those who had faced the tigers and survived. 'There was a man,' Kalpana said, her voice dropping to a whisper, 'who stood face to face with a tiger. He had no weapon, no protection, only his courage and his prayer to Bon Bibi. And the tiger . . . it turned and walked away.'

In her mind, Annu saw herself as a daughter of this jungle, a child of Bon Bibi. She imagined running barefoot through the dense thickets, her laughter mingling with the cries of the birds of the jungle. She pictured herself climbing trees to pluck honeycombs or paddling a boat down a narrow channel of water shimmering like molten silver under the sun. Even in the confines of their poor village, where the days were marked by the family's struggle to earn enough for a single meal, her imagination soared beyond the boundaries of reality. The Sunderbans became her refuge, a world where she could be wild and free, unshackled by the expectations that weighed heavily on her as a girl in rural Bengal.

Her mother's stories were not just entertainment – they were lessons in resilience. Kalpana herself had experienced the perils of the jungle. She had faced tigers, battled the biting insects and endured the swampy terrain. 'The jungle tests you,' she told Annu one evening, her voice tinged with both pride and sorrow. 'It doesn't care who you are or where you come from. If you're strong, you survive. If you're weak, you don't.' Annu would gaze at her mother in awe, seeing her not as a poor woman struggling to feed her family but as a warrior who had emerged from the heart of the Bon.

Her tales shaped Annu's view of the world and her place in it. She grew up with a deep sense of connection to the jungle, even though she had never set foot in it. The Sunderbans became part of her identity, a symbol of freedom and strength. At night, as she lay on her cot under the open sky, she would close her eyes and imagine the rustling of the mangroves, the distant roar of a tiger and the call of Bon Bibi echoing through the trees. The narrow confines of her village, the dusty roads and the hand-to-mouth existence of her family couldn't cage her spirit. In her heart she was always running through the wild expanse of the Sunderbans, a daughter of the jungle, fearless and unyielding. And though life would try to tether her to its harsh realities, Annu carried the Bon within her, a living flame of resilience and wild hope.

As a girl in her teenage years, she would race across the barren lands of her village that ran parallel to the railway station, competing with the express trains. She would defeat the boys of her village in races and bring home a fresh pumpkin or cauliflower as the first prize. The sports teacher of Bhaleya Primary School had asked Haradhon many times to get Annu professionally trained in running. But Haradhon did not have enough money for that; neither was Kalpana willing to send Annu away from home, thanks to her preconceived notions about getting girls educated or trained in anything and what she had seen happen with Devyani as a teenager. '*Maiya manusher doure ki hobe? Biya diya demu tore*,' she would often tell Annu. There is no point in a girl learning to run. They would get her married soon, she would say. But the dreamer in Annu believed she could defy destiny.

One special day remained etched in her memory: the midday sun was blazing down on the uneven dirt track of the village school, the long shadows of the eager crowd that had gathered being cast on it. The boys, a cluster of wiry limbs and competitive energy, stood at the starting line, their eyes fixed on the makeshift finish line marked by a tattered rope tied to two bamboo poles. Among them was Annu, her wild curls bouncing with every small hop she took to loosen her legs. She was the only girl in the line-up, her presence a novelty that drew whispers from the crowd. Some were amused, some disdainful, most disbelieving. What was a girl doing in a race meant for boys?

The village school's annual sports day was a spectacle. For many children it was the only escape from the drudgery of their daily lives, giving them a brief moment when they could imagine themselves as heroes. The air crackled with anticipation as the schoolmaster raised his hand, signalling the start of the race. 'Ready . . . steady . . . go!' he barked, and the runners took off, a cloud of dust rising in their wake.

Annu's heart pounded as her bare feet slapped against the warm earth. The boys surged ahead at first, their legs pumping furiously, but Annu's steps were steady, her breath controlled. She had always loved running – chasing the wind through the mustard fields, her laughter echoing through the air. It was freedom, pure and exhilarating. And today, with the crowd's noise fading into the background, she felt that familiar surge of joy. Her body moved as if it were one with the earth beneath her, the horizon ahead calling her forward.

She began to overtake the boys, one by one. First the slower ones, who huffed and panted after an early burst of speed. Then the quicker ones, whose confidence faltered as they glanced sideways to see Annu pulling ahead. With every stride she felt lighter, stronger. By the final stretch, only the fastest boy remained ahead of her, his face contorted with determination. But Annu's will burned brighter. Summoning every ounce of strength she could, she surged past him, her foot breaking the finish line just a fraction of a second before his.

For a moment there was silence. Then a scattering of applause erupted from the younger children and a few amused adults. Annu stood there, chest heaving, a triumphant smile spreading across her face. She had done it. She had beaten the boys, proven that she was just as capable as them – no, more capable than them. Her eyes searched the crowd for her parents, hoping to catch a glimpse of pride, of approval.

But what greeted her was far from what she had hoped. Her mother's face was set in a grim line, her arms tightly crossed over her chest. Her father shook his head, muttering under his breath. When Annu ran up to them, beaming and holding out the small medal she had received, her mother snatched it away. 'What are you trying to prove, Annu?' she snapped. 'This is not how girls behave. Competing with boys? Winning against them? Have you no shame?' Annu's joy faltered, her heart sinking like a stone in her chest. 'But I . . . I ran well,' she stammered, confusion clouding her wide eyes. Her father stepped in, his voice gruff. 'Girls don't need to prove they're better than boys, Annu. It's not their place. A woman's role is not to compete, but to support. You think life will reward you for this? No. It will punish you for forgetting your place.'

Tears pricked Annu's eyes as she looked at the medal in her mother's hand, now treated like some useless trinket. The laughter of the boys she had defeated rang in her ears, mocking her victory. Her triumph, which had moments ago felt so pure, so full of possibility, now seemed hollow. She had won the race, but in the eyes of her parents – and by extension the world around her – she had failed.

As the crowd dispersed, Annu trudged home behind her parents, the medal clutched tightly in her hand. A strange ache settled in her chest, a heavy, suffocating weight. For the first time she understood something she had only vaguely felt before – that being a girl meant walking a path wearing invisible chains. Her worth would never be measured by her skills or achievements but by how well she could mould herself to the expectations of others. The world had already decided that she was a lesser, a vessel meant for sacrifice and subservience.

That night, as she lay on her cot under the star-studded sky, Annu stared at the medal glinting faintly in the moonlight. The joy she had felt during the race seemed like a distant memory, overshadowed by the bitterness of her parents' words. She didn't cry – she was too exhausted even for that. But something inside her shifted, hardened. She resolved to run again, not to win the approval of others but for herself. For in those fleeting moments of speed and freedom she had felt truly alive. And no one, not even her parents, could take that feeling away from her.

Kalpana kept her word and got Annu married at the age of fifteen to Salil Bag of Hero Bhanga village, who had been projected as an eligible bachelor by the local matchmaker, Tinkori. Salil was eighteen years older than Annu, around five feet four inches tall, curly haired, dark complexioned and potbellied. He claimed he had a cloth business of his own but later turned out to be an imposter. The wedding day dawned quietly in the little mud-and-thatch home nestled in the Bengal village, with its unpaved pathways and swaying paddy fields. But within the walls of the bride's house, the air was anything but serene. It was charged with nervous energy, laughter and the occasional scolding of a distracted younger cousin of the bride's. The aroma of freshly cooked rice and dal mingled with the scent of mogra garlands strung the night before, signalling the momentous occasion. For this was the day that Annu, the rebel tomboy-daughter of the house, would leave her childhood home and step into a new life – a life bound to a stranger.

The preparations began early. Annu sat coyly on a low wooden stool, her delicate frame bathed in the first rays of sunlight streaming through the bamboo slats. Her Ma and aunts crowded around her, smearing turmeric paste – *halud* – on her face, arms and feet. The *halud* ceremony, meant to purify and beautify the bride, was accompanied by giggling and teasing as the women remarked on how radiant she looked. She smiled shyly, her face glowing with the bright yellow of the paste. But her heart felt heavy. The turmeric, soft and fragrant, felt like a mask for the turmoil underneath. Would this man she was to marry – a man she had only seen once – treat her kindly? Would he care for her as her family did?

As the day wore on, the house filled with relatives and neighbours. A large fish, its skin glistening and its head adorned with a red *alta* dot, was brought by the groom's family. It was a symbol of prosperity and fertility, an unspoken promise of abundance. The fish was presented ceremoniously to Annu's parents, who accepted it with folded hands and cautious smiles. Annu watched from a distance, her eyes darting between the ornate fish and the faces of her parents. This was the first tangible token of the bond she was about to form, yet it felt foreign, like a ritual enacted for someone else.

The village women, dressed in their finest red-bordered white sarees, which were actually quite coarse, gathered to apply *alta* on each other's feet. The crimson liquid, symbolic of auspiciousness and marital bliss, was painted on their soles and toes in intricate patterns. Annu's small feet, stained with *alta*, looked like they belonged to someone older, someone wiser. As her mother bent to apply it, a rare tenderness passed between them. Her mother's fingers lingered a moment longer than necessary, and Annu felt a lump rise in her throat. She wanted to cry, but the chaos around her left no room for any show of vulnerability.

The wedding ceremony itself was a blur of rituals, each laden with meaning, though much of it escaped Annu's understanding. The sound of the conch shell, blown in sharp, rhythmic bursts by her aunts, reverberated through the night air, signalling the arrival of the groom's party. With them came the beat of the *dhaak* drum and the shrill wail of the shehnai, all of which stirred something deep within her – a strange mix of excitement and dread. She sat in the inner room, her saree's red-and-gold folds draped carefully, her face painted with sandalwood paste and vermilion, transforming her into a bride.

The groom arrived on a cycle rickshaw with his friends. This was a common vehicle across West Bengal, used by people to ply short distances. He was older than she expected. His expression was unreadable as he was ushered to the ceremonial platform. Her heart pounded as she was led out, her friends teasing her and shielding her with a betel-leaf fan. The crowd parted, their eyes fixed on her, and she felt the weight of their expectations press down on her shoulders. The priests chanted mantras, their words ancient and foreign, while she walked around the sacred fire with the groom, her small hands trembling in his.

Each step of the ritual represented a promise: to share joys and sorrows, to support each other in sickness and health, to build a life together. But Annu, barely out of her teenage years, could not comprehend the gravity of these vows. They felt distant, like words from a play she was performing in. The most poignant moment came when the groom applied vermilion to her parting line, marking her as his wife. The bright red powder, the same colour as the *alta* on her feet, burned against her scalp, as if branding her with a new identity.

The wedding feast followed – a lavish spread of rice, dal, fish curry and sweet rosogollas, prepared with the pooled resources of the village. The men chewed paan as they discussed the weather and the harvest, their laughter hearty and loud. The women, their hands busy serving food, exchanged hushed comments about the bride and groom. Annu's cousins ran about, pilfering sweets and trying to catch glimpses of the groom, while she sat quietly, her hunger dulled by nerves.

As the night drew to a close, the final farewell approached. The bidaai, the most heart-wrenching part of the ceremony, was a ritual of separation. Annu, seated on the floor, wept uncontrollably as her family circled around her. Her father, usually stoic, wiped his eyes discreetly while her mother sobbed openly, clutching her tightly. The young girl who had spent her days running barefoot through the village, chasing dragonflies and climbing mango trees, was now leaving behind everything she had ever known.

The thought of entering the home of a stranger filled her with fear, but she masked it with a shy smile as she climbed into the waiting bullock cart. Her husband sat beside her, distant and awkward, as if unsure of what to say. The cart jolted forward, its wheels creaking under the weight of their new life together. As they crossed the threshold of the village, Annu turned back for one last look at her home. The flickering oil lamps cast long shadows on the walls, and she could see her family standing there, their faces blurred by tears.

In the quiet of the night, as the cart rolled on, she felt the enormity of her new reality settle in. The rituals, the *alta*, the promises – they were all meant to prepare her for this moment. But how could they? She was just a girl, thrust into the role of a wife, expected to navigate the uncharted waters of her future with grace and resilience. Yet, in the midst of her fear and sadness, a tiny ember of hope flickered within her – a hope that this new chapter, however uncertain, might one day bring her the happiness and freedom she had only ever dreamed of.

Within one year of the marriage, Annu was pregnant. Every night Salil would come home heavily drunk and beat her. Annu would sit in the corner of the kitchen and cry like a child. Salil's widowed mother would add fuel to the fire by complaining to Salil about how Annu had been playing all day with the local girls instead of doing the household chores. One such day, when Annu was eight months pregnant, Salil took her to Bhaleya and left her at her parents' house saying he would come and take her back soon. That 'soon' did not happen ever. Kalpana had often tried to coax Haradhon to send Annu back to her husband's place, but Haradhon refused to. Haradhon loved his daughter. By this time he had heard the truth about Salil from many people, and all he wanted to do was to protect his daughter. As for Annu, she had no will to get back to Hero Bhanga. Not even for one day had Salil been affectionate towards her. He would accuse Annu of being frigid in bed, of being abnormally thin with small breasts – a defective woman. Annu would respond with silence. She could hardly understand anything of all this. All she knew was that she has been married to a beast more dangerous than even the beasts of the Sunderbans. Still,

Annu had forgiven Salil, but the day he brought her to her parents' place, Annu wished to never see him again. And her wish was granted.

In Bhaleya, Annu was free. She gave birth to a girl, whom she named Ruma. She took care of the infant Ruma and helped Kalpana in the kitchen. Life was good and uncomplicated for her now. She would often lie on the porch of their small house and watch the stars, imagining that they were running towards the infinite.

Sometimes she would chat with her neighbour Poornima, who used to work in some big city named Bombay and would visit the village once or twice a year. Poornima was a few years older than her. She would bring rich gifts for Ruma every time she came. She was the diva of the village, a peacock strutting in a field of sparrows. One of her sarees, a gleaming emerald green with a gold zari border, seemed to catch the sun and hold it hostage, every thread shimmering as if to announce her arrival. It clung to her curvaceous frame with deliberate grace. It sharply contrasted with the faded and threadbare sarees the other women in the village wore. Her blouse, tightly fitted and embellished with sequins, sparkled every time she moved, the tiny mirrors catching the light in bursts of brilliance. Around her neck, hung a gold necklace – real or fake, no one knew, but it shone bright enough to make people believe it was the former. Her ears bore heavy jhumkas that swayed with every toss of her head, and her wrists were weighed down by glass bangles in a riot of colours, clinking musically with each step she took. Her hair, dark and glossy, was braided and adorned with fresh jasmine flowers, their scent wafting behind her like an invisible veil. Her loud attire and confident gait mesmerized Annu. She was like some forbidden song she wasn't supposed to hear but couldn't help humming along to. Annu's own saree, faded to a dull brown and patched in places, suddenly felt like a shroud of poverty. Her thin arms, unadorned except for a lone brass bangle gifted by her mother, crossed over her chest as if to shield herself from the piercing reality of her inadequacy.

Poornima's lipstick – a deep crimson – seemed to mock the soft, natural pink of Annu's lips. Her cheeks were powdered and slightly rouged, and her eyes, lined heavily with kohl, carried a sultry defiance that Annu both feared and admired. There was an unspoken power in the way Poornima tilted her chin, as though the stares of the villagers were beneath her. It wasn't just the finery she wore – it was her entire demeanour and her air of superiority that set her apart from the rest.

Annu's heart twisted with a feeling she couldn't name. Was it envy? Awe? Or something darker, a yearning for a life she didn't yet understand? She imagined herself in Poornima's place, draped in such a saree, the village boys gawking at her as she walked by, the women whispering enviously. She pictured herself wearing bangles that clinked, earrings that dangled, and a necklace that glowed like fire. It was intoxicating, this fantasy of being noticed, of being important. For a moment Annu's mind soared above the drudgery of her reality – hauling water from the well, tending to the cows and mending torn clothes. In Poornima's world, there were no cracked feet or patched sarees, only the glitter of gold and the allure of beauty.

But beneath Annu's admiration for her, a flicker of unease stirred. Annu saw the way the women of their village averted their gaze from Poornima and discerned a faint contempt in their whispers. She noticed how the men looked at her – not with respect but with a greedy hunger that made Annu's skin crawl. There was something hollow in Poornima's laughter, something brittle in her smile. Annu brushed the thought away. How could someone dressed so beautifully, with the world seemingly at her feet, be anything but happy?

Little did Annu know her envy was a premonition, a shadow of a future she couldn't yet see. Poornima's dazzling appearance was a mask, a thin veneer hiding a world of exploitation and loneliness. But to a young woman who had known only scarcity, it looked like freedom. As Poornima passed her by one day – a fragrant trail of jasmine and the sound of her bangles softly jingling marking her presence – Annu's eyes followed her with longing. She could not see the road to ruin but only the glittering mirage of a life she thought she wanted.

It was after Poornima started working in Mumbai that the financial situation improved remarkably for her family. Poornima got her brother a motorcycle, renovated their house, changing the terrace from asbestos to cement, and also got a separate and exclusive tap water line for the house. Annu admired Poornima and her dressing sense. She wore beautiful sarees and looked gorgeous. Annu wished she too could look like Poornima some day. Little did Annu know that her wish was on the verge of turning true and that providence had a far more destructive plan for her.

During the monsoon of the next year, a large flood swept away the villages of the Sunderbans. Bhaleya was no exception. There was water everywhere. The roof of Annu's house fell. Water filled the house and the family were at once homeless. Kalpana, Ruma and Beena were sent to Poornima's house while Annu and Haradhon ran around saving their livestock and the people of their village, sheltering them at the local clubs and two-storeyed houses. A flood not only brings mass destruction but also a host of diseases with it.

Soon there was an outbreak of dengue in the village. On day four of the outbreak, Haradhon was affected. Annu ran to get help and medicines, but it was all in vain. Relief was only granted to a selected few. Lack of resources, medicines and beds at the village hospital culminated in the sad demise of Haradhon. Having lost the only support she had, Annu did not know what to do. Not only was she grieving her father, she now also had the worry of finding a means to support her family. She neither had the money to support them nor the skills to get a job. Initially she bought groceries and vegetables on credit. However, as the days passed, the grocer refused to sell any more to them on credit, and survival became more and more difficult. The floods had caused severe loss to everyone and nobody was in a state to support anyone else in the village. Annu tried to get in touch with Salil but got to know that he had remarried and settled in a town somewhere in the outskirts of Kolkata. Ruma was falling sick and becoming physically weak, and so were Kalpana and Beena. Every day Kalpana rebuked Annu for 'living a useless existence'. One day Poornima came to visit the family and was moved by their plight. After some time, Poornima took Annu to the ghat near the village pond and advised Annu to take up a job. But who would give a job to an uneducated girl like Annu? She had never worked in her life. And she did not know anyone who can help her in getting a job either. Poornima smiled and said '*Tui aamar saathe Bombay chol.*' If Annu went with her to Mumbai, Poornima would get a job and accommodation in the city and she would be paid fairly for the service she would render. Annu saw a twinkle in Poornima's eyes. But what about Ruma? She was still a small child, said a clueless Annu. 'You take Ruma along. It will not be an issue. Both of you will thrive.'

Annu spent the next couple of days packing for the journey to Mumbai. She requested Poornima's mother to take care of Kalpana and Beena. Poornima gave Annu some money, which Annu handed to Kalpana, who was very happy to have it. Poornima purchased the train tickets for Annu. She took great care of Annu and Ruma on the journey. They boarded a train from Canning to Sealdah, and then from Sealdah to Dadar Junction. Annu had never travelled by train, let alone a train as fast as these. The train stood at the small station of Canning like a colossal iron caterpillar, its long metallic body shimmering under the faint morning sun. To Annu it looked alive, a machine with a hunger for people, swallowing them into its vast belly. The engine hissed and groaned, exhaling clouds of steam, as if impatient to be off. Annu clutched her infant daughter Ruma tightly to her chest, her heartbeat drumming in rhythm with the hum of the engine. This was her first train journey, but the awe it inspired in her was tangled with a thread of trepidation so tight it made her palms sweat. The cacophony of voices, the calls of the tea sellers and the clatter of footsteps everywhere created a symphony that was both intimidating and thrilling.

She thought of the life she was leaving behind – a small hut with a thatched roof that leaked during the monsoons, the fields where she had once raced barefoot, the narrow dirt lanes that smelled of cow dung and wet earth. Poverty had been her shadow, constant and unyielding, but it was familiar, a known adversary. Now, as she prepared to board this mechanical beast bound for the unknown city of Mumbai, her heart felt like it was being tugged in two directions. Hope propelled her forward, but fear dug its heels in, creating a stubborn knot in her stomach.

The scene outside the train was a blur of chaos – hawkers shouting, women balancing bundles on their heads, children running barefoot and stray dogs sniffing for scraps. The station smelled of coal, sweat and fried food, a concoction that made Annu's senses reel. Inside the train, the air was thick with human warmth, the scent of metal mingling with the tang of unwashed bodies. People were crammed into the compartments, their voices rising in a cacophony of Bengal's diverse tongues. Luggage was stuffed under seats and hung precariously from overhead racks. Annu found a corner and settled Ruma on her lap, her shawl pulled tight around them to ward off the chill of the early morning air.

As the train lurched forward with a jolt, Annu's thoughts drifted to her days as a young girl. She had been the fastest runner in her village, her feet flying over the fields like the wind itself. She had raced the boys and beaten them every time, her slender legs carrying her with a grace and speed that made her feel invincible. The train's rhythm reminded her of her own pace – steady, relentless, unstoppable. But this machine was faster, its iron wheels devouring distance in a way her legs never could. She felt a pang of jealousy, as if the train had stolen the one thing she had always taken pride in. Yet there was also a sense of exhilaration, as though she had been given wings she could never grow herself.

The countryside unfolded like a moving painting outside the window. Paddy fields stretched endlessly, their emerald green broken only by the occasional palm tree or the silhouette of a scarecrow. Mud huts with thatched roofs dotted the landscape, smoke curling lazily from their chimneys. Farmers toiled in the fields, their bodies bent under the weight of ploughs and the sun's unyielding gaze. Annu watched the scenes flicker by, each one a reminder of the world she was leaving behind. Inside the train, the atmosphere was a stark contrast – clamorous, suffocating, alive. Children cried, vendors wove through the crowd with trays of snacks, and women gossiped in hurried whispers. It was a world within a world, a moving microcosm of humanity.

Annu's heart swelled with conflicting emotions. She was leaving behind a life of penury, where every day had been a struggle to feed Ruma, to keep a roof over their heads. Mumbai, she had heard, was a city of dreams, a place where fortunes could be made and lives transformed. But it was also a city of harsh realities, where the poor were swallowed whole, their dreams ground to the dust. Annu had no illusions about the challenges that lay ahead, but she clung to hope like a drowning woman clinging to a piece of driftwood. For Ruma's sake she had to believe in a better future.

As the train gathered speed, Annu felt the knot in her stomach tighten. Leaving home was no small thing, even when home was a place of want and hardship. The small hut in Bhaleya, with its cracked walls and smoky hearth, was where she had taken her first steps, where she had laughed and cried, where she had felt safe despite everything. It was where she had buried her dreams of racing, of being more than what her circumstances allowed. Now she was leaving that behind for a city she had never seen, for a life she could not yet imagine. The weight of the decision pressed down on her, heavy and inescapable.

Ruma stirred in her lap, her tiny fingers clutching Annu's saree. Annu looked down at her daughter's face, so small and innocent, and felt a surge of determination. This journey was not just for her; it was for Ruma, for the chance to give her a life that wasn't defined by hunger and despair. But the fear lingered – an unwelcome companion. What if she failed?

What if the city proved too much for her? What if she lost herself in its labyrinth of slums and streets?

The train hurtled forward, its iron body rattling and groaning, as if it, too, bore the weight of its passengers' hopes and fears. Annu pressed her forehead against the windowpane, the cool glass soothing her fevered thoughts. The landscape outside had changed; the fields had given way to towns, the towns to factories, and the factories to a horizon that hinted at the sprawl of Mumbai. Her heart raced, a mixture of anticipation and dread.

As the train roared ahead, Annu felt the first stirrings of resolve. She didn't know what awaited her in the city, but she knew she couldn't turn back. The past was behind her, a life of poverty and struggle she was determined to leave behind. The future lay ahead, uncertain and daunting, but filled with possibilities. For Ruma, for herself, she would face it, one step at a time. The train's rhythm matched the beating of her heart, carrying her towards a new life, a new beginning, and a world as vast and unknown as the city itself. While Poornima snored in the upper berth of the compartment with Ruma in her lap, Annu watched the trees and fields and houses and railway stations disappearing after losing the race with the train. The train was indeed a great runner, thought Annu. As the train halted at Dadar station, Poornima asked them to get down. It was the early hours of the morning so the railway station was not very crowded. They went out of the station and hired a cab. '*Kamathipura lelo, Bhaiya,*' said Poornima and put a betel leaf in her mouth. After a ride of around forty-five minutes, they reached their destination. Poornima chewed the betel leaf in her mouth with great pleasure and instructed the cab driver, '*Chauda Gulli, Bhaiya.*'

4

Torn by the Hawks

The cab stopped in front of a huge building. Poornima got down with the luggage. Annu got down from the cab with Ruma in her arms and followed Poornima. The moment Annu stepped out of the rickety taxi on to the road and saw the congested, narrow lanes of Kamathipura, a wave of nausea hit her. The air was thick, heavy with the oppressive stench of urine, rotting garbage and a hint of stale incense trying – and failing – to mask the filth. It clung to her, this suffocating shroud of foul smells, and for a moment she felt the world tilting under her feet. She clutched little Ruma tightly to her chest, as if her child's innocent warmth could protect her from the chaos unravelling before her eyes. The baby whimpered, disturbed by the noise and unfamiliar smells, and Annu's arms trembled as she held her closer.

Her first sight of Kamathipura was a brutal assault on her senses. The buildings loomed tall and decrepit, their walls peeling like the bark of a dying tree. Patches of faded paint hung on to them for dear life, and most of the walls bore the graffiti of time – stains, cracks and the residue of countless hands brushing against them. Clotheslines sagged between the windows, heavy with damp, mismatched garments. Water dripped rhythmically from leaking pipes, pooling into grimy puddles that glistened under the dim, flickering streetlights. It was a far cry from the open skies and green fields of her village in Bhaleya, where even poverty seemed to wear a softer face.

The street was alive, but not in a way that brought joy. Men loitered in clusters, their eyes darting like those of predatory birds. Women leaned against doorframes, their faces heavily made up, the garish colours of their lipstick and kohl clashing with the sadness in their eyes. They chewed paan and spit carelessly, leaving red stains that dotted the cracked pavement like bloodied petals. Somewhere in the distance a harmonium wheezed a melancholy tune, which mingled with the cacophony of the vendors hawking food, the metallic clanging of pots and the sharp cries of children running barefoot.

Annu's head swam with confusion and dread. What was this place? Poornima had spoken of a better life in the city, a chance to leave behind the grinding poverty of the village. She had painted a picture of opportunity and prosperity, of bustling streets where fortunes could be made and dreams realized. But this? This was a nightmare. Her knees felt weak, and for a moment she wanted to turn back, to gather Ruma and flee. But where would she go? The village she had left behind no longer held any promise for her.

Poornima stood beside her, her face unreadable, as if Kamathipura's horrors had numbed her long ago. 'This is where you'll stay,' she said finally, her voice devoid of warmth. Annu wanted to protest, to ask why, to demand an explanation, but the words stuck in her throat. She stared at the darkened windows of the brothel that Poornima gestured towards, her heart pounding. It was as if the building itself were alive, its hollow eyes watching her, mocking her naivety.

Her mind raced with questions and fears. What am I doing here? What kind of life is this for Ruma? She thought of her village – the sprawling fields where she once raced the wind, the simplicity of life, even in its hardships. The memory of her mother's warm embrace and the familiar smell of freshly cooked rice flooded her senses, and tears pricked her eyes. Kamathipura was the antithesis of everything she had known. It was loud, filthy and unrelenting. She felt like a tiny speck in its overwhelming vastness, dwarfed by the towering buildings, the sea of faces the sheer density of life packed into these narrow lanes.

A terrible premonition began to take shape in her mind. The women leaning against the walls, their garish smiles, the lingering glances from the men . . . it all began to add up, and her stomach churned. Poornima had hinted at hard work, at making sacrifices, but she had never been explicit. Now, staring at the reality before her . . .

Poornima told Annu while walking towards their building that its name was Pilla House and this was where she and many women like her worked. The interior of the building was very shabby and dilapidated. Annu smelt a foul smell all around. She could see a mutton shop next to the building. The butcher was separating the bones from the flesh with a blood-stained knife. He looked at Poornima and winked. Poornima winked back at him. While walking into the building, Annu saw Poornima pat a man and say, '*Maya Bibi kidhar hai re, Rafiq*?' Annu could not understand a word of what Poornima spoke. It was a different and difficult language for her. She quietly climbed the stairs with Poornima. They stopped in front of a locked room. Poornima took the keys out of her bag and opened the door, saying the room belonged to her. Annu could rest there and feed Ruma and even stay there till she got a room for herself. The room was a small one; as small as their coupe in the train. The room was very damp. Annu saw that the paint on the walls had worn out and that chunks of cement were falling from everywhere. There were obscene pictures of foreign couples stuck on the walls of the room. Annu was confused. A hundred questions were rising in her mind. Where had she landed? What was the job? And many more. But before she could ask anything, Poornima told her to relax, feed Ruma and take a nap. Annu was woken up by Poornima. Ruma was still deep asleep. Annu caressed her face and kissed her. She felt a little fresh. Poornima whispered into her ears, asking her to go downstairs with her. Annu was hesitant to leave Ruma alone. Poornima assured her that nothing would happen to her. She asked a woman standing outside the room to look after Ruma. Poornima took Annu to a hall downstairs. An elderly woman was sitting there. '*Maya Bai, yeh Annu hai, mere gaon ka hai.*' Maya called Annu closer, made her sit by her side and said, 'Yeh randi khana hai, baccha' and laughed like a devil. She was as dark as a moonless night. Annu was shocked! She looked at Poornima out of fear. Poornima looked at Maya and spoke softly, '*Nayee hai, sikh jaayegi, Maya bai.*' She was new and she would learn soon. Annu could not understand their conversation. She angrily asked Poornima why she had brought her to this dirty place and what exactly the job being offered to her was. She could not comprehend what this dangerous looking woman named Maya was telling her. She felt an acute pain in her abdomen out of the terrible anxiety that had seized her. Her innocence had become her enemy. Her expertise in running and swimming through the jungles of the Sunderbans seemed of no help to her here, for she was among people whose countenance looked alien to her. A sharp slap on her tender skin, which stung like a bee, brought her back to her immediate reality. 'What do you think, Annu?' shouted Poornima, 'women born to poor fathers like ours will get sophisticated jobs and lead a prestigious life? I have been raped multiple times by the man in whose house I used to work as a maid in Kolkata and then was trafficked here five years ago by him. What would I have done apart from selling my body, to stay alive and support my family? Who will give us decent jobs? Now, at least I can send money to my mother at the end of every month and save them from starving and dying. It is completely up to you, Annu, to decide what to do.' Saying this, Poornima left.

Annu sat on the floor and contemplated the situation. The faces of Ruma, Kalpana and Beena haunted her. She had to work to feed those three stomachs. She had to work to raise Beena and Ruma. She had been a runner. It was time she ran the longest and crudest race of her life. She could not afford to stop. Yet she could not fathom making peace with what life was offering her and descend into a hell of depravity forever. She was not ready to accept the label which would be stuck to her forever.

Maya asked Chameli to dress up Annu in a saree and get her made up. Annu looked pretty, but the biggest problem was that malnutrition had made her lean and her breasts were not very full. Moreover, she was of an athletic build and had little fat. Maya ordered Chameli to stuff her blouse with scraps of cloth to make her breasts look bigger and more attractive. After the make-up was done Annu was made to stand in front of Pilla House along with several other women. Tears would not stop rolling down her cheeks. She was dying a thousand deaths, and yet there was no escape. After some time she saw Poornima too joining her. Chameli stayed back with Ruma in the room.

Rafiq was Annu's pimp. Rafiq had been abandoned in Chauda Gulli of Kamathipura by an unknown woman when he was only an infant of six months. A passing woman spotted him next to some garbage on the street. She had picked him up and taken her to Maya's den, where she had handed him over to Gulab, Maya's consort. It was Gulab who had raised Rafiq, first naming him after the most lucrative customer of Maya's. Gulab had tried his best to make Rafiq at least a generous human being, if not educated or decent, but Rafiq turned out to be a scoundrel who took Maya as his godmother. He grew up to become her constant shadow and confidant in the trade. Rafiq also grew up to look as dangerous as Maya. Rafiq had a limp and walked with a stick. The sound of his stick was like an alarm to the women, telling them it was time for work. Under the evil influence of Maya, Rafiq grew up to be the most notorious pimp of Kamathipura.

The first time Annu was sold as a sex worker, the world seemed to collapse around her. She sat in the dim, suffocating room of the brothel, its walls streaked with stains and shadows, a single bulb casting a dull, yellow light that made everything seem more grotesque. The air was heavy with the sickly mingling of sweat, cheap cologne and despair. She stared blankly at the chipped floor tiles, her hands clenched tightly into fists on her lap, trying to still their trembling.

The door creaked open and in shuffled the man – grey – haired, stooped, with the paunch of age weighing down his sagging frame. He wore a crumpled shirt that smelled faintly of tobacco, and his eyes, bloodshot and rheumy, regarded her with a hunger that made her stomach churn. He was old enough to be her father, perhaps older. The sight of him brought back memories of her father sitting on the charpoy in their village, the smell of earth and wood in the air, and the quiet dignity he carried even in poverty. But this man, with his lecherous gaze and shaking hands, was a desecration of that memory.

Annu's body tensed as he stepped closer, his presence filling the small room with a suffocating weight. She thought of running away screaming, but where would she go? Kamathipura's narrow lanes were a labyrinth of despair, and outside this room was the Madam who had already made it clear that escape was impossible. She had been bought, and now her body was no longer her own.

Her throat felt dry as sandpaper, and she fought the urge to gag. She wanted to shout at the man, at the world, at Poornima for bringing her here, at herself for ever believing there could be a better life for her in the city. But she said nothing. Her voice seemed trapped, buried under layers of fear, anger and shame.

He reached out, his coarse hand brushing against her arm, and she flinched as though burned. Her heart pounded in her chest, but her mind began to shut down, a survival instinct kicking in. She bit her lip hard, tasting the metallic tang of blood, and stared past him, fixing her gaze on the cracked wall, as though it could transport her away from this nightmare.

In that moment, she realized that to survive this she would have to become numb. She would have to lock away her soul, bury her dreams and silence the girl who once ran free through the fields of Bhaleya. She imagined herself building a wall around her heart, brick by brick, to protect what little was left of her dignity and self-worth. The act that followed was mechanical, lifeless – a hollow transaction that stole a piece of her humanity.

When it was over, she curled up on the thin mattress, her body aching, her mind hollow. Tears streamed silently down her face, soaking into the fabric, but she didn't make a sound. Crying out wouldn't help; there was no one to hear her.

She thought of Ruma then, her baby girl with the softest cheeks and eyes full of wonder. Ruma was her only anchor, the sole reason she hadn't crumbled entirely. Annu had allowed herself to be dragged into this abyss because she believed it would give Ruma a chance at a better life than hers. It was this hope – fragile and flickering – that she clung to now, even as everything else inside her felt broken.

The memory of Ruma's tiny fingers clutching at her saree brought a faint warmth to her chest, but it was quickly overshadowed by guilt. What kind of mother could she be to Ruma now? How could she look into her daughter's eyes, knowing what she had done, what she would have to continue doing?

That night Annu sat by the small window in the room, staring out at the dimly lit alley below. The voices of men and women, laughter mingled with despair, rose up to her ears like a haunting melody. The weight of what had happened pressed heavily on her chest, but she forced herself to breathe.

The world hadn't stopped; time hadn't frozen. She was still here, and for Ruma she had to keep going.

The experience had marked her forever; it was an indelible scar on her soul. It had destroyed her, but it was also an experience that reshaped her, forcing her to build a facade of strength she didn't feel. Annu realized she couldn't afford the luxury of grief or rage. In Kamathipura, survival meant silence, endurance, and learning to live with the unbearable.

And so, as the first light of dawn filtered through the grimy window, Annu wiped her tears and steeled herself for the day ahead. She told herself that she wasn't doing this for herself but for Ruma. Her daughter was the only dream she had left, and Annu vowed to protect that dream, no matter what it cost her. But deep down, a small voice whispered a question she couldn't answer: Would Ruma ever understand the price her mother paid for her future?

'Chai chai, coffee!' Annu was brought back to present by the cries of the tea seller. For the last fifteen years Annu had been a permanent resident of Kamathipura, peddling her body to innumerable men of various age groups to feed herself and her family. Adequate food and access to the necessities of life had improved her and Ruma's health. Annu had overcome the psychological trauma of physical and sexual abuse, understanding the importance of money. When Ruma was seven, Annu had sent her to a boarding school in Nashik. She was now fourteen. Annu did not want Ruma to know about her reality. Also, the vicious ambience of Kamathipura would have turned Ruma into prey for the predators. There were days when Annu would attend to customers on the bed and

Ruma would be asleep on the floor. At times, when Rafiq brought customers abruptly, Poornima would hide little Ruma under her dupatta so that she would not see anything. When Ruma was an infant, she would often be left to play in the same room where some man raped her mother like a mad dog. Annu could not risk keeping Ruma with her at Kamathipura. Thus, with the help of Aapa, Annu sent her away. Every day the mother in her would crave for a glimpse of Ruma, but she prioritized the safety of her daughter over the yearning to have her by her side.

It was late evening and the train was running tremendously fast. Annu ordered tea and a few biscuits and paid for them. Later she visited the washroom. On her way there she saw a young man and a young woman passionately kissing, completely oblivious to the presence of others. Their lips were intertwined and they were in each other's warm embrace. The man was probably in his mid-twenties. He looked devastatingly handsome and exuded a striking charm that instantly made Annu remember Rajan.

Rajan was her first love. Annu had met him on a January evening, many moons ago. Rajan was a Thakur from Uttar Pradesh and had come to deliver gout medicines to Aapa. Rajan used to work as a mason on a construction site in south Mumbai and had to perform small duties for his boss. Aapa had been a consort to this boss. That day Annu was waiting for a customer outside Pilla House. Rajan saw Annu and approached her. The first time Annu laid her eyes on Rajan, it felt as though a sudden gust of fresh air had blown into the suffocating alleys of Kamathipura. He stood at the threshold of the brothel, his tall frame backlit by the dim evening light filtering in through the haze of grime and despair that pervaded the space. Rajan was unlike any man she had ever encountered in this pit of decay. His pinkish-fair skin seemed to glow, untouched by the shadows of misery that clung to most of the men who frequented this place. His dense black hair was slicked back, thick and gleaming, as if the dirt and soot of the city hadn't dared to mar its perfection.

More than six feet tall, he towered over everyone around him, exuding a quiet confidence that set him apart from them. He had broad shoulders that stretched the fabric of his simple kurta, and his sturdy build spoke of a man accustomed to physical labour yet untouched by the weariness of hardship. His hands, large and calloused, carried the faint scent of fresh earth and wheat – a reminder of the village he had come from, far removed from the sordid chaos of Kamathipura.

Annu couldn't help but stare. He looked incongruous there, like a lotus blooming in a stagnant pond. The grime and filth of Kamathipura seemed to retreat in his presence, shrinking against the vitality and vigour he exuded. Her breath caught in her throat, a flush rising to her cheeks. It wasn't just his looks that struck her; it was the way he carried himself – upright, unbothered and untainted by the despair that clung to every corner of this place.

For a moment she felt a strange thrill. Men like Rajan didn't belong here. They didn't look at women like her, at least not with admiration or desire. And yet his eyes, dark and intent, had swept across the room and landed on her. Something about the way he looked at her – not with lust, but with curiosity, maybe even respect – made her heart race. In the silent transaction of gazes, Annu felt a spark she hadn't felt in years.

The other women noticed him too. Murmurs spread quickly, punctuated by whispers of the possibilities of wooing this man. 'A Thakur!' someone hissed, her voice laced with awe. 'What's he doing here?' Another woman, older and bitter, scoffed, 'Probably slumming it for the thrill.'

Rajan's presence was a reminder of all they couldn't have, a glimpse of the world beyond Kamathipura's narrow confines. And when his attention lingered on Annu – her slight frame draped in a saree of muted colours, her face devoid of the garish makeup favoured by the others – it only added fuel to their bitterness.

Annu felt it too, as a deep sense of pride engulfed her. She had captivated him, this man who seemed too good for this place. For a fleeting moment she allowed herself to imagine what it would be like to leave this life behind, to stand beside a man like Rajan, to escape the clutches of Kamathipura. It was a foolish dream, she knew, but in that moment it felt intoxicating.

Beneath the thrill there was also a seed of doubt. Men had come to her before, wearing masks of kindness and charm, only to reveal cruelty underneath. Was Rajan any different? Was the warmth in his gaze genuine, or was it just another illusion, a fleeting kindness that would dissolve in the harsh light of reality?

But for now she clung to the moment. His presence had made her feel alive again, like a woman, not just a vessel that had to be offered for survival. In the midst of Kamathipura's grime and despair, Rajan was a glimmer of hope, however fleeting, however impossible. Annu felt both exhilarated and terrified.

Annu's counterparts giggled and teased her for capturing a '*jawan khoobsurat murga*'. Annu was quite bewitched by

Rajan's appearance. She led him to her room and shut the door. Both were silent for some moments. The neon lights of her room bubbled flamboyantly at them. Rajan touched Annu and made her sit on the bed. He sat next to her, gazed into her eyes and smiled uneasily. Annu was beginning to feel coy. She had never seen a man as handsome as Rajan ever! Slowly, Rajan touched her and kissed her lips. She blushed like a bride and perspired even in the chill winter night. They made love wonderfully. That was the first time Annu moaned while making love and did not want it to get over at all. The feminine desires in her spread their wings wide and soared into the skies of passion. She had slept most peacefully in Rajan's embrace that night. Rajan left in the morning with a promise to come back again. Rajan was back after a week. Annu was thrilled. Rajan was terrific in bed and a master in passionate love-making. They explored each other's bodies with a magical zeal. Rajan's visits to Pilla House became more frequent as he was besotted by Annu's beauty and the delicious dishes that she would cook for him. In the past few years, having become a permanent resident of Kamathipura, Annu had turned her passion towards cooking and had converted it into an art form. Every afternoon she would lay out her canvas of spices in different colours, pick up her spatula as if it were a brush and pour her heart into the canvas of the sizzling mustard oil in the kadhai and churn out masterpiece after masterpiece. Her masterpieces included a Kolkata-style fried mutton roll, the delicately spiced meat intoxicating in its aroma, biriyani with a potato, which would have shamed the famous Aminia Biriyani of Kolkata, and an occasional hilsa mustard curry, which was so sought after that the women there often squabbled over it to partake of a morsel of it.

Annu was the master chef of the area. Perhaps that is why Aapa and Kajol entrusted her with the serious responsibility of cooking and feeding 'Officer Didi' when Kajol had invited her to their pocket-sized room during the Bengali New Year, before few months of her travel to Bhaleya. Didi was an ace Bengali and had an undying love for food. Annu had cooked a few of her masterpieces and presented them before Didi, who had feasted on them and hugged her for all the effort she had taken to rustle them up. Annu was almost in tears. The warmth of that hug reminded her of three people; her father Haradhon, Ruma and Rajan.

As the train ran with all its might, Annu drowned herself again in the thoughts of Rajan who had come into her life like a tornado. It has been many years, yet Rajan's memory lingered untouched in Annu's mind.

Rajan had claimed to be in love with Annu and told her he would marry her someday. Aapa had warned Annu; she should not weaken towards Rajan and must treat him like the other customers, without any special attention given to him. But Annu was taken. She could not resist falling head over heels in love with Rajan. She would book two tickets for a blockbuster film starring Shahrukh Khan and watch it in Maratha Mandir almost every week.

Maratha Mandir was one of the oldest theatres in Mumbai, and it had been showcasing the same Hindi film for the last twenty years. And all the women of Kamathipura nursed this Bollywood dream that someday their Raj would arrive and take his Simran away from the world of unending darkness. Annu felt that one day Rajan, like Shah Rukh Khan, would take her along in the train with him, away from the miseries and crude realities of life. While she lay like a corpse with other customers and waited for them to finish the act, with

Rajan she wanted more and more. The thought of marrying Rajan became her only escape route to break free from the world of misery she had drowned in. It seemed like a fairy tale for Annu.

Annu had always known the rules of Kamathipura, a world where love was a word bartered in whispers and betrayal lurked behind every promise. Yet, when Rajan entered her life, she had allowed herself to hope. Against the odds, against the cynicism that years in this hell hole had bred in her, she dreamed a dangerous, fragile dream. She had believed his honeyed words, the gentle way in which he had touched her, the promises he had woven of a life far from the filth and degradation of Kamathipura. For the first time she had allowed herself to imagine a future where she could be more than just a body, a commodity. But that dream too shattered like fragile glass the day she discovered the truth about him.

The morning began like any other, the dim sunlight filtering through the peeling walls of her room, the stench of stale sweat and despair hanging heavy in the air. Rajan had left her the night before, his words lingering in her mind: 'Soon, Annu. Just a little longer, and I'll take you away.' She had held on to those words as if they were a lifeline, her heart swelling with the hope that she could escape this abyss, if not for herself, then for her daughter Ruma.

But then Kajol, her sharp-tongued friend-turned-rival, burst into her room, her face twisted in mock pity. She thrust a phone into Annu's hands, the screen flashing a video. Annu froze. It featured her. She saw herself on the screen, naked, vulnerable, her body exposed in ways she had never agreed to. Her heart pounded as her brain struggled to make sense of the horror unfolding before her.

Rajan had filmed them. He had filmed their most intimate moments – the ones she had foolishly thought were born out of love – and he had sold the video to strangers on the Internet. The bile rose in her throat as Kajol spat the final blow: 'He made a fortune off you, Annu. And now he's gone. You were just another deal for him.'

The room seemed to spin, the walls closing in on her. Her knees buckled and she collapsed on to the hard, cold floor. She wanted to scream, but no sound came. The betrayal was like a knife slicing through the fragile threads of trust she had painstakingly woven around Rajan. Her chest ached, not with anger but with an overwhelming, hollow pain that seemed to swallow her whole. She had been used before – by countless men – but this was different. Rajan hadn't just used her body; he had stolen her soul, her hopes, her belief in the possibility of a better life. She had trusted him, let him into the hidden corners of her heart that no one else had touched. And he had turned that trust into currency, traded it for wealth and left her with nothing but shame and despair.

It was then, sitting on the floor of that dingy room, that Annu felt the final remnants of her faith in humanity drain away. She remembered what her father Haradhon would often say to her when she was a child. His words echoed in her mind. He would always say, that, one who fights against monsters should be careful lest he thereby become a monster. In childhood, Annu could not understand a word of Haradhon, but she has been realizing how true her father was in speaking those words! She had fought the monsters of Kamathipura for years, clinging to the belief that she was more than the life she had been forced into. But now, she realized, the abyss had claimed her.

Her tears blurred her vision as she thought of Ruma, her little girl with her wide eyes and innocent smile. What kind of life was she offering her daughter? How could she protect her from a world where men like Rajan existed, where women like her were destined to be invisible, unheard, disposable?

In that moment Annu felt not just the pain of betrayal but the weight of every indignity she had endured. She was not someone who could dream of love or dignity. She was a shadow, a necessity for men, but never an equal. She was the unspoken one, the one whose existence was tolerated only in the dark corners of society.

Rajan's betrayal had stripped her of her last shred of hope. She had thought Rajan was different, but he was just another face in the endless parade of men who had used her, discarded her and moved on. The world was not meant for women like her to thrive; it was built to keep them down, to make them believe they were less than human.

Annu wiped her tears and rose to her feet. Her body trembled, but her mind was cold, numb. The love she had once felt for Rajan was now a gaping wound, and it would leave behind a scar that would never heal. She looked at her reflection in the cracked mirror on the wall – a woman stripped of her illusions, a woman who could no longer afford to hope.

In that reflection, she saw not just herself but every woman like her, every 'fallen' woman whose dreams had been crushed by a society that refused to see them as human. Annu realized that she could no longer dream of escaping this life. All she could do now was to survive – for Ruma, in the faint hope that her daughter might one day live in a world kinder than this one.

Annu lived in mortal fear now. What if Ruma's teachers got to know about the video clips? Her daughter would be thrown out of her school for being a whore's daughter, and her sister Beena and her mother Kalpana would have to commit suicide if the video clips reached her village! For many days she could not sleep. The trauma left her severely ill and she had to be hospitalized. Poornima, Chameli, Aapa and the other women of Pilla House stood by her, assuaged her pain, took care of her and brought her back to life. A strange bond of camaraderie saved Annu from dying physically, but the woman in Annu had to die once again. There could be no oasis of hope in the desert of her life. The sticker of their identity was glued so firmly to them that it could not be peeled away until their death. '*Madam, thoda side dijiye*' Annu shuddered as a passenger asked her to move forward. Annu went to the washroom and looked into the mirror. She found herself sobbing like a baby. Rajan's had been a betrayal of the worst order.

5

Tale of the Innocent Dove

It was the early hours of the afternoon, the time when the fiery rays of the scorching sun become identical with the shimmering desert sand. The squawking of vultures echoed through the shrivelled cacti and tumbleweeds, reaching the crimson sky; the creatures were waiting for their day's meal. The desert of Jaisalmer stretched to infinity under the fierce afternoon sun, its golden expanse shimmering with an otherworldly glow. The crimson light of the sun spread like liquid fire across the dunes, creating a breathtaking illusion of millions of diamonds scattered across the sands. The heat rose in rippling waves, distorting the horizon, where the dunes seemed to dance and blur into a molten mirage. The desert was alive, pulsating with a deceptive beauty that masked its unrelenting cruelty. It whispered secrets of forgotten travellers, buried treasures and unmarked graves, its ever-shifting sands holding a thousand tales of life and death.

In this expanse of radiant desolation lay a lifeless form, a stark contrast to the vivid, pulsating desert around it. The body of a young boy, Raju, lay sprawled in the sand, motionless and haunting. He couldn't have been more than sixteen. His dirty white dhoti clung to his lifeless legs, and his once-bright sky-blue kurta was stained with the dark bloom of blood that seeped slowly into the sand. His turban, once neatly tied, now lay crumpled a few feet away, its bright colours dulled by the dust that clung to its fabric.

The blood on his forehead glistened in the sunlight, a stark crimson river escaping from the bullet wound that had stolen his life. It trickled down his temple, carving thin trails in the sand before vanishing into the earth, as if the desert itself thirsted for his essence. The faint smell of blood mingled with the acrid stench of gunpowder.

Even in death, Raju's body bore traces of his humanity. His earrings, delicate loops of gold, peeked out from beneath the dishevelled tufts of his black hair, catching the sunlight in a rebellious glint, as if defying the stillness of death. His young face, pale and dusted with sand, wore an expression of surprise frozen in time, his wide eyes staring into the endless sky above. Around him the desert offered no answers, no sympathy – only silence and the soft, dry hiss of wind brushing against the dunes.

Above, the vast expanse of the sky seemed oppressive, its blue almost cruelly vibrant in contrast to the lifeless form below. As the sun began its slow descent, the golden light turned the sand into molten amber, and shadows stretched long and ominous. The desert, timeless and impassive, began to stir with the faint whispers of an approaching sandstorm. The wind picked up, carrying with it fine particles of sand that stung and blurred the already surreal landscape.

The sandstorm came gradually, a murmur growing into a roar as the winds swept across the dunes. It began to bury Raju's body, grain by grain, as if the desert sought to claim him, to draw him into its womb and erase all traces of his existence. The sand seemed to engulf him lovingly, tenderly, as though it mourned him in its own silent way. The neat pile of his turban disappeared first, then his earrings, until only the faintest outline of his body remained visible, and soon even that was gone.

As the sandstorm raged on, the landscape blurred into a swirling chaos of gold and crimson. The smell of blood and gunpowder dissipated into the dry, searing air, leaving behind only the faint, earthy scent of the desert itself. The world seemed to hold its breath as the chaos gave way to a haunting stillness as the storm subsided. When the winds finally calmed, there was no sign of Raju's body, no trace of his fleeting existence. The desert had claimed him completely, folding him into its endless expanse, leaving only a faint indentation where he had lain.

The sun dipped lower, casting long shadows over the now-smooth dunes. The desert resumed its deceptive beauty, its shimmering sands masking the horrors it had just swallowed. For those who might pass by, there would be no evidence of what had transpired, no marker to signify the life that had been snuffed out.

For Raju, there would be no memorial, no mourning cries, no one to carry his story forward. Only the desert would remember, its grains of sand whispering his tale to the wind, carrying it across the vast expanse of Jaisalmer until it too would be lost, buried in the unending march of time.

A caravan with a small, fragile child and a menacing brute stopped in front of Jaisalmer railway station. It was dusk. Kala Shah got down from the camel, patted his thick grey moustache with his index finger and instructed Iliaz to bring the girl down. Kala Shah had turned sixty last Dusshera. He had the skin of a leopard, shinier and more polished though, an abnormally big head that housed a round face and dirty uneven teeth stained by prolonged consumption of tobacco. He was about five feet eleven and heavily structured.

Kala Shah, who hailed from Rajasthan, wore long *gokhru* earrings of gold on both ears and consciously turbaned his bald head to protect it from the intolerable heat. Illiaz asked the cameleer to make the camel sit and shouted at the girl atop it: '*Neeche utar, chhori*!' A nervous Rani got down from the camel, as instructed, with the help of the cameleer. Her face was covered with a piece of black cloth. She was wearing the colourful frock that had been given to her by Kala Shah. Kala Shah looked at her and chuckled; his ugly stained teeth shining in his dark, crude face. He adjusted his red turban and walked towards the railway station. Illiaz followed him with the girl.

The Jaisalmer railway station, though not a very big one, was built using the unique golden yellow limestone and sandstone of the area, and was a perfect blend of Victorian, Rajasthani and Jain architectonic heritage, much like the Jaisalmer Fort, colloquially known as '*Sone ka Quila*', or Golden Fort. On one side of the railway station premises, a group of gypsies was sitting and jamming to a regional folk music tune. To most, Jaisalmer railway station was a quaint but unassuming outpost, with its low archways and carved facades, a small point of connection in a vast, arid expanse. But to young Rani it was the edge of the world. Her trembling feet barely reached the ground when she sat on a wooden bench, and her small hands clutched at her dupatta as if it were a lifeline. Her heart pounded against her ribs like a trapped bird, in a painful rhythm that matched the muffled cries she dared not release.

Outside the station, Jaisalmer Fort rose like a golden leviathan, its sheer size casting a shadow that seemed to stretch across the world. The fort's vast walls glinted in the sunlight, their intricate carvings betraying no hint of the centuries they had endured. She had never seen anything so massive, so eternal. Her village, with its crumbling huts and uneven pathways, was a world of smallness, a place where even the largest banyan tree could be climbed if one was brave enough. But this fort? It was something else entirely. It seemed to her not merely a structure but a living creature, its massive walls breathing slowly in the desert heat. To Rani, it was a giant sentinel watching her plight with indifference. For all its life, it was uncaring, its cold grandeur a silent reminder of her insignificance.

The platform buzzed with life, vendors shouted as they sold chai, there was a sharp hiss of a pressure cooker, the sounds of porters hauling luggage and the clamour of passengers. Yet to Rani, all of it blurred into meaningless noise. Her world had shrunk to the cold grip of Kala Shah's hand on her arm. The air was heavy, thick with the scent of sand and despair, and the oppressive weight of her own helplessness. Every sound, every movement around her, only emphasized how small she was, how utterly incapable she was of resisting the current dragging her away from everything she knew.

Kala Shah, her captor, stood nearby, his cruel eyes scanning the platform. He barked orders at someone, his voice slicing through the air like the sharp edge of a knife. Rani flinched, her body curling inwardly, as if to make her invisible. She wanted to scream, to run, to somehow claw her way back to the safety of her village, but the weight of her circumstances pressed down on her like the desert heat, immobilizing her.

As soon as the train arrived on the platform, the passengers ran towards the train to board their compartments. Kala Shah and Illiyaz waited for the train to halt completely before them. The train snaked in and stopped at the edge of the railway station. Illiaz forcibly pushed the girl into a dark, dingy compartment. A pair of hands gave a bundle of green-coloured notes to Kala Shah. The deal was done. The train whistled and started to move after a few minutes. Kala Shah and Illiaz walked towards the desert and disappeared into the darkness of night. The train ran very fast. Someone opened the black cloth tied around Rani's face. Rani blinked for some time. Everything looked blurry and black. Rani was terrified. She did not know where they were going, where this journey would end. Rani remembered Ma and Daadi. Rani remembered Raju Bhaiya. Tears rolled down from her eyes. She recalled how Kala Shah had inflicted inhumane torture on her by imprisoning her in a room without food or water for God knows how long. She shuddered out of fear. She hid her face in the black cloth and shut her eyes.

Kala Shah yanked her to her feet and pushed her towards the waiting train, Rani stumbled, her feet dragging on the stone platform. She was ushered into a dim, crowded compartment, the air heavy with the smell of sweat and damp fabric. She was forced on to a seat by the window, where her eyes were immediately drawn to the scene outside as the train groaned in preparation for its departure.

Through the dusty glass, the fort loomed larger still, its golden sandstone glowing like molten metal under the sun. The fortress seemed alive with secrets, its labyrinthine passages and watchful turrets whispering of ancient kings and forgotten battles. It was as if the fort contained the entire history of the desert within its walls, yet offered no answers to Rani's silent pleas. Instead, it seemed to say: this is the way of things. We have seen it before, and we will see it again.

The size of the structure dwarfed her spirit, destroying the last shreds of hope she had clung to. She wondered if this was how life was like. She thought of Kala Shah's promises of safety, his oily smile as he led her away from the only home she had ever known. How quickly those promises had turned into chains.

As the train jolted into motion, Rani pressed her forehead against the window, watching the platform slide away. The crowd thinned, the cries of the vendors faded, and soon all she could see was the endless desert shimmering under the sun. The golden sand stretched in every direction – a parched ocean devoid of life. To her it seemed like the desert was consuming the world, swallowing everything into its unrelenting emptiness. The scent of its sand seeped into the train, mingling with the faint acrid smell emitted by the coal engine.

Rani's thoughts turned inward, her young mind struggling to grasp the enormity of what was happening. She thought of her village, of the narrow lanes she used to run up and down in, the cool shade of the neem tree where she would sit with her grandmother listening to stories of gods and demons. She thought of her friend who had been killed, of the blood that had soaked into the sand, leaving a mark that would vanish with the next gust of wind. Life felt as fleeting as those grains of sand, slipping through her fingers no matter how tightly she tried to hold on to it.

She remembered something her grandmother had once said: '*The world is* mrigtrishna, *child. A mirage. It draws you in, only to vanish when you reach out to touch it.*'

Now, as the train clattered through the dust-blown plains, she wondered if the mirage had finally claimed her.

Was her life nothing more than a shimmer on the horizon – beautiful, beckoning, but hollow at its core? She had chased dreams, love, certainty. But had she been running toward water that never existed?

Mrigtrishna watches them all, she thought.

The thirsty deer, the desperate traveller, the child with wide eyes. It doesn't lie. It simply reflects what they hope to find.

The thought chilled her, even in the suffocating heat of the compartment.

Was she just another seeker, fooled by light and longing? Outside, the land shimmered in the sun. Inside her, everything was beginning to dissolve. As the train picked up speed, Rani's reflection flickered in the window, a ghostly image overlaid on the vast desert. She stared at her own face, her wide, frightened eyes, and for a moment she didn't recognize herself. She had always been small, but now she felt more diminished, like a shadow of her former self. The gigantic desert, the looming fort, the relentless noise and movement of the train – they all conspired to remind her of her own insignificance.

For the first time Rani truly understood the meaning of despair. It seemed that she has grown up to be an adult in a span of only a few days. It wasn't just sadness or fear – it was the crushing realization that she was powerless, that her life was no longer her own. She looked at the fort one last time as it disappeared, its golden walls glowing like a distant sun. It had stood for centuries, enduring the rise and fall of empires, indifferent to the lives that had passed through its shadow. And now, Rani realized, she was just another fleeting figure in its endless story, a grain of sand caught in the vast, uncaring desert.

The train left the station with a gust of black smoke. Kala Shah stood on the platform and checked his pocket. Yes, he could feel the vibration of the revolver that had killed Raju sometime before. Kala Shah had roared like a lion, 'Betrayer!' He was infuriated with Raju. He could not believe that his own blood could betray him! Raju was his son from Dali, one of his multiple mistresses. Dali and Raju stayed in Jahazpur and looked after his set of illegal businesses there. Kala Shah ran a racket involving child trafficking, drugs and illegal weapons across the state of Rajasthan. His network stretched across Barmer, Jaisalmer and Bhilwara, from where minor girls were kidnapped and trafficked to different parts of the country. Dali was his most capable counterpart, way smarter and slyer than his other mistresses, but Raju had been a rebel with rotten ethics. 'The fool got a death he deserved,' smirked Kala Shah, and looked up at the evening sky to watch a giant vulture carrying a tiny prey in its mouth soaring across the sky. 'Rebels have no right to live,' contemplated Kala Shah as he took out a betel from a silver box, put it inside his mouth and chewed on it till his mouth turned red like that of a raven that has just pecked at its prey. Kala Shah was ruthless, demonic and noxious; he did not love anyone apart from himself.

Rani was born in the village of Bakhera in the Jahazpur town of Bhilwara. Jahazpur was a historic town with a legendary fort whose origin dated back to the days of the Mauryan emperor Samprati, the grandson of Ashoka. The Jain temple of Swastidham was built around this fort. Bakhera was approximately one hour from the tehsil of Jahazpur, and most of the dwellers of Bakhera were dependent on Jahazpur for their daily needs. Rani's ancestors were Banjaras, the nomadic tribe of Rajasthan. Rani had heard from her grandmother that they originally belonged to the Rajput clan who retreated to the forests to protect themselves from the Mughals and came to reside in the outskirts of the city post-Independence. Rani's father, Ratan Singh, was a puppeteer from the Bhat community of Rajasthan.

Ratan Singh excelled in the art of Kathputli, which he had learnt from his parents. Often, he would be hired to present puppet shows at the local weddings. The art of puppetry among Rajasthan's Bhat community is as colourful and dramatic as the tales their wooden characters bring to life. These tribal puppeteers, who hail from a lineage of storytellers, have been telling stories of gods, kings and commoners for centuries. The origins of Kathputli are steeped in folklore. Some say the Bhats were once royal entertainers who narrated stories of epic battles and courtly intrigues, while others whisper that their nimble fingers and quick wit were put to use in espionage. These humble performers doubled as spies, slipping into enemy territory under the guise of being itinerant storytellers. Through clever allegory and seemingly innocent performances, they relayed crucial intelligence back to their patrons, proving that even puppeteers can have a hand in politics – quite literally.

The Bhats' puppets are no ordinary playthings. Hand-carved from mango wood, the puppets are dressed in vibrant, traditional attire and have expressive, painted faces that can convey everything from royal fury to romantic mischief. A typical performance unfolds on a portable stage, with the puppeteer pulling strings from behind a curtain while also doing the narration in a rich, dramatic voice. The performances are a riot of action. Villains cackle, camels trot, and heroes swing swords that are, well, a bit too tiny to look intimidating. But the Bhats' storytelling prowess ensures that the audience hangs on to their every word, whether it's a retelling of a king's bravery or a cheeky tale about a scheming neighbour (with names changed, of course, to avoid post-show confrontations).

Their itinerant lifestyle adds another layer of intrigue to their profile. The Bhats travel from village to village, bringing their wooden troupe in compact boxes. While they look like simple entertainers, their knack for observation is unparalleled. A sharp-eared puppeteer could weave a scandalous village quarrel into the next day's performance, subtly airing grievances while everyone laughed at the 'fictional' characters. Imagine attending a puppet show and suddenly realizing, mid-giggle, that the puppet with the oversized nose is suspiciously similar to your uncle who recently 'lost' his neighbour's goat.

Then there's the spicy tale of how puppetry once saved a kingdom (or so the Bhats claim). Legend has it that a particularly resourceful puppeteer distracted an invading army by staging a puppet battle that was so realistic the soldiers paused to watch it. By the time the show ended, the king's troops had regrouped and the invaders were fleeing – not from swords, but from humiliation. If this isn't evidence of the Bhats' flair for drama, what is?

Socially, the Bhats occupy a fascinating niche. Beyond their role as entertainers, they've historically been mediators and messengers. Their performances often tackled moral dilemmas, teaching lessons in loyalty, honesty and wit. Puppet performances, though small, wielded immense power, and were renowned for both their jest and the justice they stood for.

Despite their charm, the Bhats are finding the modern world a tough stage. Their craft struggles against the glitz of cinema and smartphones. But in Rajasthan, kathputlis still twirl to the tune of ancient tales. Whether they're telling stories of romance, ribbing a greedy landlord or (allegedly) passing secrets to kings, the Bhats remind us that sometimes the smallest puppets pull the biggest strings.

Ratan was popular for his puppetry across Bhilwara and earned well to sustain his family. He had a little 'pukka' cemented house of his own. But a truck hit him while he was returning home one evening and he died even before he could be transported to the local hospital, leaving eight-year-old Rani, her mother Laaji and Daadi Jashoda behind. Rani was severely traumatized to see the blood-stained body of her dead father, to see how bitterly her mother and Daadi cried when her father's body was placed on top of a wooden pyre and cremated. Rani stood in silence and witnessed how the fiercely lapping fire had turned the corpse of her father into ashes, within a few minutes. Rani was deeply wounded. She returned home with her Ma and Daadi, but could not forget the sight of her father's pyre. It haunted her to this today. Then followed days of helpless penury and struggle. Laaji had no idea how to earn any money and feed her daughter and ailing mother-in-law. All she could do was to pawn her silver jewellery, one piece after another, to the moneylender to feed their hunger. But soon her stock of jewellery, silver utensils and domesticated animals was exhausted and there was nothing left to sell. For a few days Laaji starved, feeding the food that was left to Rani and Jashoda, but her striking physical transformation from a plump healthy woman to a woman with sunken eyes and cheeks could not hide the fact of her starvation from Jashoda. The art of puppetry had run in their blood for the last seven generations. Left with no other options to survive, the ailing, nonagenarian Jashoda decided to support the family by taking up the job of puppetry, like her dead son. However, standing for hours in the marketplace or on a highway or in front of the village school and doing puppet shows was not as easy as the Banjaran thought it would be. Although money started trickling in as spectators paid notice to the old lady, she became unconscious and fell severely ill after some days of standing under the scorching sun and from travelling far distances to ply her craft. Jashoda became bedridden, and though she had the will power to continue her work, her feeble health would not permit it. So once again they began sinking into poverty.

Two years passed. Rani was now ten. She had stopped going to school after Ratan's death since they just did not have the means to send her to school. During these two years, while Laaji and Jashoda strived to make things happen, Rani sat at home, traumatized and heartbroken. Every day she would stand in front of Ratan's picture and practise some puppetry. She had seen Daadi and her father stage numerous plays with puppets in the village fairs, and she had memorized all the scripts. Every fortnight it had been a different village, new people, new juicy stories – everything to make a young child's life full of adventure and mystery. Rani found a strange bliss in talking to her puppets and making them dance to her tune. She was the mistress of her huge coterie of puppets, who abided by her every wish and command. They made her feel like Alladin on a magic-carpet adventure! She would play with the wooden dolls, dress them up colourfully and call them by amusing names. She would beat her little dholak and start narrating intriguing tales of love, friendship and war while her fingers would hold the strings attached to the dolls and make them dance and act out the tales. Eventually, she began to put up small puppet plays for her friends and neighbours. Her audience would applaud, saying she was a worthy successor to Ratan. When Jashoda and Laaji could not earn enough for even one square meal a day, and the sight of their hungry child would not stop haunting them, Rani stepped into the show, literally. She told her Ma and her Daadi not to worry, that she would give it a good try. Seeing her confidence and seeing no other way out of their plight, they agreed. Rani started doing puppet shows at the highway that connected Bakhera to Jahazpur. Her house was about eight kilometres from the highway, a distance she mostly walked, except on the days some neighbour or other offered her a free lift on his bicycle. Tourists and other travellers passing through the highway watched her shows. They were a welcome relief in the midst of their hectic journeys, and they paid her, though very little. The man at the highway dhaba would offer her some food at times. Rani would step out at dawn and walk back home after sunset, through the desert, carrying whatever money she had earned. Daadi and Ma would be worried for her, and also ashamed that their tender child had to work so hard.

Rani looked unconventionally pretty. She had inherited the beauty of her Daadi, who used to look quite exotic in her youth, with her peach-ish complexion, thick, brown hair, a perfectly structured nose and emerald eyes, bearing an uncanny resemblance to the Romanis of Europe. Ratan Singh too had the same kind of physical features. Rani had heard from her father about the Romanis, a race that had originated from Rajasthan and had migrated westward a thousand moons before.

Just as in the golden sands of Rajasthan the Bhat tribals' vibrant puppetry breathed life into stories that had been passed down generations, thousands of miles away, in the streets of Europe, the Romani people danced and sang similar tales of exile, adventure and survival. Though separated by continents and centuries, the Bhat and the Romani people shared an unspoken bond, which lay woven into the fabric of their legends and languages. Linguistic studies have uncovered strange parallels between their dialects – words like *dori* (thread), *raja* (king), and *churi* (bangle) danced across both tongues, hinting at their common origin. A journey of discovery unfolded when a curious linguist uncovered an ancient story from a forgotten manuscript telling of a caravan that once crossed the deserts of Rajasthan, their people seeking refuge from invading forces, carrying their music, gods and myths with them as they fled westward. Over time they settled in Europe, their culture adapting to new lands but never losing its roots. The legacy of these wandering people has endured, both in the bustling bazaars of Rajasthan and in the cobblestoned streets of Europe.

Daadi would often say that Rani would grow up to be an amazingly beautiful girl! However, her long days of hard labour were tarnishing Rani's beauty. She was turning weak and her complexion was getting dulled by the dust and sun. Rani would often get blisters on her feet from the extensive walking she did every day. Her diet was not adequate to support the physical exertion of her daily work. Yet Rani was happy. At night she would sleep next to her Daadi with her dragon snores. Rani was only ten, but her hard life was wearing her down. Every day she would wake up by the first light, her body stiff from a night spent lying on a straw mat on the cold earth, as she had nothing more than a thin blanket to cover herself.

But when night fell, Rani's world transformed. Every night, in her world of dreams, the tiny puppets she brought to life each day took on a life of their own. They spoke to her, comforted her and became her closest friends. To Rani they were not just wooden figures; they were her companions, her confidants, the only ones who understood the depth of her loneliness and her yearning for a life beyond the confines of poverty.

One night, as Rani lay on her straw mat, the soft murmur of the desert winds outside whispering their stories, her puppets came to life, as they always did. But tonight it was different. Tonight, the tale they shared was the story of Lakhi Banjaran and the shepherd, a tale she had heard her grandmother tell many times. It was a story of freedom, love and longing that had always captured her imagination. The puppets danced around her in the dream-like haze; it was as though they were alive. The tallest puppet, a woman adorned in bright, flowing colours, took centre stage. It was Lakhi, the Banjaran, the free spirit of the desert, as wild and untamed as the winds that blew across the sands.

Lakhi Banjaran, in the tale Rani dreamed, was a woman whose heart was as vast as the desert itself. She lived a life of freedom, wandering the dunes, singing songs of sorrow and joy, her voice carried on the wind. She was both a symbol of strength and of loss, bound by nothing but the endless sky above and the golden sands below. A shepherd – Raghav – had fallen in love with Lakhi. He was a man of the earth, steady and grounded, with a heart full of tenderness. He had longed for her for years, knowing that her soul was as wild as the desert, but he loved her anyway. They met under a moonlit sky one fateful night, when the desert winds were calm and everything felt as if it had stopped for them.

But Lakhi was not meant to be tamed. As the puppets whispered the tale to Rani, she saw it all in vivid colours. Raghav loved Lakhi with all his heart, but Lakhi could not stay. The call of the desert was too strong, the winds too powerful. She was a creature of the earth and sky, and no matter how deep Raghav's love was, she could not be bound by it. And so Lakhi left, disappearing into the desert once more, leaving behind a heartbroken shepherd and a land that would never forget the wild woman who had wandered it.

As the dream unfolded, Rani felt both sadness and exhilaration. She saw Lakhi's spirit, untethered and free, racing across the golden sands. It was the life Rani longed for – the life she dreamed of when the sun bore down upon her and the dust of the road made her weary. In her dream, she was Lakhi, running through the vast desert, her heart light, her soul free. She was not bound by poverty or the harsh realities of her waking world. In the dream, there were no limits.

The puppets, now silent, watched her with knowing eyes. They had shared their story with her, but they had also given her something else – hope. Hope that one day she too could be free. Hope that someday, she could escape the unrelenting sun, the daily toil . . .

One evening, after Rani was done for the day and was arranging her puppets inside her prized possession, a small, well-worn bag made of camel leather, to leave for home, she saw a boy, perhaps sixteen to eighteen years old, on a motor bike waving at her from a distance. He was wearing flashy clothes and was around six feet tall and well-built. He had a moustache and beard. Rani ignored him. Daadi had warned her against the city boys after Vrinda in her village had run away with one such 'imposter'. The boy halted his motor bike and ran towards her. '*Ghano badhiyo khel dikhawe hai bainad!*' he exclaimed. Rani was relieved; he admired her puppetry and regarded her as his 'sister'; he was not one of those rogues. Rani smiled at him. He offered Rani a chocolate and said, '*Bainad, aavan ro hafta haveli mein badi daawat hai … Tu apno jod ro khel dikhawegi? Jam ke milsi dhani paisa!*' He was inviting her to perform at a party in someone's bungalow, and she would be paid handsomely. '*Kikdi haveli, Bhaisa?*' she asked. He showed her the mansion at the end of the highway towards Bhilwara and said he would pick her up from the highway and drop her at her home after the show. He gave her some money as an advance. Rani said her father never used to accept money before his work was over and that she would only take money after people had applauded her act. The boy smiled in agreement and started his motor bike. Within moments he vanished, raising a huge storm of sand behind him. Rani was exhilarated! Finally, her art had been noticed by someone worthy. She would get the opportunity to perform before dignitaries!

Rani wanted to share the big news with her Ma and Daadi but she decided to get the money after the show and surprise them. Rani thought of taking long leave after the haveli show. Her body needed rest. Her legs used to ache badly at night. She would rest well, she thought, and play with her friends. Rani looked at her father's picture hung on the wall and asked Baba to bless her. On the day of the feast, Rani wore a green ghaghra gifted to her by her father. She carefully chose the puppets and dresses for them and rehearsed all morning for a splendid show. Laaji and Jashoda asked if anything special was coming up, to which Rani said no. After a few shows, she eagerly waited for the youth to turn up. He arrived in the late afternoon and picked her up on his motorbike. Rani sat behind him and closed her eyes. She had never ridden a motorbike. The boy asked her to hold him tight. They flew away with the whirling wind. It took about two hours for them to reach the haveli. Rani got down from the motorbike and looked around in awe at the palatial mansion of yellow sandstone radiant in the golden light of the crimson sun. Rani stood in the courtyard of the mansion. It had fountains and gardens full of flowers. Rani eagerly stared at the ornate balconies, the grand pavilions and the domes resembling those of their village mosque. Rani had never seen such a big house ever in her life. The boy had talked about a feast but Rani could see no lights, no decoration, no people, apart from few men who looked scary. '*Dawaat kidhar hai, Bhaisa?*' asked Rani. The young boy winked at her and asked her to follow him. Now Rani was frightened. She did not want to go in with the boy. She looked like a tiny urchin in front of the colossal mansion that appeared to be empty. An afraid Rani asked the boy to drop her back on the highway. The boy laughed slyly and ordered the men to take her inside. Rani started to scream at the top of her voice. Two men picked her up and started swinging her by her limbs. Rani cried and begged them to let her go. The boy laughed. Meanwhile, as she was being taken in through the cast iron gates, Rani saw another boy, perhaps a little younger than the first one. He was short, fair and lean. Seeing him, the men put Rani down and stood back. The boy came to Rani and said his name was Raju and that he lived in the haveli. Raju asked Rani why she was there and why she was crying. Sobbing, Rani told him everything. Raju listened to her account and slapped the other young boy hard. The young boy turned red in anger, left the courtyard and disappeared inside the mansion. Raju asked Rani to quickly follow him. He took her to the back end of the haveli and asked her to wait till he returned, saying he would be back with his car as soon as possible. Raju was about to move away when two men, led by a woman, started to come towards them. The woman was fat, and looked ruthless and dangerous. She was wearing a black ghaghra-choli and a lot of jewellery. She had the sun sign of Scorpio tattooed on her right arm. She instructed the men to take Rani inside and asked Raju to leave. Raju protested. He shouted at the woman and asked her to release Rani, to which the woman turned a deaf ear. One of the two goons picked Rani up in his arms and took her inside. Rani cried bitterly, pleading with him to let her go until her voice faded away. The goons took Rani down almost a hundred steps till they reached a scary dark room in the basement of the haveli. They threw her in there and locked the door. Rani was terrified. She looked around to notice only darkness. She cried and cried but no one came to help. She was hungry. She missed her Daadi and Ma. They must be worried about her, she thought. She did not know if she could ever meet them again.

Rani was awakened by the creak of the door. She had fallen asleep crying. She did not know what the time was, whether it was day or night. There was absolute darkness inside the room. She saw the goons standing on the other side of the iron gates with torches in their hands. With them was another man who looked at her curiously. He was massively built and had an unusually thick moustache. His teeth were stained and he wore dhoti-kurta and a huge red turban. Rani screamed loudly, believing that the whole of the village would hear her cries, but the man just laughed at her. She realized that her screams had no sound at all. Her throat had turned into an enemy at that very hour of need. She had a stabbing pain all over her body. She did not know what these men were going to do with her. Then the iron gates were opened and one of the goons pushed Rani outside. The thick-moustached man threw a bag at her face and asked her to wear the dress inside it. Rani refused. The man slapped her pitilessly. Rani now looked like one of her own lifeless and listless puppets. She changed into those clothes out of fear. They then brought Rani outside the haveli and made her sit on the back of a camel. Her face was tied with a black cloth. Rani wished Raju Bhaiya would come and rescue her from these demons. But no one was around. The camel started pacing. Rani cried hopelessly.

Rani was shivering in the cold of the damp compartment of the train. She noticed that the man who was travelling with her was deep asleep. Rani slowly stood up and tried to walk towards the window, but she realized that her legs were tied tightly with a rope. She wanted to untie it when, suddenly, a heavy voice spoke out of the dark: '*Zyada fudak mat; nahi toh pankh idharee kaat dunga*!' This threat, to 'chop her wings' was followed by a tight slap straight across Rani's face. Her cheek hurt terribly. Rani tried to locate the man but could see nothing in the dark. Slowly, she went back to her place and sat quietly. She had cried so much in the last few hours that all her tears must have dried up and now refused to flow. Rani found herself like one of her own puppets that would act exactly the way she wanted. She felt the puppets had cursed her for making them dance to her tune. She could hear the whistle and noise of the train, which she believed must be taking her to some hell.

Rani was woken up by the man who had travelled with her. In the morning light, Rani saw his face clearly. He looked dirty. He was tall with grey hair and sunken eyes and cheeks. There was a slash mark on his forehead. He was smoking a beedi and looking at Rani. Rani was terribly hungry but didn't dare ask the man for food. After some time the train stopped. The man, after untying her feet, pushed Rani out of the train and on to the platform. He started to walk, holding her hand so tight that she felt like crying out in agony. Rani looked around. It was a very big railway station. Rani had seen a railway station only once in her life – last night, where she was forced into the train. But this railway station was far bigger than that. There were people everywhere and they spoke different languages. The sunken-eyed man was walking so fast that Rani had to almost run to keep pace with him. Rani was perspiring and breathless. Suddenly the man stopped. He hailed a vehicle and put her in it. It was a black and yellow four-wheeler. Rani sat in it, frozen. The man only spoke one word to the driver: 'Kamathipura.' The four-wheeler stopped in front of a long lane. The man pushed Rani out of the vehicle. In the dark, dim light of that sultry evening, Rani saw a busy lane with many men and women. The streets glimmered with lights that flickered like stars, dancing against the night's velvet darkness. To Rani, a girl of ten, the world she had entered felt like a fairy tale. Her eyes were wide with curiosity. Her small feet, clad in worn sandals, tapped lightly against the cobbled lane as her head darted from side to side, taking in the dazzling spectacle of colours, laughter and music that wafted through the air.

Rani found herself enchanted by the women who seemed to float about like queens. They were draped in bright sarees and wore shimmering jewels. Their faces were painted in dazzling colours. Their laughter rang out like a melody, and they strode about confidently, leaving trails of perfume in the air. It was a world far removed from the simplicity of her village life. It was a world she believed was magical.

The irony of her situation was invisible to her. She had no way of knowing that the bright jewels were as fake as the smiles that adorned those faces. The women's laughter, a practised melody of seduction, veiled hearts heavy with sorrow. The irony that Rani saw adoration where there was only treachery was as tragic as it was inevitable. Her innocence acted as a shield, preventing her from perceiving the shadows lurking beneath the neon glow all around.

The air was thick with a paradox that Rani was too young to grasp. The alleyway was alive with sights and sounds designed to distract, to beguile, to sell an illusion. To the women there, it was a stage on which they were forced to perform nightly. To Rani, it was a celebration.

As she wandered further into this labyrinth of false enchantment, a figure emerged from the shadows and stood on the doorstep of building. It was a brothel, but of course Rani did not know. Kajol, her name whispered like a secret, appeared as though conjured from a dream. She was dressed in the finery of her trade, wearing a pristine white sari that shimmered faintly under the dim light of a flickering lantern. The purity of her attire contrasted sharply with the world she inhabited, creating an image of defiance against the filth surrounding her.

Kajol's eyes, lined with kohl and filled with a strange, quiet sorrow, softened as they fell on the young girl. There was a tenderness in her gaze that Rani mistook for love. In truth, it was pity mixed with an ache born of understanding

– a recognition of an innocence that would soon be eroded. Kajol bent down, her movements as fluid as a river, and gently caressed Rani's cheek.

'Where are you from, little one?' she asked, her voice like silk brushing against Rani's ears.

Rani, shy but mesmerized, hesitated before answering. Her voice was small, as though afraid to disturb the dream-like moment. 'From my village. The city is so big and bright. Are you a princess?'

Kajol's lips curved into a bittersweet smile. Her heart, hardened by years of cruelty, softened momentarily. From the folds of her sari, she retrieved a tiny purse tucked close to her chest. With delicate fingers, she produced a small piece of chocolate, its wrapper gleaming in the dim light. She offered it to Rani, who accepted it with wide eyes and trembling hands. 'Eat, little one,' Kajol murmured, her voice a lullaby. 'You must keep your strength.'

The chocolate melted on Rani's tongue, filling her with a sweetness that seemed to match the warmth radiating from Kajol. For a brief moment the world felt perfect to Rani – a world where kind princesses in white saris gifted chocolate to strangers. She looked up at Kajol with adoration, her innocent mind crafting a narrative far removed from the reality of her situation.

To Rani, Kajol was a beacon of beauty and kindness. She couldn't see the cracks in the façade – the weariness in Kajol's eyes, the bruises covered by the saree, the emptiness behind the soft words. For Kajol, the encounter was a painful reminder of her own lost innocence, a fleeting connection to the child she once was.

As Rani walked away, her small figure disappearing into the dimly lit street, Kajol remained on the doorstep, her pristine white sari catching the light. She watched the girl with a mixture of longing and despair, knowing that the child's illusions would soon shatter. The thought weighed heavily on her, but she quickly buried it, just as she buried every other feeling that threatened to surface.

For Rani, the night was filled with wonder, but for Kajol it was another chapter in a story she wished she could rewrite.

In that encounter, two worlds collided – one of untainted wonder, the other of silent suffering. Rani walked away with a sense of amazement, her heart light and carefree. Kajol, however, stood frozen in the doorway, her pristine white, a defiant symbol against a world that had long since turned to ashes.

Rani saw an elderly woman waving at her; she was wearing a simple blue salwar kameez. Her hair was neatly tied in a bun. She made her sit by her side and asked her whether she was hungry. She gave her roti and curry to eat. Rani ate like she had not eaten for ages and was grateful to the woman for being so kind. The woman took her to a room and asked her to rest. Rani happily obeyed her. It was a tiny room on the mezzanine floor of the building with a small bed and a pedestal fan running noisily. There were no windows. The walls of the room were full of pictures of men and women Rani had never seen in her life, but the women were almost naked. Rani sat on the bed and shut her eyes. She felt sleepy. She was grateful to God for protecting her from the devils and bringing her finally to a safe abode. The horrifying incidents of the past few days had left her completely drained. Her small body had no strength left. All she wanted was to sleep. She dozed off within moments.

Rani woke up abruptly. She felt something heavy on her. She opened her eyes. To her utter dismay she saw a stranger, a man, on her body. He was smelling foul. He was aggressively trying to tear Rani's frock. Rani started to hit him but he was way stronger than she was. He slapped Rani many times and tore open her frock. Rani screamed for help, shouted, yelled, begged the man to leave her alone, but her voice was lost in the noise of the fan. The man started to bite her all over, like those jackals of her village that used to hunt by night with fiery, salivating tongues hanging out of their jaws. The jackal stalks its prey under the indifferent gaze of the wilderness, its movements fluid and calculated. The sparrow, unaware of the shadow closing in, flits about in the innocence of routine, oblivious to the doom that circles her fragile world. The strike is sudden – a flash of teeth, the rustle of feathers, the panicked thrashing of wings as they succumb to the grip of inevitability. The sparrow's confusion is brief, her bewilderment silenced as she becomes sustenance for a predator driven by instinct. For the jackal, it is survival, an act as natural as the sun setting behind the trees. For the sparrow, it is the cruel end to a world that once seemed safe.

In the civilized world, the hunt takes on a darker, more insidious form. The man, a creature bound by social rules and cultural facades, casts aside his mask to reveal the beast lurking beneath. He preys not on a sparrow but on a young woman – a sex worker who has learned to navigate the vulnerabilities of her existence but is unprepared for the feral hunger disguised as humanity. To him, she is not a person but a vessel for his desires, her autonomy stripped away in an act that mirrors the jackal's attack on the sparrow but is far more monstrous. Unlike the jackal, he is not driven by survival but by a primal, unchecked cruelty that seeks to dominate and destroy.

For the girl, the experience is shattering, rupturing her understanding of the world. She enters the encounter expecting a transaction, a fleeting moment in a day filled with many. But what unfolds is something she cannot fully grasp – a violence that transcends the physical and seeps into her very being. Bewilderment clouds her mind, the weight of the act too heavy to comprehend. Unlike the sparrow, she has a consciousness that struggles to make sense of the event, but the absence of a frame of reference leaves her adrift, unable to fathom its full gravity. She feels broken in ways she cannot articulate, her sense of safety and self-worth gnawed away by the man's beastly appetite.

The damage is profound, though it leaves no visible feathers scattered on the ground. It lingers in her mind like a shadow, eroding her understanding of trust, of human connection, of her own worth. The jackal moves on, its hunger sated, leaving behind nothing but a lifeless sparrow. The man, too, resumes his place in society, his mask securely in place, blending back into the world of civility. But for the girl the encounter becomes a haunting wound, an inexplicable moment of destruction that reshapes her life in ways she may never fully comprehend. The world, once familiar, now feels alien—a place where predators walk in human form, their masks hiding the wild beasts beneath.

Rani recalled how she and her friends had once seen them tearing a pigeon apart and feasting on its flesh. Rani cried out of pain. She was unaware of what was being done to her. She felt an intolerable pain in her lower abdomen. She lost consciousness.

When she opened her eyes she realized that she was in a different room, with huge walls painted white, high ceilings and long windows. Everywhere around was dirty, and there was a strange smell. She saw many other children of her age lying on thin mattresses, and bandaged here and there. She saw a thin tube stuck to the inside of her wrist and further attached to a bottle full of a watery liquid that hung upside down on a rod next to her bed. She noticed herself in a long, white frock. She could neither see that beastly man nor that ugly woman who had offered her food and water, rather two different women whom she had never met in her life. One elderly woman stroked her hair and said to another woman, '*Annu, doctor ko bula/bacchi ko hosh aaya hai.*' Annu replied, '*Bulati hoon Aapa*,' and went outside the room. The woman smiled at Rani and asked her to rest. Rani felt a burning pain in her lower abdomen, she yelled. The elderly woman sat by her side and consoled her. Rani's vision blurred. Everything became black.

In the tangled, breathless maze of Kamathipura, where the air carried the honk-honk of distant taxis and the tik tok of hurried footsteps, there existed an impossible bond among a band of women. It was a bond forged in the heat of survival, polished by shared laughter and sealed by a silence that spoke louder than words. They were not sisters by birth but by circumstance, each having carved out a corner for herself in a world that had tried to erase them. Their silence was a pact, a hush that wrapped around their histories, anchoring them to the present, like a Sicilian omertà. No one pried into the spidery webs of pasts abandoned; no one wanted to. The only way forward was to let those threads snap, to sweep the shards of yesterday into the gutters that ran alongside the crumbling buildings they now called home.

Eleven years had passed, like eleven moments or, rather, eleven lifetimes. Rani was twenty-one. She had spent eleven years of her life dying several deaths in the ruthless beds of demonic strangers and lived a few moments of happiness through the rare kindness of Aapa, Annu and, of course, officer Didi, who was like a ray of light breaking through the shadows of her and several other women like her's despair.

They say that Time is the best healer, but Rani always felt that Time could not heal, it just flitted past, compelling one to accept one's reality since there was no escape from it. Deep wounds never really healed, and even when they did they left scars behind as permanent reminders of the betrayals, abuse and pain, forcing one to relive those moments of anguish. Time is too feeble to mend broken souls. It only strengthens us to accept the truth, bury the pain deep inside us and walk the path of life. Time is a chameleon; sometimes life is painted with the vibrant colours of the spring, while sometimes acting like autumn with falling leaves and broken dreams.

Now Rani understood how she was trafficked from her remote village in Rajasthan to one of the largest red-light areas of the country when she was only ten. Rani understood how brutally she was raped by a man here in Chauda Gulli of Kamathipura right on the day she had stepped in. Annu Didi had told her how she was lying half dead in a pool of blood after being raped and assaulted, how Maya was thinking of throwing her away on the street, doubting if she would live, and how Aapa had arrived with Annu, Kajol and a few other women and had rushed her to hospital, and how, miraculously, she was alive despite being nearly fatally injured and had recuperated after several months under the affectionate and healing touch of Aapa. Rani remembered how she had begun work as a babysitter to the children of the women who were known as sex workers and had herself become one of them, and how this handful of women had been protecting her against the abuses of Maya and her acquaintances. There were nights when Rani would tremble in her sleep out of fear remembering her trauma and Aapa would take her in her embrace. There were days when Maya would abuse Rani for being a wrong bargain and try to hurt her physically and an intoxicated Kajol would appear from nowhere and stand as a shield before her. An annoyed Maya would hiss like a cobra and run away. There were days when Annu would hide her in the wooden cupboard of her room so that Anna Shetty and his brothers could not find her. Rani's eyes moistened whenever she thought that God had done a grave injustice to her by making her land in the pit of Kamathipura, but the next very moment she would thank God for sending her a gang of sisters, without whom she would have died a terrible death by now. Rani would amuse the children of the women of Kamathipura with her puppetry. Aapa and Kajol had got her a few wooden puppets and some accessories for them from the market. Slowly, even the women requested her to entertain them with puppet plays whenever they were depressed and felt worn out physically and mentally. The young Rani did her best to make them smile, and in return they took care of her selflessly. In a world where love was a myth, Rani developed an unbelievably strong bond of affection with the so-called prostitutes, who not only stood by her but also gave her the time to prepare herself psychologically before adopting the trade as a profession.

Rani was an adult by then. Her striking beauty became more exquisite with age. Her emerald eyes, peach-hued complexion and long, cascading curls of rich brown hair made her look like one of those women depicted in Greek frescoes. She was a vision, of the kind seldom seen in the dirty gutters of Kamathipura, and thus was 'branded', with a hefty price against her name. She was carefully peddled only to those who could afford the heavy price attached to her. She was no ordinary woman of her trade but a rarity. And her exclusivity became her power and sword with which to fight the devils of the world.

Rani lived up to her name – a queen navigating the darkness of Kamathipura, commanding respect and value even in a world designed to destroy her. She created a perfect symphony of survival with Aapa, Annu, and Kajol. On nights when the beasts roared outside their door, banging it with their fists and demanding entry, they would drown out the noise with their own music. Aapa's crack-crack laughter would start it, followed by Annu's heh-heh-heh giggles. Kajol would join in with her dhoom-dhoom guffaws, and Rani's tinkle-tinkle peals would tie it all together. They would laugh until their ribs hurt, until their voices echoed down the narrow lanes. It was a sound so full of life that even the beasts paused, bewildered.

There were competitions too, absurd and childish, but fiercely fought. Who could peel the most onions without crying. Who could mimic the shrill screech-screech of their landlady's voice the best. Who could make the loudest slurp-slurp sound while eating chai-dipped biscuits. These games, ridiculous as they seemed, were their way of reclaiming fragments of their girlhood, which had been stolen from them. In their common room, laughter rang like the ding-ding of temple bells, sacred and unstoppable.

On festival days, the women transformed. Aapa became the snap-snap of crisp saris being pleated, her sharp eyes ensuring no pleat was out of place. Annu was the clink-clink of bangles on wrists as her hands deftly applied kajal to tired eyes. Kajol's fire burned hotter, her voice the crack-crack of defiance as she joked about scaring off the rich customers. And Rani – she was the swirl-swirl of colour, her lehenga a whirlwind of red and gold as she prepared for the one thing she loved most: dancing.

No one could rob them of their laughter, their defiance, their childlike pleasures. Kamathipura might have been a cactus, its spines pricking at them every moment of their existence, but they were the desert flowers that bloomed on it. Their lives might have been painted in sepia tones, but their room was a palette of colour: the scarlet of Kajol's rage, the golden-yellow of Annu's curry, the silver of Appa's wisdom and the vivid hues of Rani's dreams. Their laughter, their games, their competitions – they were all a declaration that they were alive, that no beast could devour the essence of who they were.

And so, in the shadowy streets of Kamathipura, amidst the clang of metal, the honking of cars and the whisper-rustle of lives being traded, these four women stood as a symphony of survival. They didn't just endure; they lived, they laughed, and they danced, like the rare flowers that bloom in the harshest of deserts.

With time, Rani learnt the trade and accustomed herself to selling her body, multiple times a day, to strangers who paid money in exchange for getting their sexual desires satiated, their perverted fantasies brought alive or their frustrations let out. Rani's heart still ached for her Daadi and Ma. Rani faintly remembered the fairy tales that Daadi used to narrate to her. It was just that there were no good djinns in her life who would appear out of smoke and take her away from the hell pit to her own land. But she had indeed met a few valiant real-life warriors, like the kings from Daadi's tales, who had stood around her on guard till she herself had transformed into one of them, strong and brave.

Inauguration of the 'All Women Post Office' in Kamathipura

Aadhaar campaign for the children of commercial sex workers in Kamathipura

Yearning for childhood The paintings, by 10 children from the red light area of Kamathipura contain the young artists' visions and aspirations, that can be read via a QR code.

She is my father

A postcard-making initiative by India Post helps children on the fringes pay tribute to their mothers: sex workers of Kamathipura

SARASWATHY NAGARAJAN

A postcard featuring a woman's face with a moustache, painted by the 14-year-old daughter of a commercial sex worker from Kamathipura, Mumbai, has a message. A QR code behind the postcard, when scanned, reveals that the artist has depicted the dual identity of women in Kamathipura, who have to play the roles of mother and father to their children.

Yet another postcard, Innocence, shows a child on a swing, symbolising the innocence of childhood, which the artist says she has always craved.

Ten such postcards made by children of sex workers from Kamathipura, the oldest red-light district in Mumbai, deliver messages of hope, innocence and optimism. The names of the young artists have not been revealed to protect their identity.

The set of postcards, which costs ₹180, and contains each artist's vision in a QR code, was recently released by Bhagat Singh Koshyari, Governor of Maharashtra, at Raj Bhavan in the presence of the children, social workers and officials of India Post, in a massive boost for a demographic that is usually ignored by the public and the system.

The postcards are one of the byproducts of sustained intervention by Swathi Pandey, Postmaster General of Mumbai region, that has made a difference in the lives of women in Kamathipura.

Poonam Awasti, who works with Apne Aap Women's Collective, an NGO, says it was a grand gesture of validation for the children and their mothers. The NGO has been closely associated with officers of India Post in their work in Kamathipura. "Each mother in Kamathipura is proud of the 10 youngsters who were invited to Raj Bhavan. Their paintings will travel across the world and it has motivated the children to dream big and empower themselves," says Poonam.

Swati says it all began in 2021, during a workshop on savings and investment in connection with the Sukanya Samriddhi Yojana, a savings scheme for the girl child, in Kamathipura. Swati happened to hear the women speak in Bengali. She spoke to them in the same language and the women, though startled, gradually opened up. Swathi asked if they were saving for a rainy day or for their children.

"That is when they told me they did not like going to a bank or post office because men often look down on them and they feel inadequate and ignored," she says.

Women empower women

Although there was a post office in Kamathipura, the women told Swati that they would feel comfortable only if it had women in all the posts. Swati assured them that she would convert it into a women-only office.

"I visited the office, and saw that it was a ramshackle building. To convert that into a women-only post office would, somehow, be demeaning to the women. So, it was spruced up, upgraded and computerised. Kamathipura Gali No. 8 Post Office is now one of our best-kept post offices. It is the fir[st] 'safe space' of its kind post offic[e] branch in Mumbai."

The post office was opened o[n] December 21, 2021. Sweta Kar[...] Post Master of the branch, [...] proud to be part of an interv[en]tion to help women from dis[ad]vantaged backgrounds. "Man[y of] them have opened post office [sav]ings accounts and learnt the b[asic] steps of banking. We have [also] helped them secure Aadhar c[ards] for their children."

Article in *The Hindu* after the release of picture postcards made from the paintings of the children of commercial sex workers

An ordinary evening with the toofani girls of Kamathipura

Article in the *Times of India* after the release of picture postcards made from the paintings of the children of commercial sex workers in Kamathipura

India Post gives voice to children of Kamathipura

Namita Devidayal | TNN

Mumbai: A thoughtful intervention will take a Mumbai child's imagination across the oceans into distant lands. India Post has just released a unique set of postcards made by kids of Kamathipura's commercial sex workers. The 10 postcard set was released on Saturday at Raj Bhavan by governor Bhagat Singh Koshyari in a small ceremony attended by postal officials, children and social workers.

Each postcard carries a QR code which, when scanned, describes the child's thoughts behind the painting, although it does not reveal the name of the child to protect his or her identity. For example, a picture featuring a woman's face with a moustache, done by a 14-year-old girl, depicts the dual identity of every woman in

One of the 10 postcards with a 14-year-old girl's image of her mother— one with a moustache

Kamathipura, who has had to play the role of both mother and father to her kids.

Postcards have been packaged in an envelope which carries a QR code linked to an article carried by **TOI** last month, which reported on first 'safe space' post office launched in Mumbai's oldest red light district. Priced at Rs 180, the postcard set, the brainchild of Mumbai's postmaster general Swati Pandey, will be available at select post offices.

Candid moment in the pocket room of Aapaa A.K.A. Salma

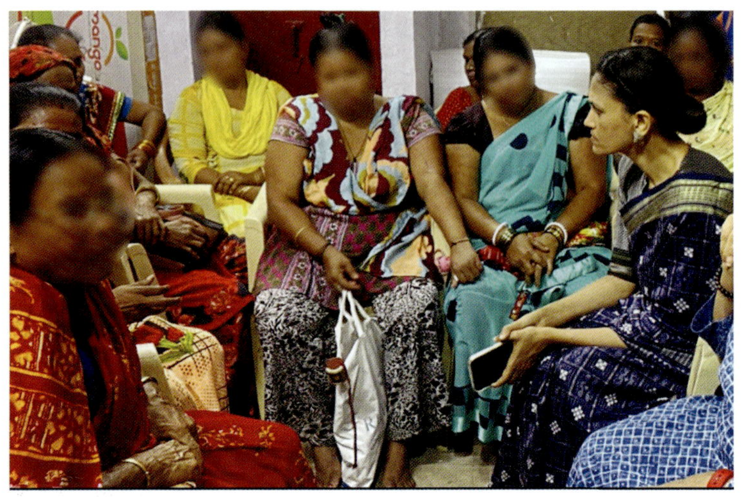

Counselling session with the commercial sex workers of Kamathipura

Aadhaar campaign and recreational event with the children of Kamathipura

Release of picture postcards made from the paintings of the children of commercial sex workers of Kamathipura. It was released by the then Governor of Maharashtra Shri Bhagat Singh Koshyari Ji.

'MILAAP' a session of interaction on mental health of the commercial sex workers of Kamathipura

A hug of warmth, empathy and assurance!

Tying the bond of love and protection. Celebrating Raksha Bandhan with the women of Kamathipura.

Raksha Bandhan with the toofani girls!

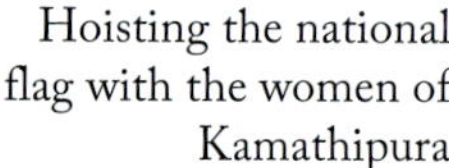

Hoisting the national flag with the women of Kamathipura

6

Into the Lion's Den

As the dawn cracks open the silence of the night, every story finds its moment of origin – a birthplace where destiny first stirs. In this chapter, the shadows lengthen over Kamathipura – that labyrinth of lost innocence where, in the late 1970s, a legend was born. Amongst the gang-wrought tumult of those years, Maya moved like an ancient serpent – silent, graceful and hypnotic. Her presence brought danger, destruction and forbidden wisdom. She was the black cat slipping between thresholds, the raven surveying ruin, the lone wolf rumoured in myth and menace; each step she took echoed a primal omen drawn from nature's most feared creatures.

To speak her name even now, decades later, is to conjure a diverse reactions among the girls of Kamathipura – shock, anger, awe, trembling silence – as if her shadow still clings to every crumbling wall and narrow lane. Maya is so feared that she has become less a memory and more a myth: genesis not of virtue, but of ruin. Through her, we explore not only where it began, but how darkness, rooted in the wild and the human alike, can haunt a place across generations.

We walk the by-lanes of our lives and find that some lanes are forbidden for entry. Forbidden worlds both excite and make us abhor them.

Our mind slips into a world of demons, ugly trolls and grotesque villains. We enter *patal lok*, where the bad and lurid rule.

This is what Tolkien means when he talks about 'sub creation'. Of course, he talks about magic, fairies and heroes. The forbidden demons and trolls are the other side of such a world.

When we 'sub-create', we are able to safely meander into a world within our wider reality and experience it vicariously. The forbidden becomes a paradox – something to be avoided and yet something to be fantasized about.

We 'sub-create' an orbit of people we can live alongside at a safe distance. We can experience the drama from outside the ring where it is happening, without dirtying our hands.

The history of Kamathipura is perhaps even darker and more gruesome than the concept of *narak* in Hindu mythology. It seems as if Lord Shiva poured every drop of the *halahala* that he gulped down during the *samudra manthan* into the grisly by-lanes of Kamathipura. Thus it is that whoever steps in here inevitably drowns in an ocean of the vicious poison, thereby transforming into 'human demons', devoid of mercy, affection or pity.

Maya was one such woman. Her journey from being a mere pawn in the hands of destiny to being the most horrific

'Madam' of the red-light district of Kamathipura unfolds like a gripping Netflix thriller, layered with intrigue, betrayal and chilling revelations. Maya was an enigma. She was savagely ambitious and loved power. She had an innate craving for sex and money. She could even walk up to and knock at the gates of hell if she thought that it could fulfil her desires. Maya embodied everything contrary to compassion and generosity. She was absolute power, desire and crudity!

Born into a lower middle-class Muslim family in Hatkarwadi, Beed district, of the Aurangabad tehsil of Maharashtra, Maya was named Asifa by her parents. The third of ten siblings, Maya inherited the barrenness of the land on which she was born. Beed, a district scorched by the merciless sun, is a land where the earth cracks like parched lips begging for a drop of water. The landscape stretches endlessly, arid and unyielding, and the colour green is a fleeting memory for the people of the land, a dream whispered by the wind. The soil is powdery, more dust than dirt, swirling into choking clouds with every gust of hot, dry wind. Wells lie barren, their depths echoing the futility of hope for its people, their walls scarred by desperate hands that have dug and prayed, only to find more emptiness. The air smells of despair; baked earth, withered crops and the faint tang of sweat from bodies worn thin by toil.

The people of Beed are carved out of this unforgiving land, their faces etched with lines as deep as the cracks in the soil. Hardship clings to them like a second skin, shaping their nature as sharply as the drought carves the earth. Kindness, here, is a luxury; survival demands steel. Children grow up barefoot, their soles hardened by the scorching earth, their hands blistered by the tools of labour long before they learn to write their names. Their laughter, if it exists, is brittle, breaking like dry twigs underfoot.

Hatkarwadi itself looks abandoned even though it is not. The houses – made of sun-baked mud and straw – sag under the weight of despair, their walls fading into the colourless backdrop of dust and stone. The few trees that stand here are skeletal, their gnarled branches stretching skyward in silent supplication, waiting for rain that never comes. Even the animals, gaunt and hollow-eyed, seem to shuffle through life as though burdened by the knowledge that there is no reprieve for them from the heat and drought.

Hardship has not only dried the land but also hardened hearts here. Smiles are rare, and words are fewer, exchanged only when necessary, as if conversation wastes what little energy remains. Survival here demands an unyielding resolve, a resilience born not of choice but necessity. To live in Beed is to understand the fragility of life and the futility of struggle, to carry on, despite knowing that the earth beneath your feet may never yield anything but dust again.

And yet, in this barrenness, there is a quiet defiance, a grim determination to exist, no matter how small or insignificant that existence is. The people endure, just as the land endures, each bearing the marks of a battle they can never truly win. If lack of rain for years has left the village of Hatkarwadi cracked, dry and parched, so has Maya been affected the same way, barren and unyielding at her core. Maya abhorred her parents and her brothers and sisters. She hated the fact that they were poor, that her father worked in a *kasai khana* as a butcher and that her mother was an assistant to the nearby tailor. Maya hated the fact that her parents could never feed them well, that they never had proper clothes to wear or a *pucca* house to live in. Maya hated the fact that every single night her father would get drunk and abuse her mother, and that her mother, instead of protesting, would bear the act with awful moans. Maya hated the fact that, despite being terribly poor and incapable of procuring the basic necessities of life for them, her parents had an immense yearning to produce more babies and dump them in the corners of their impoverished house. Maya hated the fact that she had to take care of her six siblings during the day while her parents were at work, and then again during the night while her parents were busy mating. Maya had often felt like killing her siblings when they groaned for food, and her blood ran wild with the desire to bang their heads against the ground or throw them out of the window. But, as fate would have it, she was helpless; she felt had been chosen to rot in hell along with her unbearable siblings.

Maya dreamt of a lavish life since the time she was very young, maybe eight or nine. She envied Afreen, the daughter of the village sarpanch, whose family was among the few that had hereditary wealth. Afreen had no siblings and her life was uncomplicated. She did not have to struggle for survival nor manage nagging siblings, and could thus be free and happy. However, Afreen did not symbolize the typical villager of Hatkarwadi. Rather, the poverty into which Maya was born and in which she was raised mirrored the desolation of the village poignantly. It was a land stripped of crops. Ponds had turned into empty hollows and the people into malnutritioned skeletons, often succumbing to starvation.

It was not for nothing that Maya hated her parents. Her deep-rooted hatred towards them was also because she had not inherited their physical appearance, especially her mother's. Her mother Zaika was beautiful. She was fair, had a well-sculpted face and long hair. She had a mole on the right side of her chin, which people found attractive. Maya's father Jamal was an incredibly handsome man, almost six feet three inches tall and with a heavy body but without an inch of extra flesh anywhere. He was as fair as camphor. Alcohol and poverty had failed to fade his physical charm. Only, he had lost his hair with time and was partly bald. But that had not tarnished his Casanova image or his popularity among women. This was on account of his marvellous expertise at satiating his female partners. He was still popular among the women of the village, still talked about; he had been nicknamed '*aashique mijaz*' for his sexual potency. He had helped many of his friends and acquaintances by sleeping with their wives and getting them pregnant. And they all produced healthy babies. Neither he nor Zaika regarded this a sin; rather, they felt it was an honest way of bringing new souls into this world and thus deserving of the blessings of Allah.

Jamal was extremely proud of his masculinity and sky-high libido. He had had an affair with Zaika and Zaika's mother at the same time, after they had relocated from a town following some financial problems and had happened to be his neighbours. Zaika's father was a labourer on cargo ships and seldom visited home. He had found a decent neighbour in Jamal and had requested him to take care of his family in case of any emergency. Jamal took great care of the family. He seduced Zaika's mother by day and Zaika by night.

This went on for almost five years till the mother succumbed to dengue. Jamal then married Zaika and looked after two of her brothers, who were actually Jamal's own sons from Zaika's mother. Zaika's father never returned and people assumed that he must have died in some natural calamity or been preyed upon by some sea predator. Jamal lived happily with Zaika. He was very fond of her, not because she was beautiful or because he relished his carnal activities every night but because of the intense love she had for him. Zaika had accepted Jamal the way he was despite knowing everything about his illicit affairs.

One day he brought home a girl – an infant. He told Zaika that the infant would stay with them. Not once did Zaika express any curiosity about the child's parents or demand to know the reason for Jamal's affection for her. But Jamal himself told her the child was his child from a tribal woman from Gadchiroli who had come to work as a labourer on the highway project that would connect their village to the town nearby. The woman had died while giving birth to the baby in the labourers' colony and Jamal wanted to raise the child. Jamal told Zaika that the child had inherited her mother's complexion and hair. Zaika looked at the child again. Its complexion was a polished black, and the child had voluminous curls. It seemed to Zaika that she was holding a moonless night in her arms. And she felt the presence of something very ominous in the child. She was scared for a while. However, she held the child close to her and whispered into her ears: '*Salaam alaikum*, Asifa!' The child wailed violently and that shook Zaika from within, as if apprehending some dire misfortune in her family. Yet she hugged the child close to her bosom and prayed. Since then, Asifa had stayed with Jamal and Zaika and became part of their family.

It was almost dawn. Maya was woken up by one of her siblings screaming for milk at the top of her voice. It was Khushboo. Maya understood she was hungry. But her screams set Maya's temper on fire. She felt like putting a pillow over her face and suffocating her to death. Maya lay quietly on the floor where she was sleeping, acting as if she were deep asleep to escape the toil of feeding the child.

Maya hated her siblings to the core. The exception was her elder brother Masood, whom she adored. Masood was almost five years older than Maya and the eldest of the ten siblings. When Maya was a child, she could remember Masood taking her in his arms and playing with her. Slowly, as she grew up, she developed a fondness for Masood, but it was not the usual fondness of a sister for her brother. It was rather strange. When she turned eight or nine, Maya began to feel a peculiar attraction for Masood, which eventually grew into a wild frenzy of feelings for him. As a girl of fifteen who had never gone to school, never played with her friends, had never been caressed by her parents and had never done anything but clean utensils, wash clothes and help her mother in the kitchen, Masood was like a breath of fresh air. He was someone who had not hated Maya for her physical grotesqueness, unlike the rest of the universe, which considered her awfully ugly for her raven black skin, obesity and thick, curly hair. The contrast was stark when she was seen with her siblings, who were fair and traditionally beautiful, and even more stark when she was seen with her parents. Her parents had typical Afghani features, with olive complexion, dark, almond-shaped eyes, high cheekbones and well-crafted jawlines. Maya deeply hated both, and the 'Allah' who had created her to look strikingly different from them.

It was during Eid that many people in their village used to go to the town nearby for their shopping. They'd have saved money round the year for the occasion, the festivities of Eid being a big break for them from their poverty-stricken existence. Jamal and Zaika had never gone, though. They could hardly save any money for Eid festivities. All they could afford was to make sevai and eat it together after offering prayers to the Almighty. But that year, Masood insisted they let him go to the town and buy new clothes as he had started to work in the shoe factory of the village and was earning. Jamal and Zaika did not stop him.

Shirur was the town closest to Hatkarwadi, around two hundred kilometres from their village. It took five hours to get there by public bus. Many of the villagers travelled to the city often, mostly on account of their occupational necessities, working as daily wagers and porters at the bus stops and railway platforms, or as assistants to the roadside hawkers or as labourers in the few factories in Shirur at that time. For some families, it was only once or twice a year that they would travel to Shirur to shop for 'luxuries'. For most of the residents of the village, where the land was parched and survival was a regular battle, shopping and celebrating festivals were beyond their imagination.

It was a regular day when Masood decided to travel to Shirur and buy new clothes for his siblings for the coming Eid. As he got ready to catch the bus to town, he asked Maya to get ready quickly. He said he would take Maya along and buy her a good salwar kameez, since she had only two or three, which were now torn and resembled rags.

Maya had actually been waiting for this opportunity for a long time. She readily agreed. She went to Afreen and borrowed a salwar kameez from her. Afreen gave her the worst salwar she had, saying that even the most beautiful dress would not make any difference to Maya's appearance. Maya was angry but ignored Afreen's sarcastic comment, considering that Masood had given her very little time to get ready. She wore the salwar kameez and looked at herself in the cracked mirror of their house. She could see how correct Afreen was. She looked perfectly ugly.

She quietly left the house with Masood and walked behind him towards the bus stop. Accompanying them was Masood's childhood friend Saifu, who always had eyed Maya with a peculiar hunger in his eyes. The bright sunny weather of the morn became grim within no time. Soon a mild dust storm swept the land, coating everything in its path. Maya's hair and salwar kameez were all cloaked with dust, making her look very dishevelled. Masood could not help chuckling at the sight, but briskly offered her his handkerchief to wipe the dust away. All three were huddled together close, making one feel that their breaths were in unison. Maya and Saif's hands brushed in the exchange, and a fleeting yet electric thrill ran through Maya, turning her dark face a coarse red.

It was afternoon when they reached Shirur. Maya was enthralled to see the market, with its wares of beautiful garments, foods that looked delicious, toys and balloons of various shapes, sizes and colours, and what not. Maya had never seen such vibrance – hundreds of people busy buying their desired goods. She was awestruck. She wanted to buy everything in the market – the dresses, the cheap cosmetics, the bright and flamboyant chappals that she had seen Afreen wearing, the lip-smacking food that emitted wonderful aromas, and that tangy syrup served with ice shavings – kala khatta, but all for herself. She would not share these things with anyone, she thought. 'One day I will buy them all,' she thought to herself as she walked slowly by the side of the two boys.

After roaming in the market for some time and buying a few clothes, which included a green salwar kameez for Maya and dresses for their siblings, it was almost late evening. Masood hired a rickshaw and asked Maya to get inside, saying they were going to his friend's place, where two other friends of his would also be there. They would spend the night there and start for home by dawn, fresh and rejuvenated after the day's toil. Saying this, Masood put his hand over her shoulder and cozied up against her a bit. Maya noticed a twinkle in Masood's eye, a twinkle that Maya had never noticed earlier, Masood did not look as innocent as he used to when he would sleep by her side. Maya's heart started beating faster. What did that twinkle mean? Maya was engrossed in her thoughts as the rickshaw stopped in front of a narrow lane. Masood got down and helped Maya to get down. He asked her to follow him. There was no one in the lane and it appeared dirty and haunted. A foul smell of stale food pervaded the lane.

After walking a little, Masood stopped before a small, dilapidated house with asbestos sheets for a roof and worn-out colours on the wrecked walls. He knocked on the door softly. Soon, a boy of Masood's age opened the door and smiled at him. Masood smiled and hugged him and asked Maya to greet him. 'Assalaam alaikum,' said Maya, looking at the boy. The boy was tall and lean. His hair had grown to the level of his neck, and he had a beard. He looked at Maya and giggled. Masood told Maya that he was Abu and that he was his best friend. Now another boy, who appeared to be of the same age as Masood and Abu, joined them. He was stout and bald and had a scorpion tattooed on his shoulder. He took them all inside. They were seated in a room that looked like a stable, dirty and unorganized, with cardboard boxes kept in rows and what looked like a low camp bed. Maya had never seen a bed in her life; she did not know that this specific type of furniture with four legs was meant for people to sleep on.

She looked at it astonished, hesitating to sit on it. She sat on the floor and looked at Masood.

Masood put on the ceiling fan and took off his t-shirt; he said he was feeling hot and exhausted and asked the lean boy for water. The boy gave him and Maya a bottle of water each and some bread. Maya was terribly thirsty and hungry. She ate the bread and drank the water quickly. As she drank the water, she felt dizzy. Her head was spinning badly. Unable to sit any more, Maya lay on the floor and slept.

When Maya opened her eyes, she saw Masood smiling a wicked smile at her. She looked around and realized that she was lying on the bed and that Masood was lying by her side. Masood looked at her and said, 'I have watched you all these years, where others find you ugly, I find you like a black diamond.' Saying this, Masood touched her breasts softly. Maya was trying to figure what was happening as Masood went on defiling her body. He started to undress her. Maya smiled blushingly at him. But deep within she was angry. She was agitated. Her sinister mind was weaving an extremely complicated idea, the goal of which was to ensure herself a comfortable life ahead.

Maya had no dreams of spending her time with Masood. She did not love him. But what she wanted was to conquer this man and understand the matrix of physical desires. His puppy-like behaviour and dream of their staying together annoyed her. She had escaped from her pathetic village and family, she thought. 'Now it's time to prepare for a longer plunge,' she thought. She had a Machiavellian mind, unlike ordinary teenagers and it ran ceaselessly, knitting plans for a future in which she was the queen of this world. In the meanwhile, she could feel Masood entering her restlessly. Her anger knew no bounds. She felt like pushing his body away, but this was not the time to make hasty decisions, she thought, and patiently waited for him to finish the act. She faked it with alluring moans that she had heard her mother make. Within a few minutes it was over. Forget pleasure, Maya did not even feel the passion of intercourse. Masood kissed her on the forehead and went off to sleep. The Machiavelli in Maya was wide awake. She got up from the bed and tiptoed towards the door and opened it. She saw the other boys drinking and smoking beedis. Maya was completely naked. The boys looked at her in surprise, and soon the surprise transformed into lust. They winked at Maya and called her towards them. What followed next was a bout of wild passion amongst the three. Maya imitated every craft she had heard her parents execute by night. She was enthralled by the experience and found the two boys' ways better than Masood's. Masood was just a kid, she thought, and smirked while she lay on the floor with the two boys writhing on her naked body. She overheard one of them saying to her, 'You should be in Kamathipura! You would rule the place like a queen!' That triggered a strange feeling in her. All her life she had wanted to be a queen. She wanted luxury, money and sex, come what may. She wanted to spit on her parents and run away from the sickening life of acute poverty she was living. Destiny had finally offered her this opportunity! She pulled one of the boys by his hair and asked, 'Where is Kamathipura? Can you guys take me there?' The lean boy named Abu rolled his eyes and said, 'You want to go to Kamathipura? Seriously?' And then paused and said, '*Udhar ladkiyon ko becha jata hai!*' Maya smiled a bitchy smile and retorted, '*To mujhe bhi bech daal!*' and laughed like a beast. Abu was nervous. He looked at Maya in utter dismay. But the other boy, the bald one with the scorpion tattoo on his shoulder, smiled like a knave and asked Maya, 'So, you want to go to Kamathipura for sure?' To which Maya replied with a yes in great confidence. The boy got up, put on his jeans, and asked Maya to get ready. It must have been early morning.

Maya went into the room and wore the new salwar kameez gifted to her by Masood. Masood was sleeping soundly. Maya took his wallet and came out. She told the boy that they must leave before Masood woke up. The boy smiled and said, '*Tu jitni badsurat hai usse kayi guna zyada khatarnak hai*!' Maya smiled back at him, as if it were a compliment to be told she was dangerous. They left the house silently, Maya walked behind the tattooed boy, crossing the dirty alley, as if she was gladly embracing all the filth nature had to offer her. She could hear the ominous crying of stray dogs somewhere down the alley. She felt restless. She asked the boy to increase the pace of their walk and almost ran towards the marketplace. The boy purchased two tickets from a tiny counter, after which they boarded a bus that took around three hours to reach some railway station. Throughout the journey, Maya felt claustrophobic, sitting in the overcrowded bus between two men who stared at her lustfully. She felt the poison of a million darts pointing towards her and piercing her body. Maya ignored them and looked around, only to find a few more men staring at her since she was the only woman on the bus. She felt quite excited to see the lascivious stares of the men directed towards her. She felt pride and confidence at the fact that she, in spite of being labelled as ugly by everyone throughout her life, was actually capable of triggering desire for her in men. She smiled inwardly, kept her calm and travelled in silence.

After around three hours of travel, they reached the railway station. The station looked desolate. The lone platform had an almost weathered, yellow signboard, barely legible. At the edge of this remote railway station, where time seemed to linger without purpose, stood a dilapidated tree – a monument to neglect and decay. Its trunk, gnarled and scarred by years of merciless weather, leaned precariously, as if burdened by the weight of its own existence. The few branches that remained were skeletal and bare, their brittle bark peeling away in patches, revealing the ashen core beneath. Nearby, a lifeless branch of a tree lay on the dry, cracked earth, its jagged edges browned with age and crumbling to dust at the slightest touch. Together, the tree and the branch painted a picture of desolation, as though the tree had shed one of its limbs in a final act of surrender to the forces of time.

There was hardly a soul in sight as the two stood there waiting for their train. The tattooed boy broke the uncanny silence and told her that his name was Raja and that he was from some village in Bihar, to which Maya did not react nor show an iota of interest. As the train came in, Raja pulled her by her hand and helped her to get inside. The compartment had very few passengers, mostly men, who were asleep on the berths. Maya sat at a corner while Raja relaxed on the floor of the train, where he lit a beedi for himself. The train ran very fast. Maya had never seen a train and was amused and thrilled by the experience of travelling in one. She opened Masood's wallet and counted the notes inside. It was around three hundred rupees. She thought of how Masood would feel upon waking up and finding that she had run away with his friend. She felt immensely satisfied to think of the plight of her mother and her useless siblings without a slave like her to serve them. 'Let all of them die!' Maya said to herself and closed her eyes as the train ran with all its might. She visualized herself as a queen in the kaleidoscope of her dream and felt the bliss of a lifetime.

Maya was woken by a push. She saw Raja smiling at her. 'Get up, we have almost reached our destination.' Maya woke up and peeped outside from the window. She could see the sun shining bright, a clear sky; she could hear the chirping of birds, which was way more soothing than the cacophony of her siblings that she woke up to every morning. Maya felt happy. She looked around and realized that the train was crowded with hundreds of people. Maya looked at them in astonishment. She felt amused. So many people with the same physical organs, such as the nose, eyes, lips and ears, and yet each one looked different from the other. Maya laughed. She could not wait for the train to reach its destination. After about half an hour, the train halted at a railway station. She could hear people saying, '*Bambai aa gya! Bambai aa gya!*' Raja asked her to get down. The railway station was the busiest thing she had ever seen in her life, with men and women of all ages darting about like remote-controlled machines. Maya steadily braved the relentless push of the crowd, even though she was facing a situation like that for the first time, and followed Raja with unwavering concentration. Eventually, they came out of the railway station and boarded a bus. Raja asked the conductor to give them two tickets to some place named Grant Road. Maya pulled his shirt and hissed, 'Why Grant Road? I want to go to Kamathipura na!' Raja put his hands on her lips and asked her to keep quiet. Maya was getting angry. After some time, he asked her to get down from the bus. They started to walk.

Maya walked after Raja. She was awestruck to see such huge buildings, skyscrapers, so many vehicles, so much noise and so many things happening at every corner of every street. She followed Raja hurriedly. They walked for a long time till they reached a broad street full of shops on both sides. There was a temple too, to some unknown god. Maya saw women grandly dressed in beautiful sarees and gajras standing by the side of the street. Maya wished she too could dress like them! She saw Raja talking to a very tall and bearded man who looked at Maya keenly. Maya understood she was getting auctioned. She waited patiently. Raja came back and told Maya that she had been sold to Shetty's brothel in exchange for three thousand rupees. Raja left, handing Maya over to the tall, bearded man who took her inside a very big house. He took her to another man, who was as dark as Maya and as tall as her Abbu Jamal, with large eyes and broad shoulders. The man took his tongue out like a wild dog and took her inside a room. Maya knew her task very well. She knew she had to impress this man in order to climb the stairs of success. She used her craft incredibly well this time. The pain that the man inflicted on her with his teeth and nails hardly had any effect on her. She dreamt of a lot of money; she dreamt of being the 'maalkin' of that huge house and keeping these men as slaves. Maya hated men and felt that they were best only as slaves. After about an hour, the man left Maya's body and went out of the room. Maya could hear him say, '*Yeh junglee billi ek din raaj karegi idhar!*' Maya was elated to hear this. She realized she had already climbed the first step to success. She saw the cut marks on her body and smiled. She loved the scars. The man came back to her and asked her name. Maya said her name was Asifa. The man thought for a while and told her, 'From today onwards your name will be MAYA!'

The name Maya denotes a sense of esoteric mystery in the popular culture but it also has numerous divine connotations. In Greek mythology, Maya was the eldest of the Pleiades, the seven daughters of Atlas; Maya was also the mother of Hermes, son of the mighty Zeus. The Roman civilization believed Maya to be the mother of Earth and the beautiful goddess of spring. In Hebrew, Maya denotes '*mayim*', or water – genteel, soft, aesthetic. Mythologies across the world have placed Maya on the throne when it came to anything ambrosial, deific or astral. But Anna Shetty had named Asifa Maya because he could perceive a unique ambition in her eyes and a tremendous hunger within her body. Hers was not the typical feminine sexual urge to captivate her male counterparts but something much stronger and brutal. He could see in the apparently ugly seventeen-year-old, a burning desire to swallow the entire universe. The Maya that rose out of the grave of Asifa was devilish, even darker than the murky, eerie nights when the moon hides itself, fearing a horrifying eclipse. Maya was cruel, sadistic and brutish.

Penetrating the core of the business and understanding its genesis was not at all easy. The Shettys ran their business systematically and moved everywhere together, like mute hounds; the entire 14th Gully of Kamathipura was ruled by the infamous Shetty gang of four, headed by Anna. They controlled the women who were trafficked from different parts of the country and sold to their brothels. They got them trained thoroughly in the craft, from dressing up and applying make-up to using seductive body language and voluptuous gestures to seduce customers. This they did through the more experienced women in the trade. Newly trafficked girls were first auctioned before customers at exorbitant rates, their virginity highlighted. And then, once it was tarnished, they were peddled regularly, say ten to twelve times in a single day. Once labelled as a woman of the Shetty brothels, a woman had to give up every freedom and become a sex machine.

It was more like a factory, where otherwise unskilled labour, skilled in the art of sex, was exploited every day in exchange for money. Most of the women, once trafficked and sold to the brothel, would realize that where they had landed was no worse than hell and surrendered themselves to lifelong abuse and assault.

However, there were a few who refused to get into the trade. They were mercilessly beaten, starved for days and confined to dark chambers, which some of the rooms in the area had. These dungeon-like chambers were where trafficked girls were hidden during the time of police raids. The girls were raped by the four Shettys and their rented goons, were injected with drugs and got forcibly drunk, or were threatened with death till they surrendered to do what they were expected to. With more than one thousand women slogging night and day in the district, the money came in, staggering, unfathomable figures every day. The Shettys managed the finances with great efficiency. The money earned by each woman was collected, consolidated and put into the iron vault in Anna Shetty's room. A considerable part of the money was spent on feeding the women. Food was prepared in the four-hundred-square-foot kitchen hall on the ground floor of Pilla House. It had three mammoth fireplaces, where food was cooked twice a day in gigantic vessels. It was mostly *daal–chawal*, with fish, meat or egg provided on weekends. Even after the expenses in the form of payments to the pimps, to the cops who often demanded money for the smooth running of the business, and salaries to the employees who handled legal and medical issues that often arose because of the illegal trafficking of women that was going on, or because of the physical and sexual violence and assaults on the women by depraved and frustrated customers, the amount that remained was astronomically high and was sent to the Shettys' families in Karnataka.

The Shettys ran their syndicate in the heart of Mumbai, in Kamathipura. Maya was merely seventeen years old. Yet everyone in the brothel, including the Shettys, was astounded by her proficiency at the job. Far from being depressed or scared, Maya was determinedly into her job from day one. Like the sincerest student in the class, Maya learnt every craft from Najma Bibi and Bulbul, the women experienced in the trade, and executed them to perfection. Every day she was turning better. While customers would not so much as take a second look at her when they first saw her, once they had had a session with her, they completely surrendered to her art. Eventually, Maya became one of the most desired women of the Shetty brothels. She could sell herself multiple times in a single day. While her counterparts often shed painful tears when they were physically injured, Maya celebrated injuries. She felt each of her scars took her one step ahead towards her destination. The Shettys entrusted Maya with control of a group of newly trafficked women to test her. The sight of new girls sobbing would irritate Maya, and she would settle their tears by means of a cane. If the women were older than her, she either injected them with drugs or made the goons rape them. If they turned rebellious, she would stub the burning end of her beedi on their skin or press a heated cooking spud on their bodies. She would also insert rods inside their vagina if they refused to entertain customers. Their screams amused her, and she would laugh to her heart's content. Maya slept with all the Shettys and kept a watch on everything with a hawk's eye, waiting patiently for the right moment to dethrone the Shettys and become the undisputed goddess of Kamathipura.

It was a customary ritual for the Shettys to visit the local temple of Lord Shiva every Monday morning. The three brothers would bathe, wear their traditional attire of a clean white shirt and white dhoti, and neatly comb their hair and moustache. On this day, there were no beedi, tobacco or alcohol stains anywhere on or within them. With great reverence they would bathe the idol of Lord Shiva with milk and make offerings of sandalwood, ghee and flowers, and sit for hours in the temple premises, praying. Trade would halt in all of Kamathipura during this time. If Shettys' goons noticed any of their women entertaining a customer or consuming alcohol or tobacco, or any man indulging in pimping or drugs during this time, they were tortured. But that happened rarely. The Shettys were feared by everyone and no one dared challenge them. The eldest of the Shettys, Nagi, used to say that their father, Ranga, had migrated to the city from a tiny village in Karnataka in search of a job. Ranga was an expert mason and had been appointed as a labourer on the construction site for the huge post office at the Victoria Terminus. It must have been 1904–1905. Ranga used to toil hard all day at the construction site; his daily escape from this drudgery was cheap alcohol by night and sex at the brothels of Grant Road. Most nights he would end up sleeping on the streets of the brothel, completely inebriated.

This went on till he met Moti, who had been trafficked by her brother to a brothel in Grant Road from a remote village in Jaunpur in Uttar Pradesh. Ranga would pay her pimp every night to be able to sleep with her. The heavily built Ranga would grasp Moti like a giant. One day, Moti informed Ranga that she was pregnant with his child. Ranga decided to marry her. They got married the same day at the Shiva temple in Kamathipura. Ranga rented a pocket room in Kamathipura for both of them. He never asked Moti to quit her trade, rather connected her with a smarter pimp. At times, Ranga would even refer Moti to his co-workers at a discounted rate. Ranga and Moti gave birth to three children, all boys. They grew up in the 14th Gulli of Kamathipura. Nagarajan, commonly known as Nagi, was the eldest and most menacing of the three. He grew up to be extremely shrewd and sharp. He mastered the art of the sex trade by learning it from his mother, joined a racket that operated the trade from Kamathipura across the country and eventually became one of the top traffickers of girls in the country. Their father chose his eldest and favourite son to accompany him to their native village in Karnataka. So, inspite of being born in Kamathipura, Nagi felt his roots in a pristine place where he ran along the endless rows of the paddy fields.

Nagi slowly expanded his business from his small pocket room to six buildings in the red-light area housing more than one thousand women of different age groups, trafficked from various parts of the country. Nagi sent his family back to their village and built an empire that was nearly impossible to invade. Indeed, he had the DNA of a mason to have laid such a foundation for his syndicate. He also had the brain of a corporate head. Within twenty years, the Shettys were the wealthiest brand in Kamathipura. Every time Nagi sat before Lord Shiva, the pitch-black stone replica of the deity became a metaphor for the darkness that pervaded his life. Nagi knew there was no redemption for his sins. They were grave and unpardonable. He had trafficked, drugged, abused and killed thousands of women, some of them innocent children. He had forced them into the trade, imprisoned them in dungeons and made them starve for days till they became puppets moving to his command. Nagi was now sixty-seven. He had everything that life could offer – power, money, sex and an empire that was unshakeable. Yet Nagi knew that one day he would fall, that one day someone would destroy him. Nagi feared death. Nagi feared being defeated. He believed in the transience of the world, and for the past few days the emergence of Gulab in Madanpura had been alarming him.

The area of Madanpura was a stone's throw away from Kamathipura. It had been an abandoned stretch of land in the heart of Mumbai till men from Uttar Pradesh migrated to the city in search of work and started putting up tents and staying there. Criminal underworld activities in Bhendi Bazaar, Grant Road and Madanpura area were at its peak during the late 1970s. Criminal gangs, such as those run by figures like Karim Lala and others, were deeply involved in extortion and intimidation that reached into the daily lives of common people across Mumbai's neighbourhoods. Ordinary traders, shopkeepers and even residents were often pressured to pay 'protection money' or face threats and violence. The presence of organized gangs led to increased street crime such as robberies and assaults, particularly targeting those seen as vulnerable or outsiders in the late-night hours. While many regular people were not personally involved in underworld operations, their daily lives were undoubtedly impacted by the atmosphere of fear, occasional violence and the economic pressures resulting from extortion or criminal rackets.

It was in this climate that the Madanpura men had adopted crime as their way of life, and the entire area was terrified of them. They looted shops, banks and houses, stole vehicles during the day and roamed around the port at night to capture imported goods, which they later sold off at very high prices. They would demand money from wealthy businessmen, sometimes killing them without the slightest hesitation if they refused to pay them or called the cops. With every passing day, the Madanpura men became a bigger threat to the neighbourhood and its inhabitants. Their leader, Gulab, was in his mid-thirties. He was immensely handsome. Those who had seen him said he looked like the *Qurbani* actor Feroz Khan. Gulab was incredibly built – beige-complexioned, he had what looked like an iron body and stood six and a half feet tall. Gulab would definitely have been competition for the contemporary Bollywood heroes had he been given an opportunity to audition for films. He and his men were synonymous with terror. It was a time when there were multiple mafia wars and criminal activities in the city and every mafia don was part of one or other infamous gang, but Gulab operated independently.

He and his group of men, all migrants from UP and Bihar, had their own senate and individual plans of operation. Every day, more and more men migrated from Uttar Pradesh and Bihar to Madanpura, and each day Gulab grew stronger and more powerful. His dreams and aspirations became wider and more destructive. Gulab and his gang satisfied their sexual lust by visiting the women of Grant Road. They had absolutely no access to Kamathipura. Neither did they have any urge to visit the infamous red-light area ruled by Nagi and company. Gulab's attention had never turned to Kamathipura. He didn't want to get into a rivalry and nasty battle with Nagi, that too for the sake of a few women. Gulab knew that Nagi had been in the trade for years and that as things stood, he would defeat him and his men easily, should they clash. But with time, Gulab's gang expanded. As they indulged in bloodshed, burglary, murder and similar crimes, the men needed to destress with some finer entertainment than could be obtained from the women in Grant Road. They also wanted to crush the snake called Nagi and feast on the flesh of his exotic women. Also, Gulab was not unaware of the huge amount of money involved in the trade. He wanted to invade Kamathipura, but not in haste. It called for a systematic and calculated operation. Gulab patiently waited for an opportunity.

Every monsoon, Nagi would visit his native village and stay there for some time. Unlike most Mumbai folk, Nagi hated the monsoons of Mumbai. The rains made business difficult. Also, Nagi was ageing and he wanted to disentangle himself from the trivial issues over which his brothers always fought. Nagi knew both of them wanted to sit on the throne and inherit the empire after him. In his opinion, both were also incompetent pigs and would destroy everything once he died. Rama and Teja were perfect nincompoops.

Gulab was sitting on the edge of Kennedy Bridge and watching the street urchins playing with sand. It was late evening. He lit up a beedi, inhaled the smoke and exhaled it with great pleasure. He saw his rings of smoke flying high in the sky. He felt someone jerk his shoulder. It was Rameez. He was panting. Gulab understood that he had come running all the way up to him. Rameez was part of his special network that brought him secret news of all the gangs that operated in the southern part of the metropolis. Rameez told him that Nagi had gone out of Bambai, leaving the business to his useless brothers and that this was the perfect time when they could raid Kamathipura. Gulab thought for a while and said to Rameez, '*Jayenge hum, lekin Gulab ban ke nahi!*'

The next few days were extremely crucial for the gang since they were about to enter the lion's den, and there was every risk of being caught and slaughtered. Gulab chose himself and Rameez for the first visit, since Rameez knew the layout of Kamathipura thoroughly and would help him escape if needed. Gulab let his beard grow for the next three days. He wore a baggy rainbow-coloured shirt and expensive black trousers. He combed his hair in a different style from usual to make himself unrecognizable. He carried his gun, along with a sword and a small dagger.

It was around eight in the evening when Gulab and Rameez stepped into the main street of Kamathipura. The sodium vapour lights on both sides of the street lit the stretch dimly. The garland sellers and *paan* vendors were busy since it was the most important time of the day for their trade. Peppy Hindi cinema songs were audible in every corner of the wide street. A foul smell pervaded the place, and of course, there were the Kamathipura women standing in queue, peddling themselves before their prospective customers. As Gulab walked down the street, conscious and careful, the women stared at him in amazement. A few of them passed a few seductive comments, addressing him as 'hero', '*sher*' and '*chamiya*'. Gulab walked on, ignoring them. Rameez, by his side, winked at a bald-headed man, asking him to show the way to Pilla House. The bald-headed man checked them meticulously and asked them to follow him. It had begun to drizzle now, and within a few minutes the raindrops turned bigger and drenched the street. Gulab looked up at the sky and smirked; a rain-swept Kamathipura was welcoming him, and he sensed an enigmatic suspense and thrill.

Since the time Nagi had left for his native village, Maya had been managing his affairs entirely. Nagi's worthless duo of brothers, Rama and Teja, roamed across the city during the day, watching movies, sitting in the railway stations, drinking alcohol in the bars and feasting on the girls of their brothels at night. Maya had already had a tussle with Teja; he had wanted money from the treasury to buy foreign liquor, and Maya would not allow it. Nagi had strictly instructed her to keep his brothers in control or they would wreck the business. Maya had assured Nagi she would protect his empire like a diligent soldier, but not out of any emotion or respect for him. She had not a tinge of emotion towards or respect for anyone. She knew Nagi was getting old and feeble and fed up with his brothers; she knew that Nagi loved to sleep with her and invariably did so at least once every day to feel the rush of dominating a sexually maddening woman. She kept Nagi sexually satiated and happy, but not because she wanted to ensure her survival here as the other women did. Her desire was far greater – she wanted to dethrone the king and usurp the crown. For this, she desperately needed to get into the core of the trade, a route to which Nagi had now slightly opened before her. Nagi thought Maya was an able commander, but in reality, Maya was a snake, one with the deadliest venom that could kill a person with its very first sting. She had silently learnt the ins and outs of the trade, analysed the process and network of trafficking that ran through the nooks and corners of the country. She had turned a few men in Nagi's gang into hers and was now waiting for the right opportunity to hammer the last nail into Nagi's coffin.

Evenings were usually very busy for Maya. She would monitor the movement of each woman in each of the three brothels. She had instructed her men to keep a keen eye on their activities. Maya knew that all the women were pure bitches, and that given a chance they would either hide the money they earned or try to run away. Maya herself had extracted money from inside their blouses and panties as she checked them post-trade. She had felt like killing them out of rage. She beat them mercilessly, threw them on the floor and kicked them if they were found guilty of keeping the money they earned. She treated the women like money-making machines, and machines were meant to work ceaselessly. Maya had broken the hand of a girl of twelve or thirteen. This child had been trafficked from a village in Manali. She had not been ready to sleep with a customer who had paid double to experience the 'warmth' of her virgin female parts. Maya had tied her with a rope and had beaten her till she grew unconscious. There was no forgiveness, nor any kind of humanity, in Maya's universe.

It was a monsoon evening and raining torrentially, Maya sat lazily on the couch in the hall and inspected the customers. Abdul was sending the women to the pockets. A few women from among the new lot were refusing to stand for trade in the queue, and Maya had called for the syringes. She would teach them a good lesson today, she thought. Suddenly, she heard a voice from behind. Maya saw two men standing at the door with the pimp, Harun. For a moment, Maya was speechless. Her eyes were fixed on one of the two men standing behind Harun. She had never seen a man like that in Kamathipura ever; he was perhaps the most handsome man she had ever seen in her life. He was more than six feet tall, olive-complexioned, broad-chested, had brownish curly hair and a brownish, Afghan-type beard. Maya wondered how this man would be in bed. Harun introduced him before Maya, 'This is Gafur Miya. He has come from Dubai today morning. He is searching for some really exotic "item".'

Maya looked straight into the eyes of Gulab disguised as Gafur. She was completely swayed by the temptation to take him into her. Maya went into a room and checked herself in the mirror. When Harun asked for Roshni, Maya did not like it. She replied that Roshni was busy with a customer so she herself would attend to the man. She asked Abdul to take him inside. Gulab was scanning every minute detail of the brothel set-up as he was taken inside by Abdul. Abdul led him to a long, narrow corridor with several pocket rooms, placed one after the other. Most of them were shut and he could overhear weird sexual noises coming from within. From the ground floor, Abdul took him through the mezzanine floor to the first floor of the house. It was dark everywhere. Gulab could smell the fragrance of some local perfume that he could recognize. He noticed that the rooms on this floor were larger than the earlier ones he had seen. A few of the doors were open and he tried to peep inside. The rooms were empty. They were moderately decorated with stone chips and mirrors on the walls and ceilings. Everywhere were pictures of heroes and heroines from Hindi cinema. Gulab observed everything with a hawk's eye.

He was made to sit in a room with walls that had tiny mirrors fitted all over. The walls were a deep blue in colour. He was sitting on a wooden bed. As Gulab looked above, he saw himself reflected in the mirrors on the ceiling. There were posters of nude men and women in the room. The room had only one small window with flowery curtains. A woman came from nowhere and spread some highly fragrant liquid on the bed and went away. Gulab quickly put his handkerchief over his nose, suspecting that the liquid might be a sedative. He often used these substances to make people unconscious for some time in order to rob them of their money. Gulab was getting more and more alert. No one should know who they were and that was why he had asked Rameez to stay alert all the while instead of trying to screw some woman. Gulab's scheme was now to get some information from this woman who was acting like the mistress of the house. She must be 'Maya', Nagi's vicious right hand. Gulab had heard of Maya from his acquaintances, how she was the one who controlled the Shetty brothers. She was ugly as a raven! Dark and plump, with jet-black curly hair, but there was something about this woman's eyes that Gulab noticed at the very outset. They were as sharp as a warrior's arrow, as if they would destroy anything that came between them and their object of conquest.

Maya went into a room and checked herself in the mirror. She was looking ugly as usual. She knew she looked ugly, but she wanted to rub her ugly skin on the body of that ruggedly attractive man who was waiting in her room. He was the most handsome man she had ever seen in her life. She was feeling an intense excitement, coupled with a kind of performance anxiety. She felt nervous for the first time wondering if she would be able to satisfy this customer. He was way different from the others, and special because Maya wanted him. Maya was growing restless. She pacified herself and walked towards the room where the stranger was seated.

Maya entered the room and shut the door. She saw the man seated on the bed. He looked confused and lost. Maya pulled off the curtains of the window and went towards Gulab. She sat on Gulab's lap and looked at him. Before he could do anything, Maya started to kiss him crazily. Gulab was getting highly aroused. Maya was touching him everywhere, and it seemed that she knew magic. Within moments, Maya was nude and had unbuttoned Gulab's shirt too. Gulab realized that he was carrying a *churi*, a small sharp knife, a symbol of street power, intimidation and close-quarter violence in neighbourhoods like Kamathipura. These daggers were part of the everyday arsenal for many gang members when firearms were less accessible or for attacks requiring stealth. He took it out and put it at the side of the bed and looked curiously at Maya. He was expecting her to get scared or hesitant on seeing it. But Maya was Maya, and she was not bothered about any weapon in the world at that point in time apart from her own. She stood up from Gulab's lap and started kissing his body as he opened his trousers. Gulab was in an equally maddened state now. He caught Maya by her arms and threw her on the bed.

After some time, Gulab lay on the bed pretending to have fallen asleep. He thought Maya must be some witch who knew black magic. Gulab had never had this kind of sex ever in his life. It was crazy, eccentric and bewildering. He had relished every moment of it, and he realized that he needed this woman more frequently. Not only to satisfy his desires, but also to use this woman to throw that bastard Nagi and his brothers out of their trade. Maya rested her nude body on the man's broad chest. She could hear every beat of his heart clearly. Maya was amazed by his masculinity. He was a 'one of a kind' man with a terrible hunger and aggression, and she had enjoyed every bit of sex with him. She had also already assumed that he must be part of some underworld gang that actively operated in the city. She could smell it in his body.

While at sex with him, Maya had noticed multiple marks on different parts of his body. Also, he carried a weapon that only criminals carried. Maya was sure that this man was someone different from the ordinary crowd. She had to find out the true identity of this stranger. Gulab slowly put his hands over Maya. '*Naam kya hai tera?*' Gulab's husky voice echoed around the room. 'Maya,' she replied, as sharp as a spark of light. She paused a little and asked Gulab, '*Tera naam kya hai?*' Gulab smirked and replied, 'Gafur.' He got up from the bed. Maya winked wickedly and asked, '*Tera naam kya hai, Gafur?*' and laughed like a witch. Gulab looked at Maya, laughing. He felt like kissing her, but he was running short of time. Rameez must be waiting. He must leave. He bid Maya farewell and left.

Gulab sat on the couch of his pocket room in 10, Madanpura Road. He lit a beedi and silently calculated the steps of 'Operation Kamathipura'. Apart from uncountable wealth and power over the country's largest red-light area, what the invasion would give him was a bitch named Maya, who had astounded him with her craft. Gulab had never seen a woman like Maya; ugly, intriguing, mysterious and unique. Of course, he wanted Kamathipura and Nagarajan's empire, but he also wanted the creature 'Maya' now. She would be his consort. But before that he had to utilize this woman to get to know the secrets of Nagi, and for that he needed to visit her many more times. Gulab felt an overwhelming desire for her; a raw and unfiltered craving that he could not suppress.

Maya was thinking a lot of things as she lay sprawled on her bed. She held the bed sheet tight against her bosom and felt the strong essence of that rogue man. He was one of a kind. Undoubtedly, he was a rogue, thought Maya. He had lied about his name and that he had come from Dubai. '*Harami sala!*' laughed Maya. Men could never understand what a sharp woman Maya was. Right after the two men left, Maya asked Radha to follow them. Radha was the only prostitute whom Maya trusted – not for no reason though. Radha had always been an able soldier in Maya's kingdom. She had proved her ability and integrity to Maya even in the bleakest of days when the other sluts tried to conspire against her. With the help of Radha, Maya had not only crushed the revolt of the bitches, but had also trafficked few of them to a more dangerous and inhumane brothel near Chambal in Madhya Pradesh. 'Let them either die without food or die satisfying the dacoits of Chambal!' she said, shrugging. From that day and up to this day, Radha had been her core informer.

Radha came back and reported that the two men had moved towards Grant Road and made a turn at the fifth Gully of Madanpura. Maya was scared, excited, thrilled and shocked to hear this. Men from Madanpura had penetrated the Shettys' brothel? This would be alarming for the Shettys, she thought. Maya smelt danger. She had to inform Nagi about it. She ran towards the only landline phone in their premises and dialled the telephone number that would connect her to Nagi. However, she stopped halfway and silently stood beside the telephone. The Machiavelli in her started to assert himself. Why would she inform Nagi about the impending danger? Why would she not take advantage of the situation and realize her own dream of becoming the Queen of Kamathipura? Maya was aware that Nagi was getting old and that he was terribly scared of the Madanpura gang. Maya started to plot. This game, she thought, could checkmate Nagi and company if played wisely. Maya decided to make the Madanpura men her allies and end the Shetty reign forever.

Gulab walked across Kennedy Bridge hastily. He was slightly drunk. The prostitutes of Grant Road stood on Kennedy Bridge soliciting customers. They looked lustily at Gulab. He didn't pay them any attention. He met Rameez at the dark alley that connected Kennedy Bridge to Grant Road and asked him to get his men together at their shelter in Madanpura. He would invade Kamathipura tonight. Rameez was not prepared for this. He looked nervously at Gulab. '*Jaldbaazi maat karna, Gulab. Woh saali Maya ke paas bohot aadmiya honge. Agar haar gye toh locha ho jayega.*' Gulab looked at Rameez. Nagi would be back soon, replied Gulab, and he could not afford to lose this golden opportunity at all. Hence it would have to be tonight. Rameez nodded hesitantly and went away.

Gulab had not told anyone that he had again visited Kamathipura two days ago. This time he had gone alone. He trusted no one but himself and his own instincts. It was the second time he had visited the notorious red-light area and had wild sex with Maya in her room full of mirrors. He could see their naked bodies writhing against each other's in the mirrors on the ceiling. But what was more important was that Maya had asked him about his real identity right at the time he was entering her. Gulab had been taken aback for a moment as Maya stopped her freaky moans and asked him in a sharp, hawk-like tone, '*Tu Madanpura ka Gulab Singh hai?*' Gulab was quiet. Maya bit his lips hard and asked again, '*Bol na! Tu Gulab Singh hai na?*'

Gulab was intimidated. He had wanted to utilize this woman for his own plans, and to do that he needed to disclose his identity before her. Gulab nodded. Maya looked at him like a wild cat and smiled while he held her hair tight in his fist. They were both bizarrely eccentric. After some time, Maya sat on the bed and watched Gulab wearing his shirt. Maya asked curiously, '*Tu idhar kyun aaya, Gulab Singh?*' Gulab smiled and replied, '*Tere liye.*' Maya laughed, putting her hands on her face. She laughed and laughed, and it seemed she would never stop. Gulab was flabbergasted. He did not know what to do.

After some time, Maya said, '*Madanpura ke Gulab Singh ko Kamathipura ke ek randi se pyaar ho gya?*' Maya clapped in ecstasy and laughed again. Ghulab was getting irritated and angry. He caught Maya by her shoulder and made her sit up. He positioned his revolver on her mouth and asked her to keep quiet. Maya was scared for a while. Feeling the pistol in her mouth, she calmed down and sat quietly. Gulab now told Maya that he wanted to get Kamathipura and the trade from Nagi, and that if Maya helped him in his quest, he would reward her with enough power and money. Maya too, had only been waiting for this opportunity. She removed the pistol from her mouth, sat in front of Gulab and asked him, '*Agar tu mere ko dhoka diya toh? Main kyun yakin karu tera?*' Gulab handed his pistol to her and said, '*Tu ya toh mera yaakin kar ya mere ko maar daal.*'

Maya understood that Gulab has been checkmated by her sexual prowess. He was now restless to have her again and again. Maya smiled within and shrugged. It was time to dethrone Nagarajan and his brothers. Maya opened the door and checked if anyone was around listening to them. She shouted, 'Radha, Abdul!' Within a minute both came running. Maya asked them to stand in front of the door till she either came out or called them in. The next two hours were extremely busy for Maya and Gulab. Maya gave Gulab every little detail about Nagi and the trade. She told him of the genesis of the syndicate, leaving Gulab astounded at the money, power and network involving the enterprise.

It was an intricate racket of trafficking women, operating out of every tiny part of the country, and Nagi was one of those parts. Maya informed Gulab that Nagi's men could be bought over once Rama and Teja were finished. Gulab analysed all the aspects and promised Maya to come back with his men very soon.

So, finally, it was the day of the conquest, the day of Gulab and his gang's encounter with Naagi's men, they are on verge of a gang war for attaining the control over Kamathipura. Maya had informed Gulab about every possibility of an encounter of Gulab's gang with Nagi's brothers. Gulab had explained the situation thoroughly to his men, giving them the facts and actions that were to be executed. They armed themselves as necessary.

Rameez and Iqbal would drive the two cars into which all their men would be loaded. Gulab would enter the brothel first and kill Teja while the gang would catch hold of Rama from brothel number two where he was to be generally found. It was almost eight when Gulab walked into Pilla House with Rameez and Iqbal. Abdul was waiting for them. Abdul already knew his job. He took Gulab towards Maya's room through the long, dark corridor and spiral staircase. Gulab heard the eerie noise of a cat crying. He could hardly bear the odour of urine all around. He felt like puking. But he had to complete this operation. He followed Abdul, tip-toeing all the way. They stopped in front of Maya's room. They could hear dreadful moans and sexual groans through the door. Gulab indicated to Abdul to stand at the side of the room while he cautiously opened the door. Gulab saw Maya and Teja busy in deep sexual intercourse; so deep their bodies were intertwined and they could hardly sense Gulab's eyes on them. Gulab saw Maya perched over Teja. She looked as though she was getting utmost pleasure out of it. Gulab was fiercely annoyed. He took his pistol out and aimed it at Teja, but before he could shoot him Maya took a pistol out from her blouse and shot Teja right on his forehead.

Teja, heavily drunk and dizzy with sexual excitement, died before he could even realize he was being killed. Blood oozed out of his forehead as his lifeless body lay on the bed. Maya removed herself from Teja's body, stood before the bed, licked the mouth of the pistol and laughed like a devil! Gulab entered the room and smiled at Maya. '*Chal, Gulab, tejori todte hai!*' exclaimed Maya. Gulab was now immensely aroused, but he had to get hold of the safe first. Maya took him to the second floor of the building, which was a stark contrast to the other floors. This floor was tidy and well decorated. The floor was covered with expensive carpets and had big tubs of flowers. Maya took him to a large hall. This was the senate hall of the syndicate, Maya told him. Here was where, once a month, Nagi held his meetings with traffickers from all over. Maya went towards a big, framed photograph on the wall showing wild horses in a meadow. She pushed it towards the right. The photograph moved, showing an opening in the wall that led to a dungeon-like space with a barred iron gate. Maya opened the gate and showed Gulab the Shettys' coffer. Ghulab's eyes twinkled as she opened it and they could see an astronomical quantity of wealth inside. Maya told Gulab, 'Whatever we take from here will be divided between us, but I will be the head of the trade. You give my trade protection; I will share the money with you.' Gulab nodded and then asked curiously, 'What about Nagi?' Maya laughed. '*Khabar gya bharwe ko, Woh ab idhar kabhi nahi aayega!*' Maya was correct. Nagi never returned to Kamathipura. Gulab and his people protected Maya with men and arms. And Maya became the undisputed Queen of Kamathipura!

Maya's rise to power was historic, dark and heinous. If Kamathipura was Egypt then Maya would certainly have been Cleopatra. Maya expanded the trade with her shrewd brain and became the leader of the syndicate. The highest percentage of women trafficking in Kamathipura took place during her regime. The highest percentage of commercial sex workers abused, tormented and murdered was also during her time. Maya loved power and ruled over the world of sin for a long time, as long as twenty years.

But this universe believes in change, and one reign must end and make way for a newer one. Thus, the universe conspired and brought Kajol to the shadowy lanes of Kamathipura, where she was destined to challenge Maya's ruthless reign and free the helpless women from the sway of her violence.

7
Putting Your Head Into the Lion's Mouth

It was an ordinary July evening. The monsoon was at its peak, flooding every vein of the metropolis. It seemed the grand artist had coloured the usually pastel-coloured skies a violent grey. Kajol was sitting by the little window of her room and curiously watching the drizzle. She could see the birds drenched by the rain water flying hastily towards their nests. They were flying in groups. Kajol did not know what species of birds they were, but they looked beautiful with their wide wet wings spread on the bosom of the sky, as if they were drawing out a wide ray of hope to reach home in time. After one group flew past and disappeared from sight, she noticed one little bird trying to fly alone. It was so tiny that it was finding it difficult to fly in the storm. It was there fluttering mid-sky, waiting for some unknown force to help her fly and take her to her nest. The sky had darkened and it started to rain more heavily. Kajol shut the window silently. Tears ran from her eyes, like drops of hot rain. She knew that the tiny bird could never reach her home. She knew that some predator passing by would invariably prey on her. Much as Kajol herself had been preyed on. Her wings had been cut long ago, leaving her bleeding in the middle of hell without anyone to heal her wounds.

Describing her childhood to Aapa, Annu and Rani, Kajol would often break into tears. She would go back to her native place Hasnabad, that picturesque village on the banks of the Ichamati river, which forms the boundary between the countries of India and Bangladesh, where she was born, and visualize her thirteen-year-old self racing every train that would pass by their narrow railway station in the middle of the paddy fields. She would revisit the vibrant local fair that was held on the eve of Charak. The *Charak er mela* was a folk festival held to worship Lord Shiva, and was mostly celebrated in West Bengal and Bangladesh during the month of Chaitra, which was roughly March. She and her brother Rizul would watch bioscopes of contemporary Bengali films and eat the lip-smacking *jhhal muri* and *phuchka*, only to be set jumping by the fiery spices in both, their eyes watering and their tongues tingling with delight. She would become highly nostalgic as she reminisced about the heart-wrenching Vijaya Dashami, the last day of Durga Puja, when the deities of their village were immersed in the Ichamati post-sunset.

The Ichamati river, nestled in the serene landscape of Bangladesh, was a place of great natural beauty and rich cultural heritage. This river, which meandered through both Bangladesh and India, had a unique place in the hearts of the people living along its banks. Its serene waters and verdant surroundings made for a breathtaking landscape that enchanted the soul, and all what one wished to do was to sit in absolute silence and look at the exquisite artistry of nature for hours.

This fluid boundary of the Ichamati dividing the two nations also acted as a boundary as harsh as a barbed wire fence to stop the people from crossing to one bank from the other. This river that separated the '*epar*' (India) from the '*opar*' (Bangladesh), giving rise to the eternal '*Ghoti-Bangal*' rivalry, a saga of humour, passion and undying one-upmanship so deeply ingrained in the Bengali culture that even Shakespeare would have struggled to script a more entertaining rivalry. These two factions, though bound by the same Bengali language, treat each other with the kind of affectionate disdain usually reserved for squabbling siblings. The Bangals, descendants of East Bengal (now Bangladesh), are fiery in temperament, louder in speech, and believe that *ilish,* the hilsa fish, is nothing short of divine intervention in the culinary world. The Ghotis, the proud natives of West Bengal, roll their eyes at this obsession, claiming that *chingri malai* curry, or prawn cooked in coconut milk, is far more refined than any dish from the other side, much like their own polished mannerisms and 'pure' Bengali pronunciation. The Partition of 1947 not only drew a border across Bengal but also set the stage for decades of cultural sparring. The term Bangal, once used dismissively by Ghotis to describe the newly arrived East Bengal migrants, was soon worn as a badge of honour. The Bangals retaliated by dubbing their adversaries Ghoti – literally meaning 'pot' – implying a people living a homebound, less adventurous existence. And thus the battle lines were drawn, ready to be played out over dining tables, at family gatherings and, most ferociously, on the football field.

Nowhere is this rivalry more intense than in Kolkata's football fever, where loyalties are permanently inked in red and gold for East Bengal (Bangal pride) and green and maroon for Mohun Bagan (Ghoti honour). Every East Bengal vs. Mohun Bagan match is a spectacle of unbridled passion as fans hurl creative insults at each other, invoke ancestral culinary superiority, and sometimes even boycott meals, depending on the match outcome. Picture this: an elderly Bangal grandfather, having witnessed East Bengal's historic 5-0 victory over Mohun Bagan in 1975, still narrating the tale to anyone who would listen, with the reverence usually reserved for epics like the Mahabharata. His Ghoti neighbour, meanwhile, refuses to acknowledge that match ever happened and instead waxes poetic about Mohun Bagan's legendary 1911 IFA Shield victory against the British. The rivalry even infiltrates households – imagine a mixed-marriage scenario where a Bangal husband and a Ghoti wife engage in Cold War tactics during football derby season. The wife subtly serves prawn curry before the match, trying to tilt fate in Mohun Bagan's favour, while the husband retaliates by placing an ilish head on the dinner plate as a good luck charm for East Bengal.

The Icchamati river's beauty was especially evident during the monsoon season when it swirled with the rainwater, bringing life to the surrounding fields and villages. The banks of the Ichamati, lined with lush greenery, tall grasses and vibrant flowers, often created a tapestry of colours, a delight to the eyes. The reflection of the sky and clouds on the river's surface added to its charm, making it appear like a ribbon of blue weaving through the green landscape. During the Vijaya Dashami evenings, Kajol would stand in the bank of the river, teary eyed with the villagers, bidding farewell to Ma Durga and her children with brightly lit clay lamps. They could clearly see the immersion on the other bank of the river by people of the neighbouring country who also carried clay lamps as a symbol of wishing 'Subho Bijoya' to their fellow human beings on the other side of the river. It was worth watching how the deities immersed by the two countries, that were once one, travelled crossing each other to reach the other country and blended with its water and soil.

Despite being a devout Muslim, Kajol had always revered the stories of Mother Goddess, that she used to hear from the '*buri ma*' (old woman) of their village, captivated by the tale of her divine emergence and manifestation. She marvelled at the immense power she wielded, the fierce valour with which she vanquished the invincible demon Mahishasura, restoring peace and equilibrium in the cosmos. Moidul chacha, who was the Dhaki who played the '*Dhaak*' (a traditional Bangali musical instrument played during Durga Puja, especially during the major rituals) every year during Durga Puja to invoke the Mother Goddess, also narrated Kajol stories about the great Goddess. Kajol used to visualize the entire process of Durga Puja metaphoric to the eternal cycle of creation, preservation and destruction in its realest form. Just as the human body is formed from the five elements – earth, water, fire, air and ether – and returns to these same elements after death, the idol of Ma Durga too follows a similar cycle – creation, preservation and destruction; an expert artisan creates an idol made of soil, a prudent priest invokes life in it by chanting holy mantras, the idol comes to life and is worshipped unanimously across the earth for four days with all devotion and reverence and finally on the fifth day the idol is immersed into the water where it melts and gets blended into the five elements of the universe. Each human being, thought Kajol, was comprised of the same epiphany, each of them melts into the same elements after death, yet while living they are judged on the basis of their social stature, their occupation, their genders and the material wealth they possess.

Later in life, Kajol laughed on the paradox of a country that revered a female goddess as the supreme being, yet simultaneously subjects women to hate, abuse, and extreme agony. They are pushed to the depths of hellish torment, stripped off their dignity, and violated until the very goddess within them is shattered. Yet Kajol was deeply spiritual. She never missed her namaz and did *ibaadat* (prayer) every single day, her faith a quiet but powerful presence in her life. Festivals brought out the warmth and kindness in her, she celebrated Eid with as much enthusiasm and zest as she did Diwali and Ganesh Chaturthi, joining Aaapa, Rani and Annu in every shared moment of festivity.

During Eid, she would lovingly prepare *sevaiya* in generous batches, ensuring every narrow by-lane and pocket room of Kamathipura received a taste of her affection. Her famous Eid *halim* and *sevaiya* were awaited eagerly by her Officer Didi, who would savour them with heartfelt gratitude and love!

Kajol held Officer Didi in deep regard, she adored her not just for her magnanimity, but for all she had done for them. Her heart brimmed with quiet thankfulness, rooted in the dignity and hope Officer Didi had helped restore in their lives.

Being the second generation of expatriates, Kajol had heard stories of the Partition of Bengal from her Boro Abbu (grandfather). It was a time when several Hindu and Muslim families in Bangladesh were attacked and had to leave their homes and assets in that country and move to West Bengal, where they had to begin life from scratch. Kajol's grandfather was one of the migrants who had witnessed this turmoil. He had been twenty at the time. Kajol had also heard how rudely and heartlessly they were treated by the people of this country, who had used disparaging terms like '*Molla*' and '*Bangals*' for them. It was not easy to live the life of a beggar when one had been born into wealth, to be marked as 'refugees' and to struggle every day against hunger, betrayal and poverty, her grandfather used to say.

Kajol had often heard her grandfather and his friends bad-mouthing all and sundry as they chatted under the hundred-year-old banyan tree in their village. That banyan tree which was a spot for the 'adda' of the senior citizens, had witnessed unnecessary brawls and nasty arguments over everything under the sun. The adda is an inseparable part of life in Bengal and one of the most important features of 'Bengaliness', deeply ingrained in the Bengali culture. It could take place under a tree, in street-side cafes, tea stalls, or at railway stations and even bus queues. 'Adda' was not just talk but thoughts, laced with philosophy, puns, nostalgia and 'what ifs' that formed to be an indispensable part of Bengali lives and is prevalent till today.

During winters, Kajol would feast on the sumptuous *peethe puli*, *paati saapta* and *doodh pithe* made by her Boro Ammi and

Ammi, especially on Makar Sankranti day when the Bengalis celebrated Poush Parbon, a festival welcoming *Poush*, or the month of December, which marks the winter season.

Kajol did not like studies at all. She would laugh as she described how the old, lanky *pandit moshai* of their village school had caned her for stealing fruits from his garden instead of studying, and how she had run away telling the *pagla buro* she would not return to the school ever again. Kajol would climb trees, prance around in the fields and swim in the ponds of their village.

Kajol was as wild as a hurricane. She was dreaded by the boys and girls of her age across her village and even across the other neighbouring villages. She had a track record of beating up boys. She would participate in all kind of masculine games with the local boys and end up wrestling with them if they played foul. Once Kajol broke a boy's leg in a nasty fight over a guava. The boy was Gopal, son of the wealthiest man of their village. Gopal and Kajol had formed an army of children to invade the garden of Binoy Khuro, which had the tastiest winter guavas. Kajol, being the leader, climbed the trees, plucked the guavas and threw them down while Gopal and the other children stuffed them into their kurta pockets. The idea was to feast on the guavas together, post the invasion. But all of a sudden Binoy Khuro appeared out of nowhere with his *neri kutta* and chased the boys away. Kajol, who was on the tree, could not get down and run away as fast as her soldiers. An enraged Binoy Khuro snarled like his pet and threatened Kajol with punishment. Unable to find any other way out, Kajol jumped down from the tree, ran towards the wall of the garden, climbed it and escaped to the other side. It all happened within the blink of an eye and Binoy Khuro and his dog were left flabbergasted.

Kajol escaped but could not forget the betrayal of her soldiers, especially Gopal, whom she had awarded the stature of her commander-in-chief! '*Hala Chucho*!' hissed Kajol, and ran towards Palter Math, the village playground where they used to assemble after an invasion, only to see Gopal and company feasting on the stolen guavas! 'Betrayers! 'Ungrateful rats!' screamed Kajol, and pounced on Gopal. The bulky Gopal fell on the grass and struggled to free himself from her grip. The other boys, terribly scared, stood in terror and watched Kajol in action. In order to win her solidarity, Chuni threw a piece of wood at Kajol, which Kajol used to use as her royal sceptre. Kajol hit Gopal's right leg with that piece of wood till he screamed and begged for forgiveness. Kajol kept hitting him till she was tired and bored and walked away after some time. Gopal lay there screaming, till his father came and carried him to the hospital, where it was found he had a broken limb.

Gopal's father complained to Kajol's Abbu, Shirajul about it. And Shirajul in turn scolded Kajol, but all in vain. Kajol had her reasons for what she did. She could not forgive betrayers, and being the king she had to punish him to set an example before her men. Kajol was indomitable in spirit and often tried to teach such lessons to those who were wanting in loyalty and integrity.

Kajol was a free soul, a wild bird who was never tired of flying before her wings were burnt and she was thrown into a pit of darkness from which she found no escape.

Kajol hailed from a family that could be said to be well off in comparison to their neighbours. She belonged to a Bengali Muslim 'Bangal' family. They spoke their mother tongue of Bangal Bengali with a unique accent. They and the Bengali Hindus lived in great harmony, valuing each other's rituals, cultures, religious customs and ethnicity, and would celebrate the festivals of both Eid and Durga Puja with the same zest and enthusiasm.

The elder of two siblings, Kajol's father was predominantly a weaver. In the 1950s, Bengal's weavers were the backbone of its rich textile tradition. Known for their expertise in artistry of weaving and craftsmanship in handloom weaving, they produced muslin, jamdani, and tant sarees, often using cotton spun by hand. Many of them being Muslims, these artisans worked from their homes or small family units, passing down skills through generations and helped preserve a heritage that continues to define Bengal's cultural identity. Kajol's father Shirajul, along with his brother Khaled, ran the business and divided the profit between themselves. Khaled was in his mid-forties and unmarried. He respected Shirajul and Amina and adored Kajol and Rizul.

When she was a child, Khaled would make Kajol sit on his shoulders and roam around the village. He would tease Kajol, saying he would marry her off to some old, toothless man, and Kajol would cry loudly. He would then buy her biscuits to make her stop crying. She would then be happy and smiling again. Kajol loved her Chacha more than her life. Since Shirajul was always busy with his work and was also a little serious by nature, Kajol enjoyed the company of Khaled. And so did Amina. Kajol would often see Khaled lying lazily on their bed chatting with Amina while Shirajul was away in town. Amina would cook the most delicious *luchi aloor dum* and *pathar mangsho* for Shirajul. Another reason why Amina like Khaled was that he was outstandingly handsome; he was almost six feet tall, pink-complexioned, and had thick hair. Khaled was undoubtedly attractive. Since he was member of the yoga club of the village and an avid swimmer, he had a perfectly toned body with a broad chest, a complete contrast to the thin, short Shirajul whose face was wrinkled and who was nearly bald. Shirajul was nearing sixty. There was a striking age difference of twenty years between him and Amina. He loved Amina dearly and fulfilled all her desires, yet there was a huge communication gap between them, and Amina used to look to Khaled to fill that gap. Amina would stealthily watch Khaled as he massaged his body with mustard oil before diving into the local pond for his bath. She would purposely go to the pond on the pretext of washing utensils or clothes and watch him swim across the pond, naked. She would wait for Khaled to finish his swimming and climb back on the bank, when he would request her to wipe his wet back with a red *gamcha*. Khaled too liked his Bhabi, who was astonishingly pretty, and would spend a lot of time with her on the pretext of teaching her to read the newspapers. He would bring lipstick and nail polish for her whenever he went to the town or to Kolkata, or ask her to massage his head when he was tired. One night, when Shirajul was away in town for business and everyone in the house was deep asleep, Amina was not able to sleep. She felt a strange longing for sex and wanted Khaled to make love to her.

Her desire for Khaled grew so uncontrollable that one night she tiptoed to Khaled's room and knocked on the door lightly. The door was open. She stepped into the room. It was all dark. Amina could not see anything. She was a little scared that Khaled might wake up and ask her why she was there. As she stood hesitantly and thought of going back, she could feel the touch of strong arms behind her. No sooner had she nervously turned around than Khaled kissed her lips. He took her to his bed and they made mad love in the darkness of night. A few moments before dawn, Amina silently went back to her room. The next day was as ordinary as any other. Shirajul came back from the town in the morning, ate breakfast and went into his room for a nap. Shirajul and Khaled's father – Amina's father-in-law – fought with another old man of thier village on some trivial issues and sat angrily on the podium with a bowlful of puffed rice for hours together, looking at the sky and shedding tears for his fatherland. Kajol went to play with her friends and Rizul went to school. Amina sat in the kitchen and remembered the incident of last night. She saw Khaled looking at her lustily from the window of the kitchen. Their eyes exchanged amorous glances. Both wanted more.

Amina and Khaled were waiting for the right opportunity to get together in bed again. But in a family of so many people it was not so easy. One day, while Amina was combing her hair, Khaled caught her from behind and tried to kiss her. Amina moved his hands away angrily and ran away. She could not afford to take a risk. She could not be a fool. No one should have the slightest hint about their equation. She had to be very cautious.

A few days after that was the 'jatra night' in their village. Jatra or yatra, which meant 'journey', is a traditional folk theatre form that has a phenomenal journey of evolution. Its origin goes back to the Bhakti movement propelled by Chaitanya

Mahaprabhu, a Hindu religious leader widely worshipped as a reincarnation of Lord Krishna, and thus belonging to the sect of Vaishavism. Jatra was his way of spreading the name and celebrating the glory of Krishna amongst the masses, roaming from place to place in processions while singing and dancing to the tune of religious songs. Eventually, Jatra became the most popular form of theatre across the villages of West Bengal, Odisha and Tripura in India. In an era when women and children were not supposed to visit theatres and watch cinema, Jatra presented them an escape from the mundane world to a world of pure entertainment and was a welcome relief from the monotony of homemaking. Once or twice every year, the Jatra groups visited the villages and enacted plays in the village playgrounds, mostly during the nights. Tickets had to be bought for these shows. Jatra was considered as one of the finest forms of art, it was in its own unique genre and was greatly popular across the villages of West Bengal. Shirajul and his father loved to watch Jatra and waited for the time of the year when it used to happen in their village. Amina too would wait eagerly for the event. She relished the performance of the beautiful actors on stage. Kajol and Rizul were also crazy about Jatra. Kajol loved dancing and singing, and greatly enjoyed the fun, frolic and drama onstage. She would perform snatches from the plays later before her friends with great enthusiasm. So, on Jatra nights, Shirajul would unfailingly take his family to their village playground, which looked vibrant, with a large, beautifully decorated stage and all lit up with halogen lights. There were hawkers and tea sellers everywhere. During Jatra time, their village looked like a grand fair. But this year, surprisingly, Amina requested Shirajul to go along with his father and the children and excuse her from it. She said to

Shirajul that she felt a fever coming on and would prefer to stay back. Shirajul, who had never forced anything on his wife, went to the show with his father, Kajol and Rizul, leaving Amina back in the house with Khaled. Amina had her own plans for herself and Khaled after everyone left. She waited till Shirajul, her father-in-law and the children set off for Nobir Math, the playground where the shows were staged. After they left, Khaled came to Amina's room. He saw her lying on the bed. Her long hair was touching the floor as she lay gazing at the ceiling fan. Khaled climbed on the bed and lay by her side. Within moments they were cosy in each other's arms. Khaled restlessly undressed Amina and himself. Holding her body tight against his, Khaled sucked her lips passionately. Soon their bodies were writhing on the bed as they indulged in intense sex. Amina moaned out of pleasure as Khaled entered her. They panted, now completely lost in each other. Little did they realize that the window of the room had opened with a gust of wind and that Kajol was watching them with burning eyes. They were interrupted mid-way as Kajol shouted, '*Ammi!Chachu! Ki kortaso tomra esob?!*' and ran away towards the terrace.

Kajol was shocked, appalled and thunderstruck to see her Ammi and her beloved chacha jaan that way. As Kajol remembered the scene she felt disgusted and annoyed. She locked herself in the small room on their terrace. The scene of Khaled making love to her Ammi not only irritated her but also triggered tremendous anger in her. She had come back from the Jatra because her stomach had started to ache badly and she wanted to sleep. She had come back and knocked on the door of their house. But when her mother did not open the door, she thought she must have slept off and tried to call her from the window, only to see her mother and uncle at the nasty act. She was flabbergasted. She puked. She cried. She did not know what to do. A thirteen-year-old Kajol would never ever be able to fathom what she had seen some minutes before. She was crying like a small child when she heard a knock on the door. Khaled called out to her: 'Kajol, please open the door once. Please listen to me.' Kajol shouted at him, 'You go from here, Chachu! I do not want to see your face! I will tell everything to Abbu and Boro Abbu once they come back!' Kajol heard her mother's voice. She spoke softly; 'Kajli, please listen to us once! I can explain that it is not the way you are thinking about it. *Ek bar dorja ta khol Ma*!' Kajol was feeling claustrophobic. Her head was spinning like a top. She opened the door and fell unconscious.

Kajol opened her eyes and saw Khaled and Amina standing in front of her. Amina sobbed while Khaled stood in silence. Both apologized and requested her not to disclose what she had seen to anyone. Amina said Shirajul would throw both her and Khaled out of the house and her father-in-law would kill them. Khaled touched her and promised to leave the house forever. Kajol saw tears in Khaled's eyes. She loved her chacha more than anyone else in the world. It was her chacha who had named her Kajol despite the kazi naming her Nafisa, since Kajol had unusually beautiful and bright eyes that looked resplendent when kohl was applied to them. Khaled was educated up to matriculation level and believed that all human beings were equal. He would often speak of Hindus and Muslims being two sides of the same coin. He had always encouraged Kajol and Rizul to befriend other children irrespective of their religious identity. Kajol has always considered him as her ideal. Kajol could not take the pain of her dearest chachu and his tears melted her heart. She asked both to swear on her name not to repeat what they had done ever. They swore on her name. Kajol forgave them and asked them to forget the episode.

Almost three months passed since that incident and Kajol had not opened her mouth in front of anyone about the incident and acted as if she had forgotten it. Sometimes she visualized her mother intimate in bed with her chacha. Khaled had gone nowhere and only talked of leaving the house and creating his own business whenever he saw Kajol. Amina remained quiet and performed all the household chores. There was no synergy between Amina, Khaled and Kajol. And then it happened.

Kajol must have been sixteen or seventeen when she fell seriously ill post her menstrual cycle. She had frequent cramps and intermittent phases of abdominal bleeding. The hakim advised Shirajul to take Kajol to the big hospital in the city and consult a gynaecologist. Since it was the crop season and Shirajul was busy in the fields, he asked Amina and Khaled to take Kajol to the city hospital. The three boarded the express train from Hasnabad in the early morning of the following day. It was raining cats and dogs when they reached the city railway station named Sealdah. Kajol walked uncomfortably while Amina and Khaled held her on either side. When they reached the bus stop, Khaled hired a yellow taxi and asked Amina and Kajol to get into it. He sat beside the driver. As the taxi ran through the wide street it started raining torrentially. Amina wiped Kajol's face with the end of her saree affectionately. Kajol felt sleepy. She slept off in Amina's lap.

On opening her eyes, Kajol saw herself in a dark room. There was a foul smell that made her feel like vomiting. She could feel an excruciating pain in her stomach. She saw a woman standing next to the bed and giggling. She was very fat and ugly. Kajol was scared. She asked for her mother and chacha . The woman laughed like a devil and said, '*Tor aami r chacha tore 20,000 takaye Sonagachir te beche geche re meye!*' Kajol could not believe her words. Her mother and uncle had sold her to a brothel? She yelled in anger and called for her mother and uncle, but no one came. Kajol shouted again and again, but her voice was too feeble to reach her mother or her uncle, who had perhaps run away after selling her to the brothel. Kajol closed her eyes in fear and hatred. It was all dark.

'Kajol O Kajol!' Aapa's broken voice woke up Kajol from her slumber. Last night had been a riot as all of them had partied wildly under 'Kanada Bridge' (Kennedy Bridge) till dawn. Kajol needed a break, and so did Aapa, Annu and Rani. It was not that she enjoyed spreading her legs before strangers, but Kajol always felt that women, no matter how educated they were and what jobs they were in, must spread their legs. Either the world fucks them or men do. Kajol did not regret being a slut in Kamathipura. Rather, she felt proud and held her head high. It had been more than two decades since Kajol's mother and uncle had sold her off in the brothel of Sonagachi in Kolkata. Kajol had tried every means of escape and revolt. She had refused to be a slut and had got beaten mercilessly by her Madam, Shona. She was raped numerous times by every man who visited the brothel. Her hands were tied with rope and a hot iron rod was inserted into her innards till she was half dead and had to be hospitalized. In the hospital the ward boys raped her at night and left her in a pool of blood. Yet Kajol survived. She was a survivor. She returned to Sonagachi after a few days as an absolutely transformed person. Once she owned the profession of prostitution and spread her legs before men, she realized that she need not starve and get beaten. She became a different human being, or rather a species different from a human being, a half-dead, half-alive demonic entity with not a drop of mercy or forgiveness in her. After spending ten years in Sonagachi, Kajol was sold in Mumbai by her Madam and started working in Kamathipura under Maya, the matre dame of this world of sin. Had Kajol not been around, Maya would have tormented and silenced a lot of women with her perversions and sadomasochism. Kajol had become that strong wall that stood against the wickedness of Maya, for Kajol believed in a code, a code to keep the women in the trade safe from perverted attacks. All was not fair game in her world. While it was true that they were sex workers, Kajol believed that they should have the dignity of a human existence. Kajol had dethroned Maya and had freed the women and herself. No one owned them now. They were free. They traded as per their own convenience and stood by each other. Whenever they were not in the mood for work, physically or psychologically, they sat back in their pockets and relaxed. Dethroning even an old and aging Maya was not easy. Maya was a living devil, a horror who had threatened and tortured hundreds of girls, compelling them to sell their bodies against their will. Maya's partner in crime, Gulab, a local gangster from Madanpura under whose empowering blanket Maya operated, had died by suicide after being betrayed by Maya with multiple men. Gulab had fallen in love with Maya and had mistakenly thought she loved him too. He had lived under that false happiness. But alas! Maya had never loved anyone. Her soul only craved power, money and sex. She had stopped resembling a human long ago. She had turned into an agency for profit.

For quite some time after Kajol came to Kamathipura, she had tolerated Maya's abuses. But Kajol was the queen of her own whims and refused to work under Maya's fascism. Consequently, she was forcefully drugged by Maya. Kajol had been forcefully fed every substance imaginable! But she was the deadliest kid of the lot! Intoxicated, she peddled her body twenty times a day. Kajol was a workaholic in the truest sense of the term. She never procrastinated and was always in high spirits. She was always looking out to catch hold of the most lucrative customers. For Kajol it was her job. She believed in working hard and earning money, and did it with utmost dedication. At the same time she hated being exploited. So she only worked as much as was commensurate with her remuneration. It was twenty years since Kajol's mother and uncle had turned her into a whore, perhaps to get rid of her permanently so no one would get to know about their secret affair. Kajol could never forgive them. She cursed them every single day of her life. She hated the terms 'Ammi' and 'Chacha' and abused them with the worst slang for being betrayers of the worst order. Kajol became pregnant from some customer of hers at seventeen. She badly wanted to kill the child, but Aapa stopped her. Aapa tried to take care of her while Kajol peddled her body throughout her pregnancy. She charged her customers double her usual amount, considering that from '*gaai*' she had become '*doodh wali gaai*'.

Kajol was high on drugs, beedi and country liquor all nine months of her pregnancy, hoping that someday the creature inside her would get poisoned and die, but god works miracles and had different plans for her. After nine months and seven days, Kajol delivered a healthy son. What was more astonishing was that the child looked like an angel. It was as if he had lit up the tiny, shabby pocket room of Kajol's with his divine presence. Every woman of Kamathipura wondered how this was possible and thanked the Almighty for blessing the kid while Kajol brooded over this added responsibility in her life and cried loudly. This made people mistakenly think that she had produced a baby with whom something was wrong. So bitter was Kajol's agony that Aapa and Annu assured her they would look after the child. Later Kajol gave birth gave birth to one more son, unwilling and repulsed as she was about it. She abused her customers for not using condoms and for creating never-ending troubles for her. Sadaab and Shoib were raised by Aapa. They knew Kajol as their mother and adored her. Their love transformed the eccentric firebrand Kajol into a quieter person. She cured herself of her severe addictions with the help of doctors and psychiatrists, though much later. By then she had thrown the infant Sadaab and Shoib many a time, out of intoxication and rage, so that they would die and end her troubles. However, destiny and the gods being too kind ensured the two children were unhurt. Kajol would then abuse the gods for being brutal towards her. The more the children tried to get close to Kajol, the more ruthlessly she would beat them up, calling them bastards and sons of bastards. But Aapa's affection and the children's innocence eventually brought a change in Kajol and she truly became a mother. She realized what the essence of motherhood was and protected her children like a tigress protects her cubs. Sadaab and Shoib turned out to be good at academics despite the ambience in which they grew up. Aapa admitted them in the local school run by a social worker. They attended school during the day and studied in the nearby church in the evening. The best part was that

Sadaab and Shoib loved each other, despite knowing that they were not sons from the same father. They also adored and respected Kajol in spite of knowing her ways and what she did for a living. There were days when Sadaab would see his intoxicated mother in a by-lane of Kamathipura, decked up in a saree, jewellery and gajra, waiting for customers. But that did not have any effect on him; rather, he noticed how beautiful his mother looked in that attire. He looked at her radiance in awe and promised himself he would buy her many sarees when he grew up. Unlike Sadaab, Shoib never allowed his mother to lock her room when she was with some unknown uncle or grandfather-like person. He would always scream and try to hit the men, till Kajol banged his head against the door and Aapa would come to the rescue. Kajol would rave and rant at Aapa and Shoib saying '*Duty ke time mein kuch lafda nahi!*' Kajol considered her job as ordinary and as stereotyped as any other job in the world and would often regard it as 'duty'. Also, she had the fire of ten street brawlers and the heart of a lioness, never one to back down, always ready to rise and retaliate when wronged. She had an intolerably loud voice, which disturbed and distracted every woman in Kamathipura, and yet they could not protest. You protest and the tigress eats you up with her horrendous vocabulary and verbal violence. Well, her means of violence even became physical, depending on the gravitas of your crime. Men often left Kajol's room seriously wounded, with a broken hand or an injured penis. She claimed to have taught them a lesson for being over-smart. Being Kajol was not easy. Had she not been what she was, she would have either been a very popular leader or a very notorious criminal.

All of Kamathipura knew her as the rebel kid. Even Maya was in awe of her temper. Initially she had starved her, made her addicted to drugs, kept her captive in the dungeons for days, made her sleep with the worst of customers, and yet she could not bring down Kajol's temper. Kajol waited to inflict revenge on Maya, and the day Maya snatched the two-year old Shoib from Aapa's arms and tried to burn his tender cheek with a ball of burning coal, Kajol rose up for her child. She was inebriated at the time. As Maya tried to put the ball of coal in Shoib's mouth, Kajol finished her bottle of alcohol in silence. Then she stood up, much like an Amitabh Bachchan, the *numero uno* hero of Indian cinema, full of wrath, looked for a while at the picture of Durga Ma on the wall of her pocket room, and ran like a mad bull towards Maya and kicked her in the abdomen. Maya was no less than Kajol when it came to physical violence. Within a moment Maya stood up and kicked the tender Shoib, who screamed out of pain and fell unconscious. Aapa nervously picked up Shoib and ran away. Kajol was furious. Her eyes burned like the third eye of Shiva. Maya hissed like a snake and giggled at Kajol. Within no time, Kajol pushed Maya to the ground and started to kick her. She would not stop, and no one stopped Kajol that day as they witnessed the fall of the tyrant. Maya yelled and howled like a devil. After some time, her voice came down. Kajol spat on her and walked into her own room. She could hear Maya's men threatening to kill her, but every woman of Kamathipura stood in unity with Kajol that day. It was as if they were expressing their gratitude to her for rising on behalf of each one of them against the terror called Maya. Maya was taken to hospital, where she fell into a coma and died after four days.

Kamathipura celebrated her death in the most gallant way by not peddling themselves for one entire day and lauding Kajol for her bravery. She was served plates of sumptuous *hilsa* and rice cooked by Annu. They partied till late night under 'Kanada Bridge', shedding tears of happiness and celebrating freedom!

With Maya's death, the situation in Kamathipura changed. Now every woman ran her own business, traded on her own terms. Kamathipura was now devoid of a corporate structure. The women were immensely grateful to Kajol for freeing them from their state of servitude. Eventually, Kajol and Salma did something phenomenal, which the hell pit of Kamathipura had never seen in the last hundred years. The craze for dance had stayed hidden in the innermost chambers of Salma's heart all these years. In the ball game of life, all Salma did was to dance helplessly to the tune of her barbarous destiny. But her passion for dance was still alive, and now she felt she could allow it to safely emerge again. One autumn evening, while casually chatting with Kajol, Annu, Rani and few of her other kith and kin in Chauda Gulli over cups of cutting chai, Salma hesitantly expressed her time-worn desire to organize a Garba in Kamathipura, at least once. Salma had watched Garba numerous times in films, in daily soaps and on the streets of Mumbai during the Navratri festival, when groups of men and women encircled a statue or picture of Durga, the fierce goddess who rode a tiger and carried a royal trident meant to destroy the asuras or evil entities. They danced expressing their reverence for the goddess, wearing gorgeous traditional Gujarati costumes, brightly coloured chaniya cholis and lehengas with mirror work. The Garba, said Salma, would not only be a break from the kind of work they did but would also instil a ray of hope and faith amongst the women that there was light at the end of darkness, that each could burn themselves and evolve into a newer version of themselves. Prostitution as a profession no more perturbed them as they had undergone a treaty of understanding with fate; what disturbed them was the thought of a bleak and uncertain future for their children, who were not even considered as part of the society. The label they carried as children of commercial sex workers chased them wherever they went. These children, most of whom were born and brought up in Kamathipura, witnessed recurring sexual abuse and exploitation of their mothers and were almost blind to the other tastes of life such as freedom and joy. Salma, being '*maasi*' to those children, wished to bring them together with their mothers and help them spend a few moments of carefree joy through the event of Garba. At first Kajol was sceptical, speculating on the astronomical expenses involved and the legal complexities of getting the required permissions for the event, but later she became enthused as Salma disclosed before her the real motive behind her suggestion. Annu, Rani and the other women supported the idea and felt it would be a welcome relief from the claustrophobic circumstances of their lives. They even decided to pay for the expenses from their own pockets. More money could be obtained by collecting money from the local vendors and customers who would visit them, in the name of the goddess. Kajol uttered, '*Joy Maa*' and gave the green signal to what would be the most pathbreaking event of their lives. The next few days were tirelessly busy for the women of Kamathipura. Kajol, who would have been an outstanding leader had destiny done justice to her, divided up the work among the women. They would report to Salma every morning and brief her of the progress. The Garba would be conducted for one night, on the ninth and last night of Navratri, which was also the most auspicious night. The permissions came easily after Kajol went to the local leader and cop and explained to them their idea and assured them of no chaos. The tigress in her roared fiercely as she said that if the Hindu religion made it imperative to use the soil of a prostitute's house and blend it with the soil out of which the structure of the deity is moulded during Durga Puja, then it is purely the goddess's blessing to make them put up the act of Garba, which comes from the original term '*garbha*' meaning womb, to purify the accursed lanes of Kamathipura, a place routinely witness to crime, abuse and rape. The Bangal in Kajol still remembered a few teachings of her village '*buri ma*' and thanked her. Kajol at her best and Kajol at her worst were equally indomitable. The women heaved a sigh of relief as things began to take a positive turn. Now, it was over to Shamim for putting a touch of glamour and finesse to the upcoming festivities. Shamim was the patent tailor of Chauda Gulli who stitched dresses for the women. Immensely popular among the women of Kamathipura, Shamim, a man of twenty-five or so, had inherited his father Riyaz's tailoring shop and expertise after his death. Shamim's shop was housed in a small room in building number thirteen of the northern-most corner of Kamathipura. His shop was full of colourful posters of actresses from Indian cinema, and each woman of Kamathipura had her personal favourite whom they followed in terms of dress and make-up. Annu adored Madhuri Dixit and wore a lot of the *Hum Aapke Hai Kaun* ghagras and lehengas in orange, purple and green, and wore her hair in a stylish bun or in braids with which she played casually while peddling herself. Rani, who was a little younger, found her diva in Vidya Balan, and thus made it a routine to deck her hair with gajras and wore beautiful sarees to work; and Nisha, an even younger girl trafficked in recent past, looked up to Dipika Padukone and often appeared in flamboyant one-pieces with deeply kohled eyes and open hair. Shamim was the man who made all the designer dresses and stunning blouses as desired by the women, since looking attractive mattered a lot in the profession that earned them their daily bread and butter. Shamim was also their most trusted confidant and dearest friend. They could easily crack the most vulgar of jokes in front of him and tease him while he took their measurements. Shamim would simply respond with a smile, every time. He was of medium height, with a cute face and wheatish complexion. He would never disrespect or ignore his customers. He would listen to them patiently and deliver them the best dresses, done perfectly and on time. So Shamim had a hectic schedule before the Garba event, so hectic that he had to call his cousins over from Bihar to help him out with the stitching and knotting. Shamim earned a lot of money, out of which he donated a lump sum to the Garba fund.

On Garba night, Chauda Gulli of Kamathipura looked completely different from what it did on ordinary days. The entire lane was decorated with vibrant torans, colourful lanterns, hanging lamps and flower rangolis. The women had poured their hearts out in doing this and were surprised at their own hidden talents. The foul odour that pervaded the place was kept in check by the use of incense sticks and perfumes. For one night, customers were not allowed to cross the premises of Chauda Gulli, and women who wished to trade were asked to go elsewhere with their customers. As the sun moved westwards and the full moon rose, Salma worshipped the picture of the deity with flowers, lamps and fumigating incense, and offered the prasad to the women, thus marking the beginning of the event. Soon, the music played and the women gathered in their magnificent dresses, all well made-up. They encircled the picture of the deity and started to tap their feet. The event celebrating the victory of womanhood became synonymous with the triumph of these women, who had defeated providence and were snatching a few moments of happiness for themselves. As they danced in heavenly bliss, tears flowed ceaselessly from their eyes, and they wiped each other's tears and hugged. It seemed that the universe had united them in some spiritual bond of womanhood, irrespective of their caste, creed, religion and thousands of other differences that bred taboos in mainstream society. The spirit of Garba ran so high in their veins that at the end of the event, Kajol announced their collective decision to bring home the great Ganpati and start Ganeshotsav in Chauda Gulli of Kamathipura. The Ganeshotsav held every year in the third gulli of Kamathipura was one of the grandest in Mumbai. Popular as Kamathipura Cha Chintanmani, the trader association and cloth merchants brought home the 'Vignahartha' to demolish the obstacles that hindered the growth of their business and to earn the blessing of prosperity round the year. However, the commercial sex worker fraternity was not allowed to worship the deity or step inside the holy premises. They and their children had no right to participate in the festival. Once or twice some of them had tried to conceal their identity and seek the blessings of the deity, but so familiar were they across Kamathipura that they were shown the exit. They were told their presence might annoy the god and a deadly curse might fall on them for breaking the norms of worship. Kajol, Annu, Rani and many other women of Kamathipura, who carried the tag of 'commercial sex worker' always wondered whether this was indeed the truth. Whenever and wherever they went asking for their rights to be granted, they were either abused, exploited, ignored or thrown out. No schools admitted their children, no hospitals treated them with care, no banks and no post offices guided them on how to build a safer and better future for their children and protect them from falling prey to poverty and circumstances that would lead them to adopt prostitution or pimping as means of livelihood. A few so called 'social workers' started to operate in the area and ensured the women got support and aid. More and more women began to enrol with these social workers, hoping for a better quality of life.

Kajol and her acquaintances did not associate with any social workers but at the same time did not stop anyone from doing so. However, one such philanthropist was beaten very badly by Kajol after she got to know that they had printed their pictures on websites and magazines and were earning donations from foreign countries at their cost. An old customer of Kajol's had shown her the pictures. Kajol and her group of women raided the office of the philanthropist and created havoc there. Not satisfied with that, Kajol beat the trustee with a chappal, put a garland of sandals around her neck and paraded her all around Kamathipura! In the end, she made her sit on a donkey and cast her out of the area. Asked about this unique punishment, Kajol explained that when she was a child, her Abbu had told her tales in which kings and sultans punished offenders in this way. Indeed, Kajol was the king of Kamathipura; a king in the best sense of the word, a protector, a saviour, a human being who rose out of a pit of mud clean, who did not turn out to be a goddess and expect worship, but who neither turned out to be a villain like Maya. Rather, she was a benevolent dictator who preserved her empire with great care and affection. Kajol still remembered a song her chacha used to sing while playing with her, '*Aamra sobai raja aamader ei rajar rajotte*!' We are all kings and equals in this kingdom. She adored the lyrics. Kajol also still remembered the statue of the elderly man with a long, white beard, known as 'Robi Thakur' that stood in front of their school building. He was the one who had composed the song, and on certain special days they were instructed to honour his memory by offering a garland to the statue.

Finally, Chauda Gulli of Kamathipura did bring home the auspicious elephant god. This they did with enthusiasm and reverence. The chant *Ganpati Bappa Maurya*, which echoed through the by-lanes of Kamathipura, was a cry to the world bringing attention to the most tragic tale of unity in diversity, but also a tale of strength and determination. These women, outcast and abhorred by society, had created a different world for themselves, where they could breathe free and create a safe space for themselves, at least for few moments. People detested them for peddling their bodies without even trying to know the circumstances that had compelled them to do so. No woman in this world sells her dignity willingly, unless society forces her to, only to later shun her for her promiscuity. Some entirely succumb under all this pressure and some, like Kajol, stand out as rebels, making their own paths and guiding a thousand more victims like themselves towards a new dawn.

8

The Warm-Nested Pigeon

The average middle-class Indian child who grew up in small towns would certainly remember the thrill of summer vacations. This was the time when children in India visited their 'native place', became familiar with their roots, got overfed and pampered by their grandparents and spent a lot of time outdoors, possibly in the fields or woods. It was a time of discovery and escape after several dreary months of school.

However, one child, a curly-haired, dove-skinned girl with an ever fertile brain and a twinkle of naughtiness in her beautifully expressive eyes, shuddered at the thought of summer holidays. For she had no 'native place' to go to. Of course, her maternal grandparents lived not far away in a beautiful village beside the mighty Mahanadi river, but she was not particularly welcome there. In the patriarchal structure of her community, she was the daughter's daughter to those grandparents, and so not the granddaughter of choice. That exalted place was kept for the children of the sons. Her mother was the only one among the siblings who had gone to school in their Odisha village, where it was mostly the sons who were expected and chosen to be educated. In the 1960s, her mother had aced all the exams in her tiny village school. She had also sailed through the medical college entrance tests with flying colours. But the young village belle with big dreams in her eyes had unwilling parents who did not want to spend money on educating a female child. But the girl went off to the nearby town which had a government medical college and educated herself to become a doctor. She promised she would not be asking for monetary assistance from her parents but would fund herself by getting a scholarship. And she did become a doctor, spending her initial years in jungles, in the most inaccessible terrain of Odisha, serving the tribal population and the newly displaced 'refugees' from Partition-hit Bengal. These events were probably the genesis of the rebellious streak the young, curly-haired developed.

This curly haired dove-skinned girl explored the jungles of Dandakaranya, in that part of India which was known as Kalinga in ancient times, the same Kalinga that was invaded by the greatest of the Indian emperors, the Mauryan king Ashoka. It was the same Kalinga that saw the ruthless slaughter of millions of her sinless children, whose blood flowed in the river Daya. It was the same Kalinga that had transformed the murderous ruler into a humanitarian Buddhist. Kalinga taught Ashoka the most invaluable lesson in humanity. It was a land of ancient knowledge, of great religion, music and dance. Yet there was something rustic about the land, and the people were gentle and kind.

On one hand, this girl was born in Kalinga, and on the other she was being raised in the jungles of Dandakaranya. While Kalinga was synonymous with creativity and peace, Dandakaranya, a land of dense forests, had forest dwellers or the 'adivasis', and was full of flora and fauna. It was the land of the ferocious Royal Bengal Tiger (Panthera tigris) and the ever-fragrant Mohua tree (Madhuca longifolia). A land of both intoxicated men and bears. For this was the land she identified as home from the time of her childhood, though there had been no one there to call her own – no battery of cousins, no doting aunts, no disciplinarian uncles, no one. Of course, she had people who had become her 'relatives'. They were unique. There was Meera Didi's family. Meera Didi was a rather contrite Adivasi girl from the gorgeous Muria Gond tribe, a woman who dictated this young girl's life and her world view.

This area had a unique history of its own, one that takes us back to the times of the Ramayana. In that Indian epic, this mystic land was home to the deadliest creatures and demons known for the atrocities they committed against the sages and deities. They were killed and the land sanctified by the princely brothers of Ayodhya, Lord Rama and his brother Laxmana. She was ignorant of history and mythology till adolescence, when her father used to narrate the old stories of the land to her during the vacations, a time when she had nothing to do and nowhere to go, unlike her counterparts who had their 'native place' to go to. When she was around seven or eight, she had once asked her father why she and her sister had no native place to visit during the summer vacations. Why were they always taunted by their friends for being 'rootless'; and sometimes they ordered her to go back to the country their father came from if they lost a game of marbles or something, or when they collected more mangoes from the neighbour's fruit-laden tree than their friends. Why did they have to roam directionless in the village in the hot summer afternoons without anyone to play with them; why did they not have a desh? She felt claustrophobic and nervous every year the teacher announced the summer vacations, unlike the rest of her class, who would dance in excitement at the thought of being free for a few months and meeting their grandparents. She simmered with anger and demanded a convincing answer from her father. The whys never stopped; and the answers her father gave were just not satisfactory.

Often, she was greeted by a tight, sharp slap across the cheek by that gigantic 'woman'. Meera Didi forbade her to irritate Daktar Babu who had come back after a hard day's work. Meera Didi was the whole and soul of the Roy household. Her words were etched in stone and her view point was the only thing that mattered. If Meera Didi called a watermelon an orange, then that was the gospel truth. There was no making her see reason, for there was no truth other than her truth. It was this Meera Didi who took care of these two young girls as both her parents were government doctors in a small town in Odisha. Her mother would be out treating patients from the early hours of the morning till the time she dozed off to sleep in a tired stupor. Their home was a free medical clinic for all the sick and wanting. Such was the culture of those days. The lines between medical dispensary and home stood blurred. The typical government doctor's pay was average, and the doctors were certainly overworked. Taking care of the ill and the needy around them also ironically meant that they hardly had time to take care of their own young daughters.

Our curly haired girl could not exactly remember when she had seen Meera Didi for the first time but her first memory of her is of Didi carrying her in her arms and running across the woods. She would be swinging like a little monkey in Meera Didi's arms. She could remember those thrilling afternoons when her sister would be taking a happy nap after an entire day at school while she would be running around the trees and climbing them with Meera Didi as her companion and guardian. She was around seven then. Meera Didi screamed at her sometimes to not to stray too far from her sight. And in the evening, when Daktar Babu would return home and ask Meera Didi the reason for his beloved elder daughter's cut mark on the hand or sunken eyes, Meera Didi would instantly blame the child and act innocent. She would complain that the child was wild, untameable and disobedient. She would not stay back in the home and rest post-lunch, unlike her thoroughly obedient sister, and would follow her into the woods. Before his daughter could defend herself, Daktar Babu would shut her up with a stern look, and she would see Meera Didi giggling behind his back. After Daktar Babu went to his room, Meera Didi would come to her and say 'chorry', caress her and explain that she could not have lied to Daktar Babu or Ma, as she would call the little girl's mother. Eventually, the girl started to like Meera Didi, in spite of her being a perfect snitch. Her younger sister, docile and cherubic, was the apple of Meera Didi's eye. Her baby sister was her anti-thesis. Where she was wild, the young kid was the ideal daughter, and everything about her was neat and orderly. She was the perfect child – at least that was what Meera Didi declared constantly. Even though our girl was very fond of her baby sister, she would harass her just to spite Meera Didi. She would pull her orderly hair, dirty her white dress, or snatch the food on her plate. But her sister was so placid that none of this seemed to affect her. But affect Meera Didi it did, and a huge battle royale would soon ensue.

There was something unique about this lady, and there developed a wonderful bond of camaraderie between the girl and Meera Didi. Meera Didi herself was very young, and found a friend in her. She would play with her and tell her tales from her life and the intriguing experiences she had undergone in her life of merely twenty years. Meera Didi was short and dark. She had a blunt nose, round, swollen cheeks and thick, curly hair. She told her how the city people had tormented and outcast her people, despite them being the original inhabitants of the earth. Her Gond blood would roar talking about the abuses they had been taking from the so-called civilized world since time immemorial. God had not been kind to them, she would say, and frequently blame god for the plight of their race. Little did our girl understand Meera Didi's complaints and grievances, but she promised to stand as an exception among the so-called elites, whom Meera Didi abhorred, when she grew up. Meera Didi would hug her every time her young charge wiped her tears as she recalled how her father was killed while protesting for his rights. The girl sensed the pride in Meera Didi's eyes when she spoke about the tribe she belonged to. She adored the way she embraced her community and yet had a yearning to learn, know and explore things. She would sit with them in the evenings after all the household chores and listen to them as they studied, reading their lessons out aloud.

'Daktar Babu', as everyone in their locality would call her father, was a reserved man. When our girl made all those complaints to him about not having a native place, he smiled at his child who was agitated and depressed and demanded an answer to so many things. He pacified her with a deep hug. She started to cry in her father's embrace. 'Yes, today we do not have a desh, but once we had,' said her father in a low but proud tone, and continued. 'We had a desh, a royal bungalow, many acres of land, farms and the title of Talukdar Zamindar, or kingly landowner. We had our zamindari at Mymensingh, which was on the banks of the Brahmaputra north of the city of Dhaka. We were part of the elite Roys who ruled over the estate diligently and were known as benevolent rulers. This we did for seven generations, till the tyrannical British Raj passed the command for India to be partitioned and broke the country into pieces.' Tears rolled down from his eyes as he said this. Our girl lifted his glasses off his face and rubbed his tears with the end of her frock. She felt a strange pain deep within her heart to see her father weep. This conversation inexorably moved to the topic of 'Her Highness' the great Kumuda Kamini Devi, the fearless matriarch of the Roy household. Tales of her were staple dining table discussion in the tearaway faction of the grand Roys. Of her running her zamindari in the spirit of a benevolent taskmaster, of her funding the anti-British revolutionary martyrs Masterji and Surya Sen. Of the widowed woman in her white khadi saree and tonsured head riding a horse, looking after her fields and holding discussions with the cantonment British officers about the rate of taxation and often disagreeing with them and walking away in a huff. Of her swimming across the rain-swelled river in her saree to save an errant boy or two on the verge of drowning. And the rebellious child always sat wonder-eyed, hoping to emulate the great Kumuda Kamini Devi in order to make her Baba proud. Daktar Babu paused for a while and said, 'The Partition may have culminated in independence for the country but it has left hundreds of families ruined, destroyed and devastated. The exodus took away thousands of lives as we were forced to leave our motherland during the Partition. As a boy of thirteen, I had to walk all the way from East Bengal, no East Pakistan, to India, abandoning my home, my people and my roots, with only priceless memories left to carry. My journey from Bangladesh to India was not on a path of roses but terribly thorny, I have spent foodless nights in refugee camps, did not know whether I would see the morning sun the next day or be caught in some religious violence.

'After ten days, my journey from East Bengal to West Bengal ended as I reached the city. I felt that was the end of my troubles too, but I was wrong. There was no food, no water, no shelter, and as a boy of thirteen I was scared, panicky, frightened and lost in the labyrinth called Kolkata. I started to beg for alms before people. The Bengalis of Kolkata ridiculed us calling us "homeless beggars" and "Bangals", and threw us out wherever we were. I realized how the British idea of "divide and rule" had penetrated deep into our psyche and made us abhor our own people. I would have died of starvation had not the monks of Ramakrishna Mission picked me up from the streets and given me refuge. I lived with them and learnt the real meaning of life. Adopting the principles of Swami Vivekananda and Ramakrishna Parahamsha Dev, eventually I grew up to be a doctor with the sole aspiration of serving my lesser privileged brothers and sisters who form the major populace of this country. I believe my struggle was way easier than the unending struggle of numerous people of this country, who live all their lives in immense pain and die untreated,' Daktar Babu stopped. The girl looked at her father in awe and curiously asked, 'Baba, did you get back to desh after that?' Daktar Babu rose up to leave. He faced the wall and said, 'No, I never went back to desh. I could not see a broken country, see my farms being tilled by strangers. I could not listen to the sounds of those flamboyant rivers and grasslands that used to smile at me, and incessantly lament the deaths of their loved ones. I could not see those vibrant yellow mustard fields where we used to hide and play – now barren, carrying the corpses of my brothers. I have never gone back. It is better to be rootless than to witness your roots cut off pitilessly by intruders. Hence, I decided to live here, serve the people, and keep my promise of selfless service that I made to those monks of the Mission who had saved my life. I have learned to be a refugee in this country, make this my country and started loving it with all my heart. And believe me, it is the same rivers, the same streams, the same boundless fields of mustard, same language here with a different accent, and the same skies. It is the same sun that rises and sets every day in my country and this country. So I belong to it and it belongs to me.'

Having said this, Daktar Babu went out of the room to the little courtyard of their house and disappeared within moments. She sat on the bed, stunned. She loved her father more than anyone else in the world. She could not fathom her father carrying all this pain. She felt proud of her father and vowed to love him more and more with every passing day. Yet, deep down she knew that here stood a broken man, though a strong man, a man who had bled all his life and was still bleeding. His story also made her the person she was, one who wished to protect those who were bleeding, carrying pains that were not visible but who were being attacked by predators every moment of their lives. A foolish saviour complex had deeply set in.

9

The Mongoose on the Loose

The Sun is perhaps the most peculiar element in the universe, bringing out the loner in each of us. But then, whoever has tried to touch the Sun has been inevitably fatally burnt or has tried to escape its fiery rays. But have we ever thought about the plight of the Sun, which has been standing alone in the solar system for zillions of years, despite being the brightest, despite having the most regal aura of all the celestial bodies, despite being surrounded by so many promising companions who stalk it from a safe distance without taking the risk of approaching it and coming closer? All of them were afraid they would be destroyed, turned into ashes within a moment of their happy union with the Sun. Such is the trajectory of growth for a family without roots, which yearns for some identity or belongingness.

As she grew up into a lady from a wild, naughty, eccentric child in loose shirts, her transformation was as unbelievable as the metamorphosis of a caterpillar into a butterfly. Gone were her loose shirts, funnily trimmed hair, lanky legs and her innate madness that made people regard her a menace and fear her. While she was in school, the other students and her teachers found her an absolute pain because of her non-conformity. The boys would not accept her as part of their league, nor the flirty teenage girls as part of theirs. She did not give a damn to either group and walked about with her nose in the air. For, not fitting in and being the one who could not be categorized was what she was most comfortable with, and which she was defiant about. But when this girl grew out of her peculiarities and embraced femininity the change was startling.

During her teens, she often wondered what it was that kept some of the girls of her age group so cool-headed in spite of the boys quite clearly not treating them as equals. They could very well fix the punctured tyres of their bicycles, but why was it that they acted completely helpless about it, as if they would faint from the effort of taking it to the nearest cycle repair shop a mere five minutes away? But they would seek a boy's help for that. Such was the life of popular girls in the slow, small town of Bhubaneswar. So much effort went in to ensure that one was called a girl. But she realized that it was indeed time to become a girl. She quite loved her wild self, but hormones set in at that unique time when you are neither a teenager nor quite a woman, and it was indeed nice to be noticed by the opposite sex. And for sure, no one was doing any noticing, for either she was asked to join a gang of boys in their fight with a gang from another college, or she had to accompany some of the girls when they would sneak out of college with their 'boyfriends' for the inevitable matinee show. It was assumed with her around no one would approach them with any romantic intentions. So, instead of adopting any of the popular means of style she created her own and thus began to look a cut above the giggly band of college girls. Only the wild passion for pushing the envelope and questioning the norm that shone through her eyes which gave her tomboyish roots away.

Her family now also relocated to a different city where no one was familiar with the earlier version of her. She had developed a '*zamindari mijaz*', the temper of the royals, and a sense of righteousness, undoubtedly inherited from her forefathers. This worried her professors a bit. In college she studied anthropology and was greatly keen to study human societies and cultures. Her deep study of the evolution of human beings brought her a gold medal when she graduated. She immediately received an appointment letter for a job with the UNICEF to work among tribal communities. It was the kind of work she had craved all her life. After all, she was a child of the jungle, having heard so much tribal folklore from Meera Didi. She was always aware of the alternative storylines that existed in the world. She was aware that the opinion of the majority was not the absolute truth and that there could be different versions of the truth. In many ways she was like her father. She could not understand the social taboos and norms, and the reasons for differentiating between the 'civilized' and the 'uncivilized'. She did not believe in the desirability of social stature and did not approve of a society that had hierarchical structures distinguishing between the privileged and the less privileged. She was a revolutionary at heart who enjoyed breaking the stereotype, much like Nemo of Satyajit Ray's *Agantuk*, a movie that she and her father had watched several times. She could sense Nemo's emotions as he described the actual concept of civilization and its conflicts with more innocent tribal cultures, the pain of being rootless, the stigma of being a social outcast and the peace of being a recluse.

10

A Monkey in the Wild

While working for UNICEF she had her first interaction with the tribal communities. Studying their lifestyles and natural ways of living, she wanted to involve herself more deeply with the real natives of her country. Her job with UNICEF was a good opportunity to study in-depth the Santhals, Totos and Bhils of the region. She would frequently tour the states of Bihar, Jharkhand, Odisha and West Bengal to understand the Santhals and their languages. Their exploitation by the so-called 'superior' races went back a very long time. She discovered that the Santhals were great fighters. Their bravery was astounding and they were passionate about their motherland. Perhaps it was this passion that had led them to revolt even against the mighty British empire years ago. In recent times, they had transitioned from hunting to agriculture as their chief occupation and source of livelihood. They had a unique flair for music and played unusual handmade instruments, one of which was the *tamak* or *tumbak*, which were cylindrical drums. They also had flutes, pipes and cymbals. Music was their prime leisure-time pursuit. UNICEF once had sent her to a remote village of Jharkhand to study malnourishment among lactating mothers and young children there. Here she had the rare opportunity of staying with the Santhal tribe and watching them at their everyday activities. Men and women both participated in agriculture and homemaking equally. The Santhals were immensely warm towards her and took care of her as a guest, though sceptical of her in the beginning. But she, who was born in the wild and brought up by a tribal woman, won their hearts with her simplicity and warmth. She would play with the Santhal children, accompanying the boys when they went fishing and hunting for rabbits and wild pigs. Soon she became part of their lives, eating what they ate and living with them in their tiny huts. She also witnessed a traditional Santhal wedding, or the *Bapla*. She learnt about Pilchu Hadam and Pilchu Budi, who were the first Santhal couple to get married, according to Santhal folklore. Both monogamy and polygamy could be found in the tribe, yet marriage was a sacred ritual, backed by exchange of vows, the custom of applying vermilion on the bride's forehead, known as *itut*, and the compulsory bride price that the bride's father must pay to the bridegroom. What she liked most of all was the Santhal dance, which not only showcased the talent of the tribe but was also a symbol of their unity. The dance was dedicated to their traditional gods and goddesses. The women would dress beautifully in white and red sarees, with strings of wild flowers tied around their heads, while men performed with bows and arrows. Typical Santhali music could be the sweetest balm to heal the wound of a bleeding heart, she thought, as she watched the people perform, completely mesmerized. The more she learnt about this so called 'uncivilized' tribal community, the more she started to adore them. Life with them was easy, free from all the complexities of city life. While on a data collection journey to the interiors, she received an urgent message from the postmaster of a post office nearby, saying her parents wanted to talk to her urgently. As she worked as a field anthropologist, she did not have a permanent work address, and she had requested the local postmaster to receive messages from her parents and convey them to her. This was her only means of contact with her earlier world. For she had gone 'native'. By the time she received the message from the postmaster, it was already four days old. Her parents had been calling the postmaster repeatedly every day, in the hope of talking to her. Those were the pre-mobile phone days. Telephone lines often went dead and one was lost to the world without any connectivity. So to be able to contact her parents in Nagpur after a mere four days of their relaying their message was a big thing. Usually, she would hear the same refrain from them – to resign her job and to come back home to the safety of the city. This time she was surprised at the excitement in her mother's voice. The entreaty to resign her job remained the same, but the reason was one that took her by surprise. She heard that she had qualified in the Union Public Service Commission exams and had been selected to the elite administrative services that were the steel frame of India, commonly known as the bureaucracy. This was her first attempt at the exams. One was allowed four attempts, and one often heard of aspirants holed up in various parts of Delhi for years together preparing for the exam. And here she was, having written her preliminary exams from Nagpur, gone on to join UNICEF, written the subsequent levels of exams while working as a full-time anthropologist, her preparation being almost a part-time hobby, and clearing them effortlessly.

She had not been particularly interested in a job in the coveted administrative services. So imagine the surprise she felt on knowing she had made the cut. She was all ready to offer some excuse like having to solve the issue of malnourishment among children at her job. But the gentle voice of her father made her drop her defiance. He said, 'Shona, it's time to come back and take on a greater role.' That was enough for her to change her mind, for his wish was her command. She now felt intimidated about moving out into the world. She was stepping out of a world that had become her second skin. She wanted to get to know the Santhal tribe more intensely; she wanted to complete her project on them; she wanted to find a way to solve the issue of malnourishment among the Santhal children using the Santhals' own local food practices.

But she joined the services, going for her initial training to the lake city of Bhopal. Here she was introduced to a world she was not even aware of! Here she realized that the bunch she was part of were the chosen few, those who would go on to become the future policymakers of the country. That was all good, but what hit her was the sense of entitlement that was part of the ecosystem. There was a belief among them that they were the special ones, having made it past the post. So, all day the talk was of the great powers that would be bestowed on them in the near future. She was considered as belonging in a rare tribe of those who had knowledge of the world beyond what was contained in books. She was now almost an expert in herbal medicine, a raconteur of wonderful tales about the different indigenous peoples of the forests, a well-travelled person with a window to the world beyond the dingy by-lanes of Mukherjee Nagar, that area of Delhi where UPSC hopefuls holed up in sub-minimal living conditions to train for the exams.

11
The Flight of the Eagle

'As flies to wanton boys, are we to the Gods/They kill us for their sport.'

The gods had never been generous to her. They had been testing her mettle and strength ever since she was a child. They had been inflicting pain on her soul every time this girl from a very patriarchal part of eastern India felt happy; they made sure she fell every time she tried to soar high; it seemed that the gods derived immense sadistic pleasure from spoiling her plans and putting her before opponents who seemed almost invincible. But every time they conspired against her, she came out triumphant, defeating them. Life was never a bed of roses for her, rather a relentless battle which she fought in the fiercest way. She believed that if at all reincarnation was true, she must have been a classical warrior in her past life, devoid of rest, ease and sleep. While the other candidates who qualified the coveted examination chose convenient postings, she chose to work in the districts of Chandrapur and Gadchiroli in Maharashtra, exactly at that point in time when the districts were torn apart by Naxalite agitations. She chose this place out of love for the forests, love for the monsoon streams, love for the Gondi song sung by women on their way back home after collecting firewood, love for the abundant deer that had became her travel companions. It was a difficult posting, entailing a very hard life of more than seventeen hours of work a day, often without electricity, only very basic amenities, a grocer with very limited stocks, a rustic single-theatre cinema hall (a necessary, must-have lifeline for her) and loneliness, for there was hardly a single soul she knew, and a very vast area to traverse, crisscrossing 500 kilometres of terrain.

The districts of Chandrapur and Gadchiroli were united as brothers from the same mother, divided only by the flow of the Wainganga River. Chandrapur, earlier known by the names of Chanda and Lokapura, was known chiefly for its massive coal reserves and its traditional industry of cotton weaving. There was evidence in Gadchiroli of the reign of the Rashtrakutas and Chalukyas, who were succeeded by the mighty Gond rulers. The Gonds of Gadchiroli took great pride in their royal ancestry and valour. Many forts of the erstwhile Gond kings stand testimony to their glorious past, though the structures are in ruins today. This is why the people call themselves Raj Gonds, or Gonds of royal descent. Both Chandrapur and Gadchiroli are symbolic of Nature at her most beauteous, with miles and miles of deep, once-upon-a-time impenetrable, mysterious forests containing rare species of agrestal plants. This is the most densely forested area of Maharashtra, also well known for the very exclusive Vidarbha teak, its quality only surpassed by the precious Burmese teak. Needless to say, the forests are often exploited for the commercial value of this teak. The teak forests of Vidarbha are among the most enchanting and ecologically significant landscapes in the region and are deeply intertwined with the cultural and ecological fabric of the area.

The forests here are vibrant ecosystems teeming with life, their dense foliage providing a perfect habitat for a variety of wildlife. The sight of a tiger moving silently through the underbrush or a sambar deer grazing at the forest's edge adds an element of wild majesty to the already stunning landscape for the lucky visitor. The forests are also alive with the sounds of birds, such as the Indian grey hornbill and the Malabar pied hornbill.

It is also a region of the tendu tree, the dry leaves of which are used in the manufacture of the indigenous beedi. The collection quota for this leaf also leads to strife between the forest officials and the local tribal populace. Perhaps that was one of the many reasons why the 'Naxalites', or the 'left-wing extremists', as they are known as today, chose these-difficult-to negotiate jungles as their safe refuge, from where they could operate their missions smoothly. This strife had led to an atmosphere of violence in these areas, and the lines between the wrong and wronged were blurred here.

Naxalism, an insurgency that advocates for the rights of marginalized and landless peasants, became particularly rampant in Vidarbha because of a combination of socio-economic, political and geographical factors. The movement, which began in the eastern state of West Bengal in the 1960s, spread to various parts of India, including Vidarbha.

The tribal communities in Vidarbha have historically faced displacement and exploitation as a result of the establishment of mining projects, deforestation and large-scale industrial activities in the region. These developments, often carried out without adequate compensation or rehabilitation, led to significant resentment among the tribal population. Naxal groups were able to tap into this anger, positioning themselves as protectors of tribal rights and resistance against the encroachment of corporate and government interests on tribal lands.

Vidarbha was also infamous for its agrarian distress, particularly among its cotton farmers. The region had witnessed a high number of farmer suicides, largely attributed to indebtedness, crop failure and the collapse of traditional farming systems. The failure of government policies to adequately address these crises further fuelled discontent among the rural population. Naxal groups exploited this distress, positioning themselves as champions of the rural poor and promising a more equitable distribution of resources.

Many people in Vidarbha felt politically alienated, believing their voices were not being heard in the corridors of power. Centralization of political power and decision-making in Maharashtra's more developed regions like Mumbai and Pune often left Vidarbha's specific issues unaddressed. This sense of political exclusion contributed to the appeal of Naxalism, which offered an alternative political narrative that focused on empowerment of the marginalized.

The roots of Naxalism in Vidarbha can also be traced to earlier social movements and struggles against feudal landlords and colonial exploitation. The region has a history of resistance, which provided a cultural and ideological foundation for the Naxal movement. The Naxals were able to build on these historical narratives, aligning themselves with the region's legacy of struggle and resistance.

The day she left for Chandrapur to join duty as an Indian Postal Service officer for the twin districts, the older officers warned her many times to put in a prayer for a simpler posting in the ministry. Her mother, whose exuberance and pride on her daughter's clearing the toughest and most prestigious examination in the country, had now changed to fear and panic after seeing what her daughter's appointment letter warned of. She scolded her and pleaded with her not to accept the posting, but in vain. Her sister, friends and acquaintances too suggested she refuse the posting. Daktar Babu was the only person who maintained a stark silence on the matter, perhaps because he knew his daughter too well. If you asked her not to do something and provided the logic for it, she would go ahead and do that thing, no matter how difficult it was, to prove that nothing in this universe was impossible. A fire to transform the impossible into the possible ran twenty-four seven in her belly. Satyajit Ray's *Agantuk*, which she had watched many times at different stages in her life, had sparked in a wanderlust to travel and explore. Daktar Babu knew her well and only smiled as people tried to convince her not to accept the posting.

'Madam, this place is not at all safe and involves the risk of losing your life. It is better that you go back and take some other job.' These were the first words of the postmaster, Prashant Bhide, of Chandrapur Post Office to her. Bhide was a lean and short man, likely in his mid-fifties – a generous-natured man who made the effort to warn her again and again, briefing her about her zone of operation before she deep-dove into work. She was provided with hundreds of files about the physical, political and present anarchical scenario in the districts. She went through a few of them. Her background in anthropology had made her a field person and urged her to do some practical analysis. So every second day the new Senior Superintendent of Post Offices, a misnomer as there wasn't any Junior Superintendent of Post Offices in the postal system, was seen roaming around in the town, walking through the villages and interacting with the local populace. Her ever-present driver, Pathan, was by her side at all times. Pathan, a devout Muslim, hailed from the temple town of Markanda. This temple complex is dedicated to Lord Shiva of the Hindu trinity. However, the name Markanda derives from the rishi Markandeya, associated with a region which would now be the Indian state of Haryana. The rishi was an ardent devotee of Shiva. He went into penance for years on the banks of the Markanda river and finally tried to offer his head to Shiva, which was when Shiva appeared and stopped him. He blessed him with a temple in his name. Pathan was more than six feet tall, more or less fair and curly haired. He was an adept story teller. He knew practically everyone in all the villages of the district, or at least this is how it appeared to the newcomer who was still getting used to the dialect of Marathi spoken in these areas and the Gondi dialect of the tribal people of the area. What was indeed striking about Pathan was the devotion with which he prayed to all the gods of Hinduism and also followed Islam. He would stop by the local mazhar and offer prayers there, and would also drag her to the small local temples on the way to the post offices she would visit. He too would offer prayers there, making the customary offering of flowers and coconut to the deity. This was indeed what the heart of India looked like.

Within a month of her posting, she observed that though there was an abundance of raw materials in both districts to create effective infrastructure for both, and the region's wealth of handicrafts, cotton and coal could be put to very good use, there was also the rising threat of Naxalite extremism, which was a severe challenge to the administration. Stories of killings and encounters between the police and extremists had become common news. Women were widowed and children orphaned. There was an atmosphere of gloom and depression everywhere. People lived in uncertainty, fearing either imprisonment or death. The small towns looked like green oases in a blood-stained desert. As she studied the situation, she realized that the bulk of the population in these areas consisted of the tribal communities of the Gonds and Madias, who were the original inhabitants, or Adivasis of the area. They had little to no education but were aware of their rights to the forests and its bounties. But complicated forest laws did not allow them the right to what they thought was rightfully theirs. So there was always conflict between the forest guards and rangers and the 'rightful' guardians of the forests – the local populace. They felt they were victims of exploitation. Mortality among males in the region was quite high due to the armed conflict, often leaving their families in acute poverty, lifelong debt and penury. She wanted to break this pattern of life. The first step towards change was to improve and secure the economic situation of the people here. To that end, she started her operation of financial inclusion through the Rural Postal Life Insurance Scheme of India Post, which guaranteed financial security to citizens upon their making modest deposits, offering beneficial life insurance. But the real challenge lay in counselling and educating the people about the importance and relevance of financial stability in their lives, especially for their children. She called for a meeting in one of the village post offices to begin the process. The meeting was scheduled for 11 a.m. However, not a single person arrived until evening. She had eagerly waited with her staff officials for people to turn up but had to return to her government guest house, dejected. When this pattern repeated at three post offices, she decided to change her strategy. From the next day onwards, she, along with her dedicated band consisting of the local postmaster and postman, who was from the community, started visiting the homes of the villagers. They tried to cover every possible locality and every possible house. In the beginning the villagers ignored her. Either they would not open their doors or would shut them in her face. They refused to talk, forget agree to being counselled, and asked her not to disturb them. Seeing her relentless, selfless efforts, the ever-clever Pathan came to her rescue. He talked to the villagers and managed to convince one woman to talk to her. Namita was a very young girl, not more than twenty years old, married to Bhima. They had three children together. Bhima was a worker in the coal mine nearby and was severely addicted to alcohol. Namita found it very difficult to feed her children. Namita herself worked intermittently in the fields, collecting tendu leaves to supplement the family income. Pathan took her to Namita's house, believing that whatever the postal woman intended to do was best begun with Namita. She explained to Namita the necessity of financial security and helped her open a postal savings bank account in the village post office. She taught Namita the value of thrift, and how money would grow through the magic of compounding. Namita was issued a passbook. That was the first bank passbook issued to a villager and the first success for her. On a whim, she made Namita fill out a Rural Life Insurance Policy of one lakh rupees with a very small premium amount in the name of her husband Bhima. That day, in the shade of a mighty mohua tree, which threw its sweet, intoxicating fragrance all around, she and her band of men in the khaki uniform that employees of the postal department wore, celebrated. They shared a frugal meal cooked by Namita, eating off sal leaves that served as their plates. This simple meal tasted more delicious to her than the food in the big city restaurants, which she was quite fond of. Her men were hesitant and uncomfortable about sharing a meal with 'Officer Madam'; indeed, such a thing was a taboo in their villages.

But her world recognized no such boundaries. She considered her men her family and life support in this unknown land, and was grateful to them. The days passed at lightning speed and her battle was only growing harder. Yet, every day she visited the hamlets in her districts and tried to talk to the villagers. She realized that they were not the dangerous or misguided people they were labelled to be. They had no malice in them but were just pawns in the hands of circumstances. She was still determined to inform them of the local moneylending system, which kept them stuck. During the lean agricultural season, the tribal people often borrowed small amounts of money from the local moneylenders, sometimes using their silver jewellery as collateral. But the interest they were charged was so exorbitantly high, sometimes more than 100 per cent, that they often not only lost their collateral but also could never be free of debt. Their constant borrowing of small sums of money ended up putting them in enormous debt. Such was the economy of the place. This led to very deep angst among them. She was determined to break this vicious cycle by introducing them to the formal banking economy through the post office. She taught them to save small amounts of money during the periods of harvest and to withdraw it when they were in need.

In this journey she was more an anthropologist and less a bureaucrat. She stood alone in this journey, for it was not what was prescribed to her. She was expected to sit in her room in the district headquarters and 'administer' by pushing files. She had no complaints about being alone; rather, she enjoyed her solitude. At times, she would sit by the river and write poetry or simply take in the beauty of the scene, thanking the universe for creating the rivers, the fountains, the hills, the trees and the forests. During these times Pathan would rest in the jeep. She was especially fond of the palash trees. During that time of the year when all the teak trees were bare, the palash would look splendid with their red blooms. The palash tree, scientifically known as Butea monosperma and often referred to as the 'flame of the forest' is native to the Indian subcontinent and holds a significant place in the people's folklore, art and rituals.

Its vibrant flowers are its most captivating feature, and they bloom between late winter and early spring. The flowers are a brilliant shade of orange-red, resembling flames that seem to set the tree ablaze against the backdrop of the dry, leafless forests. The flowers, which appear in clusters and cover the branches, have a unique shape and are often compared to the beak of the parrot. Once, while lost in the wonder of a grand landscape in the district and oblivious to everything around, she sensed that there was someone around her. She turned around to see she was surrounded by nine to ten people, all masked, with red cloths wrapped around their faces. All of them were armed. She was preparing herself for death and took a deep breath. As the leader spoke to her, she understood that it was a woman. But to her surprise, the leader spoke in a soft but resolute tone. She told her that they were aware of each of her activities and had no complaints against her. Saying this the woman patted her on the back and left in the blink of an eye, the gang disappearing with her. She was astounded! Within moments she saw Pathan running towards her. He was checking on her to ensure that she was not harmed in any way. He was as shocked as her to realize that the so-called dangerous Naxalites had left her uninjured, and after some banter with her. It was unbelievable. She asked him not to disclose this incident to anyone and thanked the woman leader from within for motivating her.

A few days later, there was a petrifying blast in the coal mines resulting in the death of five workers. Namita's husband Bhima was one of them. As soon as she received the news, she rushed towards the spot of the blast. She saw Namita and her children crying before the lifeless body of Bhima. There were other women and children too crying in front of the dead bodies of their husbands and fathers. Seeing her, Namita fell at her feet and wept. She hugged Namita and consoled her. She stood there with the families for a long time and left with a heavy heart. On the following day, she went to Namita's hut and gave her a cheque for rupees one lakh, the sum assured in her life insurance policy, and told Namita that she would arrange to have the money deposited in the local bank so that she would receive money every month as interest on the amount. In the beginning, Namita could not understand anything of this and broke down in tears. She could not thank her enough to have saved her children from starving and her from being exploited and enslaved by men. Namita's father, who was probably of her own father's age, fell at her feet and thanked her for being their saviour. She could not hold back her tears seeing the plight of these people. When she returned to office, she called up Daktar Babu and cried silently while telling him what had happened.

The Namita incident left a great impact on the people. There was a kind of awakening amongst them, and elderly villagers now started approaching her to visit their locality and explain to them the benefits of postal life insurance. She made a record-breaking number of insurances, where not even one family across the districts of Chandrapur and Gadchiroli was left uninsured. Simultaneously, she explained to them the significance of education and the good things that would result from sending their children to the village schools. Eventually, she became family to the tribal people, who now respected and adored her as they would their own daughter or sister.

During this period, a new Superintendent of Police was appointed for Chandrapur. Coincidentally, he turned out to be her fellow trainee. He was handsome and suave, soft spoken yet stern, a man with a vast understanding of the world and one who could speak in Prakrit (though she could not understand a single word of it but that was the charm). Born and brought up in the industrial town of Ranchi. Diwakar Pandey was completely self-made; his rise from a humble background to being a diligent civil servant was talk of four districts of his state, such was his name. But more than his depth of knowledge and serious demeanour, what attracted her towards him was his innate kindness, compassion, and deep sense of humanity. She was overwhelmed by his philosophy of life as a shared journey, where every human being is a fellow traveller deserving empathy and affection. His constant support towards her, soon turned their friendship into courtship and they ended up as husband and wife. Together hand in hand they went exploring this mystical world of the forest and its dwellers. He emerged not only as her most worthy but also as the closest friend who handled the chaos in her in the most beautiful way. He gave her space yet protected her with all his might; he never encroached on her freedom yet stood by her side at moments of desperation and distress. Together, they escaped to the bowels of mother earth where mysteries unfolded only to the seeker. They enjoyed immersing in the festivities of the forest dwellers who in turn opened their arms and love towards the couple. They explored each other and found two similar peas of a pod with raw passion towards nature, love and life. Of course, challenges were there but with each other by their sides, they even relished the challenges and drew immense happiness in overcoming them. Over the year, she was blessed with a son and Diwakar was transferred to a big city with a promotion.

Diwakar did not want to leave. A strong sense of apprehension raged within him. Thousands of thoughts meandered his mind relentlessly. How could he walk away, leaving behind his beloved wife and infant child among the unknown tribals? He remembered how she used to panic, every time he departed for the long-range patrols into the core Naxalite areas and would return after days. Every time he hugged her while leaving, he could see the silent terror in her eyes. He knew that while he was performing his duty, she back home was spinning nightmares of his safety in her mind and would be restless till he returned.

The world of the nineties was not as fast as today. No instant messages, no call backs. The internet was a myth, mobile phones and pagers fantasies. There was no means of contact once the person was out of sight apart from letters which were not to be written, at least in the zones where every moment survival was a challenge.

Diwakar did not agree to leave them until each villager vowed for the protection of her and her child. Phulkari, a local tribal woman, was the self-appointed caretaker of her baby and took utmost care of the boy while she was at work. There were days when she used to carry the baby on her shoulder while visiting the post offices in the villages and the baby had fallen ill. In the absence of a certified medical practitioner or paediatrician in the area, the baby was routinely checked by the local tribal doctor, called 'shaman', and he had often cured him of his ailments using medicines made from the local plants and herbs. The baby grew up in the midst of the villagers and soon became the apple of their eye. He played with the tribal children and started speaking their language. She could not have been happier. She would cross the dense forests with her baby in her car accompanied by Phulkari. Pathan would be driving. She had always felt a presence protecting them while inside the woods, and always remembered the masked woman. With time, her tenure ended and she was given a different posting, this time in the city of Mumbai. Instead of the rejoicing that would have followed in any family, she sank into a deep gloom. She was to be parted from her forests, her rivers and her people and countless memories. But she had also developed an element of detachment, having worked so far away from everyone she knew and in solitude for so long. She saw the people crying for her. She heard the men of the village say they would not let her go and would fight to keep her there. She promised them she would return, sooner or later. Pathan, in a rare show of affection, hugged her and wept. Each man and woman of the villages expressed their gratitude towards her for transforming their lives. When she boarded her car to leave, holding her baby boy on her lap, the child cried. He did not want to leave. He extended his arms towards his beloved Pathan Mama. He wanted to be picked up and taken into the jungles, something Pathan did when they played hide and seek. The boy had the spirit of the jungle within him, very much like his Ma. He preferred to be amongst his cows and pigeons than with other fellow humans. Such is the pull of the wild for the free spirited. It silently takes possession of you and alters your core forever.

The baby hated the chauffeur who now drove their car. He felt he was taking him and his Mamma away from their home to some unknown cruel land. He saw his Mamma's eyes moisten, rubbed them with his hands and lay quietly on her bosom. His Mamma caressed him softly. He closed his eyes. She turned back and saw human beings of all ages bidding them adieu with wet eyes. She felt a lump of pain in her heart for these people who had become an indispensable part of her life, who had once threatened her to stay away from and yet over time had opened their hearts to her. She realized how these people had always been misunderstood by society and labelled as uncivilized misfits. She knew now that their external ferocity was only a weapon with which to protect themselves from the unceasing exploitation and humiliation that they had been subjected to by the 'civilized' world. She would remain forever grateful to these people, who had become her family, who had showered her with love and had taken care of her and her child. She smiled at them and asked them to stay well. As her car sped ahead, she turned back and looked through the rear window to say a last goodbye. She saw a middle-aged woman waving at her from amongst the crowd. She had never seen her before. But then she noticed her eyes. She had seen those eyes before, once.

After she relocated from Chandrapur to Mumbai with a much easier and comfortable posting, life was supposed to be smooth for her. But a far more elite job profile and a far more luxurious lifestyle in a city known for its glitz and glamour seemed not to make her happy. Luxury never had any attraction for her. She valued simplicity more than sophistication and felt alone in that labyrinth of a metropolis, where everyone appeared to have a hidden agenda. It was a world completely unknown to her and she felt a misfit amongst people who seemed fake. Their emotions were fake, and their relationships too. Her much more practical husband tried to get her to understand the rhythm of the city, but every moment here she felt out of place. This concrete jungle was full of species way deadlier and more dangerous than the jungle she had lived in the last four years. There humans were mistaken to be beasts, while here beasts roamed around disguised as humans.

The city of Mumbai indeed has a unique charm that is distinctly different from that of any other city in the world; Mumbai is high-spirited and is a city of phenomenal contrasts. There is the whooshing of the waves against its shores and the savoury aroma of street-side vada pavs;

there are the spectacular posters of Bollywood films on the highways, the overcrowded local trains, the rich architectural legacy left by the British and the grimy slum of Dharavi, where people live in pathetic conditions but also display fine entrepreneurship.

At times her wearied soul would seek refuge from the chaos of the city in the sight of the shimmering expanse of the sea. She would sit on the sandy shore at Chowpatty and watch the restless canvas before her.

Another feature of the city that she loved was the Mumbaiya language, its accent and dialect, which were strikingly different from any other tongue in the world. It was a fascinating blend of various languages that Mumbaikars had created and adopted to make communication lucid and effective across the city's diverse population. The people of Mumbai mostly spoke in an amusing Hindi that had evolved out of multiple Indian languages as well as English. It was a soothing cocktail of Hindi, Marathi, Urdu, Gujarati and many more languages. It sounded like casual street chat; it was both playful and flamboyant, and was owned by everyone living in the city. It gave birth to amusing phrases like '*watt laagega*', '*aisi ki taisi*', '*band baj gya*' and ebullient terms like '*apun*', '*bole to*', '*rapchik*' and countless more, which had no deep meaning but sounded warm and were used and spoken universally across the city.

She adored this language. She could hear it everywhere, in boardroom discussions and at the vegetable sellers.

Eventually, she fell in love with Mumbai. She learnt the art of survival here, and over the years Mumbai became home to her as she outshone her counterparts and stood as the brightest star in each of the projects she undertook. Now she was given the post of Postmaster General of Mumbai city and its suburbs, to boost postal operations in the commercial capital of the country.

On the personal front, she had gone through an extremely difficult phase. She had witnessed her beloved father Daktar Babu dying from cancer. She had felt a throbbing pain when she saw the lifeless body of her Baba turning to ashes within minutes on the funeral pyre. How futile human existence was, she thought to herself. The gripping darkness of the cremation ground was symbolic of the darkness of her heart, mind and soul. To this day, she carried the pain deep within, of not being able to protect the most adored person of her life from the scourge of cancer, despite having all the power, money and resources required for so many other things in life. Thus, all her life she strived to find her Baba in everything she did.

While attempting the arduous job of making a documentary film when she did not have any expertise or experience in film-making, the only element that kept her going was the fact that the film centred on Netaji Subhas Chandra Bose, whose character intertwined with that of her nonagenarian protagonist Rama Khandwala. Rama had been a cadre of the INA and the documentary had her reminiscing on the larger-than-life figure of Bose, of whose life Khandwala remembered snatches. *Elephants Do Remember* brought her the prestigious Rajat Kamal (National Films Award 2021 for best documentary film), but what healed her inner wound a little was the ode to her Baba in the film, which showcased a slice of this freedom fighter's life before the world audience. His bravery, his love for his motherland and the sacrifices he made for it, and his pain of never being able to go back to the land of his birth, were captured in that film.

She felt the presence of Daktar Babu in everything she did; his voice still echoed in her ears; his principle of 'giving back to the society' enthused her to work for the people, selflessly; his instinct of standing by the underprivileged made her a lover of the underdog, of victims of oppression and exploitation. That was why, after she met the gang of those rowdy women screaming, shouting and abusing the postal clerks demanding post office accounts for their children, at a time when the deadly coronavirus had just started ravaging the city, when it was not yet an epidemic, she decided to find out why they were so angry with the postal officials.

She recollected her first encounter with the gang while she was on an official visit to the Mumbai Central Post office, one of the post offices with the maximum number of footfalls in the city, to check the precautionary measures that had to be undertaken to protect her officials and visitors from the coronavirus. While she was talking to the postmaster, she overheard the security in charge shouting at a bunch of women whose faces were hidden behind masks. Hearing the chaos, she got up and walked towards them to understand what was wrong. The security men were shooing them away now.

'*Madam ji, yeh kharab auraate idhar aaye the khata kholne; humne nikal diya.*' She winced at the phrase '*kharab auraate*'. '*Dhande wali hai Madam ji,*' said another, explaining to her that they were from the sex trade. She overheard one of the security men say to another, 'These prostitutes too want an account?'These women were no less abusive when they spoke, using very vulgar phrases and gestures as they talked back to the men. She was taken aback initially, but what caught her attention was the dialect in which they were speaking. It was the same dialect her Baba spoke when he met people from his 'native place'. It was the 'Bangal' dialect. She was so thrilled she could not resist going up to them and talking to them. As she stepped out of the office premises and approached them, speaking in their language, they paused for a while, surprised by her dialect, then yelled, '*Boro didi, moni tomar oi kutta guli aamader taariye dilo*!' 'Madam, your dogs have thrown us out.' She instantly apologized before them for the rudeness of her security men and requested them to calm down. It worked, and they stopped their shouting. One of them took a deep breath and said, '*Didi, moni aamra post opishe aamader bassa der khata khulte sayi, kintu jekhanei jaayi aamader randi bole taariye daaye*.' Whichever post office they visited, they were being thrown out. Saying this, she broke down in tears. '*Didimoni, daaho bechi bole ki aamra manush noy*?' Weren't they human beings, even if they lived by selling their bodies? '*Doya koro, Didimoni, aamra rendi bole aamader bacha guli re saza dio na; ora toh chele manush didimoni*.' They begged that their children must not be punished, for they were innocent. They stood in front of her in silence with folded hands.

She did not know what to say but she felt the weight of a great pain in her heart. She assured them of help and asked for their address. They said together, 'Chauda Gulli, Kamathipura.'

After they left she walked up to her cabin, wearied and exhausted. She had promised to help them though she did not exactly know how she would keep her promise. Sitting quietly in her palatial office, she contemplated the naked brutalities of the world. Kamathipura; the name itself evoked a sense of deep abhorrence, so intense was the stigma associated with it. 'Civilized' society made it a point not to step into this zone of the metropolis, and if they had no option but to drive through then they rolled up the windows of their cars. It was almost a sin to talk to the women from here. Whether it was Sonagachi in Kolkata, Grant Road or Kamathipura in Mumbai, these places evoked the grim, undeniable crudities of society that mainstream humans had not been able to overcome. She had never been to Kamathipura ever in her life, but she had heard and read about the place. The faceless women she met were its real-life inhabitants, the so-called 'commercial sex workers' who had used the term 'Didi' to address her. She could see the pain in their eyes, smell the stench of anger, misery and utter helplessness that emanated from them, despite the smell of local, cheap perfumes, which too they exuded. She knew to the core how it felt to be helpless, to not be able to do anything about certain things despite having all the resources in the world, and for these women the struggle was far more tough. Theirs was a struggle for identity and acceptance. They faced the abuses of the world silently.

'Give back to the society what you have taken from it, Munu.' She closed her eyes and remembered the last words of her Baba. She stood up from her chair and came out of her cabin. '*Sanket, mera gaari nikalne ko bol; Kamathipura jana hai*,' she said to her peon. The word 'Kamathipura' set his eyes rolling; indeed, it set all eyes in the office room rolling. There was curiosity and apprehension among the staff. For one second there was complete silence. Sanket asked worriedly, '*Kidhar jana hai Madam?*' '*Bola na Kamathipura*,' roared the tigress, striding down her lavish office towards the royal staircase that led to the portico where Deva was waiting for her in the car. As her car entered the 10th Gulli of Kamathipura, she saw a dilapidating building with a faint board which said 'Kamathipura Post Office, Mumbai-400008' on it.

As soon as her car stopped, two officials nervously ran out from inside the post office and saluted her. Both looked like 'losers'. She got down from the car and walked towards the office. The two men hastily followed her. To her utter surprise, not only was the post office building dilapidated, with cracked walls and a leaked ceiling, but the officials here were completely clueless about postal operations. She asked one of them whether any woman from the 14th Lane had come to open accounts recently. '*Aayi thi, Madam, do-teen kharab auraate; hum ne data ke nikaal diya.*' Two or three 'bad women' had come and had been rebuked and sent away. She lost her patience, immediately asking her number two to suspend the postal officer who was in charge of the area along with the two officials for negligence. She left the post office and asked her driver to take her to the address those women had given her. As he drove her to the area, she felt nervous. She got down from the vehicle at the mouth of the lane and stood still. Her refined and 'cultured' world would have winced at the sight. She saw groups of two to four women standing huddled together every ten paces apart, dressed in a cheap finery, low-cut blouses showing a lot of cleavage, over-painted red lips and a vacant stare, without any soul to the eyes. Some were busy on their mobile phones, tapping away. That was a national pastime. Some were in poses of enticement, while some just stood there looking washed out, as if they were mere dead bodies propped up. Some of them looked at her, but the majority ignored her. She was not a person of interest to them. They looked like poorly made mannequins to her, hardly human. Their poses were so caricatured. This area was off bounds to people like her, even uttering its name would have invited smirks from her friends. This place had drawn many a researcher, filmmaker, student and the odd curious passer-by just because it was a red-light district. The name bore the burden of a million sins and no one from a 'good family' in the city wanted to even acknowledge the existence of this place in their beloved Mumbai. As she contemplated her next course of action, she saw one of the five women whom she has met, the elderly one. She was dressed ordinarily in a simple salwar kameez. She was bargaining in a street shop that was selling gaudy lehengas. She walked towards her and approached her softly 'Kaisi ho, Aapa?' The woman looked at her with a face full of surprise and dismay. Within moments she turned the other way and walked hastily without answering her. The Postmaster General was clueless as to what has happened. In the meanwhile, she saw another from that group on the other side of the street. She was dressed gaudily, in a colourful lehenga-choli, a garland of mogra in her hair. An overdose of cheap make-up had entirely transformed her persona from the day she had seen her for the first time, when she had appeared as an ordinary woman next door. Today she looked raw and vulgar. She greeted her with folded hands and requested her to go with her to her room, but she was already nervous so politely rejected her request. She said she would meet them soon and left the place.

From the next day onwards, it was all an action-packed movie. Step by step, she worked out the sequence of scenes. The first step in her new project was renovation of the dilapidated post office of Kamathipura into a new one. She deployed the ablest officer in her department to supervise this work so it was done as soon as possible. In the meanwhile, she put together a team who would prepare data on the number of commercial sex workers in Kamathipura, and the age and other details of their children. She went back to the 14th Lane of Kamathipura and held numerous meetings with the women who lived there, trying to understand the ground reality. Mainstream society had never tried to analyse the reasons why women became sex workers and what compelled them to sell their bodies in exchange for a pittance. Society had never thought rationally – to understand that each time they peddled their bodies, they peddled their dignity, self-respect and morale too before the man who feasted on their flesh. Every day was a battle, every day their bodies were 'vandalized'. '*Didi moni, kono meye nijer icche te kharap hoyna go*!' No woman on earth becomes a sex worker out of her own wish, was what Kajol had told her.

Questioning these women on their pasts or even initiating a conversation with them was the most difficult task in the world. They would grant no one a ticket to their lives. They would abuse outsiders with the most uncouth language and chase them out of their area. They would scream and shout and howl together like a pack of wolves if they understood that an outsider is trying to intrude into their world. Years of exploitation and abuse have left them with such a keen understanding of human behaviour and intentions that they would not allow anyone to exploit them in their journey towards fame, success and money. But the postmaster general belonged to a different tribe. All her life being the elder daughter, elder sister, mother, and a guardian to thousands of people who looked up to her as a guide, the only instinct that stirred in her was of protection. In the beginning when she visited these women, there was a ray of doubt and apprehension in them for her. They would not allow her to their pocket rooms. They would even check her mobile phone to ascertain that she is not recording their conversations. They tested her by asking her for help to read their letters that they received from their natives or calling her during her office hours and checking whether she would receive their call or merely avoid them. She passed all her tests, without even understanding that she was being tested! Eventually they opened their doors to her. She would often go to meet them, sit with them, and have cutting chai or a bottle of cola that Aapa would affectionately treat her with. She would feast on the lip-smacking delicacies cooked by Annu. She would help Kajol's sons with their studies and Reshma's daughter in brushing up her communication skills. She would bring medicines for Surekha, who suffered from tuberculosis, and take Guriya to the rehabilitation centre to help her quit alcohol. She would fight against their landlord when he wanted Kajol and Rani to leave their pocket rooms since they could not pay the rent on time and ended up paying it for them. And she did it all in silence. Her only agenda was to protect these women, to empower them, to make them understand the importance of education and financial independence, and to protect their children from the living beasts of the society. She sought for their friendship, and they did not let her down.

Each of them opened their hearts out to her. Their stories led to several sleepless nights, her pillow the only witness to the tears she shed thinking about the grave injustice meted out to the women by destiny, the universe . . . whatever one could call it. She had sworn to let the world know about the circumstances that transforms an innocent girl into a so called 'sex worker' and make the civilised society realize the pains, the abuses, the assaults which these women undergo every single day. The world has no idea about their tears, their screams. The world is completely oblivious to all of it. She had sworn to herself to protect their children from also falling prey to the nasty desires of men. She was determined to help them live a normal life. She knew it was not going to be easy; she knew she would be criticized and judged for choosing to stand by these women instead of enrolling herself in the elite clubs of the city. But what was the point in having power if it could not be put to use for a right cause? She decided on her plan of action and, get set go, she was to ignite a revolution that would turn her world topsy-turvy. She held her flow chart ready. Then followed many meetings with her own subordinates and with the officers of the Aadhar authority of India, the Bombay Municipal Corporation and other connected organizations to find a hack that would at least help these faceless women get some proof of identity to show they were residents of this country. She knew the pain of rootlessness only too well. Her own pain had now merged with the pain of these women, and both had become one.

It took days for her to read the clauses related to Aadhaar, and finally she got a breakthrough.

She learnt that if a trustee of a recognized non-governmental organization or a local corporator stood as guardian of these women or their children and signed a consent form, they could be issued Aadhaar cards. But it was yet another colossal challenge to convince people to appoint themselves as the legal guardian of these stigmatized women. But she was not there to lose.

She coordinated with the local corporator of Kamathipura, who was a guardian to the citizens of his area, and asked him for support. She explained to him the importance and relevance of the Aadhaar card, one of the most important identification documents in India. Issued by the Unique Identification

Authority of India (UIDAI), it served as a unique proof of identity and address for residents of the country. It was a universally accepted identity proof across India. Aadhaar was essential for availing government subsidies and welfare schemes. It was used to ensure that benefits reached the intended beneficiaries, reducing fraud and leakages. Aadhaar was linked with bank accounts, facilitating the direct transfer of government subsidies (DBT). It also simplified the KYC (Know Your Customer) process, making it easier to open bank accounts and access financial services. It was often used to obtain mobile SIM cards and for obtaining connections for electricity, gas and supply of other utilities, making the process faster and more secure. It served as an official document for identity and address proof, making it vital for various legal and administrative procedures.

Javed Shiekh, the local corporator, had of late returned from Haj with his family. He was in his mid-fifties, thoroughly spiritual and a staunch believer in God. Javed welcomed her in his office and listened to her proposal carefully. He agreed to be the signatory for the Aadhar forms for Kamathipura's women and their children. She was most surprised at his willingness to do this and could not believe it. Before she met Javed, people had told her that he was conservative by nature. She stood in front of him, stunned for some time, but she composed herself and expressed her gratitude to the man with moist eyes. Javed smiled at her and said, 'In my fifty-seven years of life, I have never seen anyone standing up for these women Mohotarma. I have only seen the society abusing them, exploiting them, labelling them as 'commodities' and completely ignoring their existence. People of your social stature do not even look in the direction of Kamathipura if they are passing by. You are the first person to treat them as human beings, to think about their well-being without any vested interests, and I wish you all the best in your endeavour.' She controlled herself from bursting into tears and left Javed's office feeling triumphant. Now she was determined to break the Chakravyuh and bring her Abhimanyus out of Kurukshetra.

The children of Kamathipura held a special place in her heart. Despite being born in what resembled the pit of hell, despite not knowing the real identity of their biological fathers, most of them were incredibly talented, had fire in their belly and dreams in their heads of living a decent life. She started to get the children groomed to make them presentable in mainstream society. She organized computer coaching and art therapy for the children. Every day two of her staff would impart them this training. After a few months, many of the children could operate a computer. She liaised with the local computer training school and enrolled some of them for advanced courses. One child turned out to be a fantastic artist and won admission to the leading art college of the city with her help. The women could not thank her enough for what she was doing for them. She realized that all other identities of a woman fall short before motherhood. Her heart ached for them. She felt like crying every time she thought of them. She could not see any reason why they were grateful to her. This was the minimum one could do after knowing them, especially if one had a bit of power.

Finally, the day came. After about a month of her first visit to Kamathipura, the renovated post office was inaugurated by her. She invited all the women inhabitants of the locality to be part of the inauguration. They were ecstatic. For the first time in their lives they were at a celebration meant exclusively for them. She not only gifted the new post office to them but also converted it into an 'all-woman post office', to be run only by women officials so that the local inhabitants could visit the post office without any hesitation to get their postal needs met, and to be assured that they would be taken care of rather than abused, humiliated and shooed away.

She personally trained her women officials in the elements of empathy and compassion before deputing them at the Kamathipura post office. She personally visited each and every pocket room in 14th Lane and other nearby lanes, speaking to the women and making them understand the importance of documenting their existence officially for a start, and the sense of pride it would bring them and their children. She often faced the wrath of the pimps, criticism from her counterparts and hesitation on the part of her subordinates to accompany her to Kamathipura. One day, when she asked one of her subordinates to call Aapa on the telephone, the subordinate reluctantly told her that she would not like to store the contact numbers of such women on her mobile phone since that could affect her personal life if her in-laws and husband found out. She did not speak a word, but took out her own mobile and dialled Aapa's number. It astonished her staff to see her talking to a commercial sex worker in the same tone as she talked to her own family. They soon realized their mistake and apologized before her, at which she only smiled and forgave them. She knew that in a country like India, sex work was not illegal but was a terrible taboo. The social stigma the sex workers were met with wherever they went could not be wiped away so easily. It would perhaps take ages to transform the society so they accepted these helpless women for what they were. They did what they did to survive; to feed their children, quell their hunger and to live for one more day. In a society that refused to even acknowledge their humanity, branding them as harbingers of misfortune and ill fate, they would never get their share of respect, never be treated as equals. That would require a massive revolution – to wash away people's current mind-set and replace it with rational thinking. But when would this take place, and who would initiate it?

She could not find any promising answer to her question, barely realizing that the revolution has already begun. As the women assembled every day at the new post office to get themselves and their children enrolled under the Adhaar mandate, they were taking one step forward towards progress. She left no stone unturned to educate them, to counsel them. Her battalion comprised five daring women named Aapaa, Kajol, Annu, Rani and Guriya! They encircled her and protected her like furious warriors as she roamed around in the red-light district searching for women to enrol them for Aadhaar cards and explain to them the benefits of financial inclusion. She was even insulted by some of the women, who asked her not to disturb them and shut their doors in her face. But the overall response was more than remarkable. There was a record-breaking number of Aadhaar enrolments at the post office. The number of new savings accounts too rose sky high. Her phone was flooded with appreciative texts. Press and media skulked around to cover the story.

She remained indifferent to all the fame though. She was still under the trauma of knowing how terribly unfair life had been to the women of Kamathipura. She knew she had a long way to go with these women who called her 'Didi' and wrapped her in a strange bond of love and affection.

12

Kamathipura; A Jungle Within

Countries are like packs of cards; they fall if not handled with prudence.

The traumatic Partition of India in 1947 drew lines of separation between brothers, in the name of India and Pakistan. The state of Bengal was split into two. One became East Pakistan while the other remained in India as the state of West Bengal.

As a part of the massive population transfer initiated by Partition, millions of Hindu Bengalis migrated from East Pakistan to India and ended up settling in West Bengal, Assam and Tripura, the majority settling in Kolkata and other places with West Bengal.

The large-scale entry of the Bengalis from East Pakistan into West Bengal was not welcomed by the people of West Bengal, where they were detested. They were considered as beggars who asked for food, shelter and work. They were held in contempt for speaking in an accent that was different from that of West Bengal. Even today the terms 'Bangal' and 'Ghoti' are used as jibes by the two groups against each other.

Kajol, who was a hard-core Bangal had inherited all the Bangal characteristics, be it her loud voice, her aggression or her command over cooking. On the other hand, Annu was a Ghoti, predominantly meek, soft-spoken and more of a sober breed. Every single day, the 14th lane of Kamathipura became a war zone with Kajol abusing Annu's Ghoti forefathers for being cowards and misers, and Annu ridiculing Kajol's ancestors for being beggars. The more Kajol raised her voice, using the most offensive slang she knew, the softer Annu spoke, and with sharper sacasm, making Kajol burn with rage! All of Kamathipura watched on as the two women who had the same mother tongue raved and ranted against each other's ancestors.

One day they had invited their officer Didi for a lunch of *macch bhaat* to their place, and Bangal-Ghoti riot broke out between the two over what was to be cooked. Kajol said it had to be *hilsa* fish while Annu argued that the tastiest of seafood was prawn. Kajol told Annu that Bangals had big hearts and they loved to feed people, unlike the 'kanjus' Ghotis, whose small heartedness reflected in their choice of seafood. Annu went all red and hot at this ridiculous comment. Silently, she walked into their room and threw the bowl of hilsa fish into the drain that ran by the side of their house. As she did that she smiled sweetly at Kajol and said, '*Oi daakh bangal, tor ilish guli nordomaaye sataar kaatche re.*' Saying this, she burst into laughter. Kajol took a moment to realize what Annu had actually done, and ran towards her like a lioness with her kitchen knife. Annu was scared now. Kajol screamed, '*Ei aash boti diye aj tore kupiye maarbo.'* She was threatening to injure Annu. Realizing that Kajol was unstoppable, Annu ran into her room and locked herself in. But Kajol decided to sit near the door till it was opened. '*Aaj tore dekhe nebo ghotir bachai! Aami bangal aami baagh re toder ghoti guli sob chucho hala!*' roared Kajol!

For the next two hours the scene remained unchanged – till Officer Didi arrived. She was hungry and straightaway entered their tiny kitchen to take a look what had been cooked for her. Seeing the kitchen in a mess, she came out, only to see Kajol sitting with a kitchen knife at Annu's doorstep. Hearing Officer didi's voice, Annu shouted, begging to be saved from being killed, '*Didi, aamake ei bangal maagir hath theke bachao! E aamake mere felbe!*'

Officer Didi, thoroughly enjoying all this, asked Kajol to calm down and Annu to come out. She was briefed about what had happened. Controlling her laughter, she made them understand that the Bangals and Ghotis both belong to the same lineage and must be cordial and affectionate towards each other, but all in vain.

Every mortal life makes a journey – an extremely unpredictable journey. It could be a journey from rags to riches, or from the material to the spiritual. Centuries ago, Plato analysed the plight of human beings chained in a cave, living in a state of absolute imprisonment. The only thing visible to them were any shadows thrown on the walls, which they thought were the only things that existed in their universe.

And then, when these humans were set free, they hesitated, faltered and sank as they tried to blend into the mainstream in their newly emancipated existence. The curse of slavery and confinement had hit their brains and hearts so strongly that they were convinced that being chained was the way of life. Failing to settle down in their new world, they returned to their state of darkness and pathos on their own.

Likewise, the concept of emancipation was not easy for the women of Kamathipura to understand. India, being a democratic country, has never encouraged her citizens to seclude or isolate a fellow human being from mainstream society. However, a country with a culture that has been lauded for producing a liberal encyclopedia on sexuality and desires, the Kamasutra, centuries ago, has somewhat failed to own and accept these women who have been trafficked and forced into the trade of prostitution. They have remained invisible at plain sight since Time immemorial. They have been so tabooed, abhorred and despised by the society that, going out into the crowd and claiming to belong to regular human society is perhaps the biggest challenge for these women.

So when Didi brought them a degree of much-delayed and hard-earned independence, they were scared, shocked and terrified. Forget the other women, even the otherwise courageous Kajol would refuse to walk to the nearby bank and demand services, afraid of the response she would fetch from the so-called literate people. A tigress by nature, she would tremble to walk out of the jungle of Kamathipura and face regular society. The weight of being labelled as 'social outcasts' was too heavy to throw off their bruised bodies and souls, and that was perhaps the toughest challenge for Officer Didi to get them to overcome.

But she belonged in a different league, she was in a unique orbit where the impossible didn't exist. She had a strange power within her that would transform people to attempt the new and difficult. She was determined to release these women from their state of slumber, ignorance and thraldom and introduce them to the possibilities of a greater universe.

Accordingly, she instructed the staff in post offices that lay in the vicinity of Kamathipura to be soft-spoken and courteous to these women. This took time, as the staff were initially agitated about this, given their strong revulsion for these women. Even looking into their face was considered as something that boded ill. However, change occurred when they witnessed their apex officer walking on the road holding their hands, head held up in pride, during the Independence Day celebrations. They were dumfounded to see their super boss casually chatting with the accursed and stigmatized women of Kamathipura and sharing cups of cutting chai and vada pav with them. They were unable to say anything when this officer asked them to ponder on whether those women were also not born of a human womb, like themselves, and whether the colour of their blood was also not the same as theirs.

Change is the only constant in this universe, it has been said. But change comes slowly, tiptoeing to the door of conventional, age-old systems before knocking on it and then destroying those systems with new sets of principles.

During the event of Raksha Bandhan, when the country celebrated the divine bond between brother and sister, the lady officer arranged an event in Kamathipura in one of its streets. Initially, the officials who represented her department were sceptical about participating and did not want to get a rakhee tied to their wrists by sex workers. They stood to one side and watched flabbergasted as all the women of Kamathipura tied a rakhee on the wrist of their superior officer. She hugged them affectionately in return, promising them a lifelong commitment of a sister, to stand by them in their hour of need and protect them from demons disguised as human beings. Her officials had never seen anything like this in their lives. They could not bring themselves to change their mind though.

Kajol and her gang mustered up the courage to step into the grand old palatial post office, the Mumbai General Post Office, the largest post office in the country. It was a grand building with a huge dome, among the largest in the country, and had giant pillars and minarets. Their hearts pounded as they entered, fearing humiliation and abuse. The memory of their last visit to the place was still fresh in their minds. They had been chased away like stray dogs, and that was the time when Officer Didi had appeared out of the blue and saved them.

They saw the security guards at the lion gate of the building. Kajol frowned at them, clenching her fists. '*Ebar gaal dile mere debo aami, Aapaa*!' This time if they abused them, she would beat them up! Aapa calmed her down. But the security guards smiled at them, cordially wishing them good morning. Aapa and Annu wished them back with folded hands. Rani, standing behind them, imitated the gesture while Kajol ignored their salutation completely and walked ahead, nose in the air. But she too was actually full of fear – that she might be mistreated or assaulted.

Showing a lot of confidence, she talked to the man at the counter, enquired about her passbook and her account. The three women following her did the same. The person at the counter replied to each of their questions patiently and with a smiling face. The universe witnessed a very ordinary yet extraordinary conversation. The four women stood with moistened eyes and listened to the counter man, not able to believe if all this was for real or the best dream of their lives!

In the middle of the conversation, Kajol turned around and saw their Officer Didi standing at a distance and smiling at them. Kajol smiled back at her. It was a smile of gratitude, a smile that carried a thousand unspoken emotions that soothed the bleeding injuries of her past. Tears of joy gathered in the corners of her eyes, which had seen only betrayal, abuse and despair. For one fleeting moment, the darkness of their lives was replaced by a glimmer of hope and humanity.

Good can defeat the Bad; it is just that good has to be stronger and more powerful in order to break the chains of evil and set itself free.

13
How the Beginnings Are

It was one of those frenzied monsoon evenings when the rebellious rain had washed the classic promenade of Marine Drive in Mumbai squeaky clean. The rain had just begun to ease over Marine Drive, leaving behind a glistening sheen on the sweeping curve of Queen's Necklace. The Arabian Sea, grey and silver a while ago, now shimmered, reflecting the city lights, its waves rolling lazily on to the promenade's weathered stones. The scent of wet earth mingled with the salty breeze, and the rhythmic hum of the waves competed with the distant honking of taxis weaving through the slick streets.

Couples huddled under shared umbrellas, their laughter mingling with the soft drizzle that still lingered in the air. Street vendors resumed their posts, their carts brimming with steaming bhuttas crackling over open flames, the aroma of their charred kernels filling the air. A chaiwala, standing beside his bubbling kettle, poured fragrant, cardamom-laced tea into tiny clay cups, the warmth of the brew a welcome contrast to the evening's cool embrace.

A sudden gust of wind sent a spray of sea mist across the promenade, making the children there squeal in delight as they danced through the puddles, their reflections rippling in them under the golden streetlights. Office-goers, their day's work behind them, leaned against the broad sea wall, shoes in hand, toes curling over the edge as they let the waves kiss their feet. A lone guitarist strummed a melancholic tune, his notes carried away by the wind, merging seamlessly with the soft murmur of the city.

As the evening deepened, Marine Drive became a living canvas of light and motion – cars glided past, their red tail-lights stretching like molten rubies on the wet asphalt. The Art Deco buildings lining the boulevard stood tall, their facades washed anew by the rain. The city, always in a hurry, seemed to pause here, if only for a moment, as people lost themselves in the symphony of waves, rain and neon reflections.

She, humming, was sitting on a tetrapod by the sea getting drenched in the rain and watching the four women who had come with her dancing in ecstasy like unbridled children. She noticed that the rain water had washed away the stains splashed on their dresses by the busy vehicles that passed them while they were walking down the pavement just a few minutes ago. She wished the rain could magically wash away the stains that had been splashed on their lives by destiny, by society and by so-called civilized humans, or the babus of the Bankim Chandra novels. These four women, of a rainbow of ages, looked no different from the common multitude of women thronging the 'open space' of Marine

Drive, just to get away from their pigeon coops that were their homes for a whiff of fresh air. But this lively band was from the infamous red-light district of Kamathipura, a place they called home.

They were officially known as commercial sex workers, commonly referred to as *dhandewalis*. Every day, they committed the unpardonable and abominable sin of selling their bodies in exchange for money. Every day, they died a different death, only to become 'undead' the next morning. These women shared a strange bond of trust and affection with her. A most unusual camaraderie. It was an accident of fate that had brought them here. They had stumbled into this by-lane of life. '*Didi, tum toh pura bheegi huyi Madhuri Dixit lag rahi ho*!' Didi frowned at Kajol, who was naughtily giggling at her. '*Didi, tumhe bukhar aayega, chalo abhi nikalte hai*.' Didi smiled to be warned she might catch a fever. Slowly, all five walked down the long pavement of Marine Drive. It had stopped raining. It was time to get back to the world of urine and sweat. This band of girls had to melt back into the night. She looked up at the night sky and filled her lungs with the earthy petrichor. A family perplexed by her ways awaited her. She walked along with the girls down the bustling Marine Drive, her gaze fixed on them. Once unseen and invisible, they now stood before the world; their existence undeniably visible.

Their journey from invisibility to visibility had been a fierce battle, one they fought with tremendous resilience and unyielding spirit, demanding acceptance and equality from an apparently blindfolded society that had never acknowledged them. And though they had emerged triumphant in the battle, was this truly the end of their struggles? Or just the beginning of their rebellion against a society that stereotyped them, made them a taboo? There were miles of road yet to be walked and far more furious battles to be fought and won. But in the meanwhile, she thought, they would live with the thread of hope that now held their lives together amidst all the hopelessness and despair. Their silent hope for a better tomorrow would keep their hearts beating through the darkest and grimmest of nights. She believed that hope was not a simple word, but bore connotations of great power that one was not aware of! It was a disruptor.

A strange silence pervaded the atmosphere, muting the roar of the sea and the incessant clamour of the sprawling megapolis. For generations, these women had been forced into silence, carrying the pain of being unheard, the torment of being unable to speak, protest, or assert themselves to get even the most basic rights for themselves and their children. Cast into the abyss of an unending exile, they had been banished to *patal lok*, to be tormented by numerous *rakshasas*; their cries dissipating into nothingness.

It had taken her nearly fifty springs to accumulate the courage to speak to them about their trauma, to understand and break through the walls of their infernal silence, and to hear what had long remained unheard. She knew what they had told her was only the tip of the iceberg. There was still a lot to uncover, a lot to unlearn and relearn about them.

She remembered something her Baba would often repeat to her: 'So much to do/so little done/hurry up/hurry up/ hurry up.'

Epilogue

Not every story is told. Not every story is heard. Unseen, unheard, and unacknowledged, innumerable lives emerge survive and vanish in the vastness of this universe.

My account of these women—Salma, also known as Aapa, Kajol, Annu, Rani—and of several more whom I have seen, interacted with and understood, and still in the process of understanding, is not a work of fiction, rather it is based on real life human beings and their experiences, which I had while serving as Postmaster General of Mumbai city and while initiating a socio-financial inclusion project in Kamathipura, the red-light district in Mumbai, a name that sent shame down the spine of many a two respectable women.

However, what started merely as a job to be done gradually transformed into a poignant journey filled with emotions. A journey of both hope and despair at the same time.

Through the project, I was drawn into a world I had never really experienced before, one that contained not the 'immoral women', but rather real, resilient, and immensely courageous women who are warriors; for whom life has been synonymous to a nasty bloody battlefield where they are forced to fight every single moment in order to gain another piece of bread, in order to ensure another day of survival.

I encountered fighters, mothers, and daughters; ordinary women survived by extraordinary events. In actuality, the so-called 'bad women' were just human beings, just women, just like the rest of us, with deep humane emotions, dreams, pain, and humour. Since many of them speak the language that happens to be my mother tongue, our connect happened by two common identities: the identity of mother tongue and the identity of motherhood.

The fact that destiny has not been fair to them is not overrated nor a myth. They had been grossly unlucky. Their lives were endured rather than chosen. But they learned to endure, to fight, to cling on in that gloomy, oppressive darkness.

When the official power bestowed on us is applied for the benefit of others, it takes on significance. To break the cycle, I used my professional standing to not only bring about reform but also to inspire hope for them, and more importantly, for their children. What I achieved from it was a strange yet serene satisfaction that I have never had earlier in my so called 'privileged' life.

At times, when I sit with them in their tiny rooms today, enjoying puffed rice and lemon tea while having open discussions and they hug me out of the gratitude of hearing them, I call that, true emancipation.

I have realized that they will not be able to quit their occupation and merge into mainstream ever, as we, the mainstreamers will inevitably hesitate to live with and accept them, after knowing about their scandalous past, no matter how gruesome it may be. But then will things not change for them? Will they continue being invisible in plain sight?

The epiphany perhaps lies in their silent metamorphosis – from the depths of murky obscurity and imposed silence to a fragile, flickering visibility. It is though, just the beginning – delicate, uncertain, yet momentous.

Today, I no longer look away. I no longer raise the tinted glass of my car while passing through the by-lanes of Kamathipura. Instead, I pause. I look. I see. They are no longer ghosts meandering through the margins of my consciousness. They stand, bruised yet breathing, scared yet visible. And in that act of seeing, I too, am seen, no longer a social predator, but as a friend, as an elder sister, as they call me, 'Didi'.

I live with the quiet hope that I will not be the only one. That slowly, steadily, others will choose to see, to listen, to recognize their presence in this vast and restless megapolis. That one day, the veil of invisibility will lift not just in fragments, but completely in the beaming light of empathy and awareness.

Today, I see them.